THE HISTORY

OF

THE 7th LIGHT HORSE A.I.F.

DEDICATION.

TO the Heroic Dead of the Regiment—those true, brave comrades, so many of whom lie sleeping on far distant battlefields—this book is reverently dedicated.

Blow out, you bugles, over the rich Dead!
    There's none of these so lonely and poor of old
    But, dying has made us rarer gifts than gold.
These laid the world away; poured out the red
Sweet wine of youth; gave up the years to be
    Of work and joy, and that unhoped serene
    That men call age; and those who would have been,
Their sons, they gave, their immortality.

                                        RUPERT BROOK, R.N.R.
                                            (Died in Ægean, April, 1915.)

THE HISTORY

OF

THE

7th Light Horse Regiment A.I.F.

BY

Lieut.-Colonel J. D. RICHARDSON, D.S.O.

WITH AN INTRODUCTION

BY

Lieut.-General Sir HARRY CHAUVEL, K.C.B., K.C.M.G.

The Naval & Military Press Ltd

Published by
The Naval & Military Press Ltd
5 Riverside, Brambleside, Bellbrook
Industrial Estate, Uckfield, East Sussex,
TN22 1QQ England
Tel: +44 (0) 1825 749494
Fax: +44 (0) 1825 765701
www.naval-military-press.com
www.military-genealogy.com
www.militarymaproom.com

In reprinting in facsimile from the original, any imperfections are inevitably reproduced and the quality may fall short of modern type and cartographic standards.

DEPARTMENT OF DEFENCE.

Inspector General.

Army Headquarters,
MELBOURNE.

Introduction.

I have been greatly honoured by being asked to write a few words of introduction to the History of the 7th Australian Light Horse Regiment.

Raised in New South Wales in 1914, the Regiment was early in the field, and took a prominent part in all the important operations in the Egyptian Theatre of the War. It first came under my command on Gallipoli in November, 1915, and continued therein until the conclusion of the War. At the Battle of Romani it was largely due to its stubborn defence and spirited counter-attack, under the leadership of Lieut.-Colonel (now Brigadier-General) G. Macarthur Onslow, that the victory was so complete. At the first Battle of Gaza it was this Regiment that led the Anzac Mounted Division through the night to its position in rear of the city, and which captured the new Commander of the Gaza Defence, who was on his way to take up his command. During the Battle of Beersheba and the pursuit which followed, the Regiment sustained the fine traditions it had already established for dash and gallantry. In the raids across Jordan and throughout the long summer of 1918 in the Jordan Valley, it bore its share of the fighting and the hardships, from the bitter cold of Gilead in mid-winter to the scorching heat of Jericho in July. Under Lieut.-Colonel J. D. Richardson it played a brilliant part in the final victory, which destroyed three Turkish Armies and brought Germany's Allies out of the War.

The Regiment suffered many casualties, in battle and through the ravages of disease, and those of its numbers who are left are scattered throughout Australia, though many are still serving in the Militia Forces. I congratulate them all on their achievements during the War, and wish them every success in whatever spheres of life they are now engaged in.

Harry Chauvel

Lieut.-General.
late Commanding Desert Mounted Corps.

Abreviations and Unusual Words.

R.H.Q.	Regimental Headquarters.
B.H.Q	Brigade Headquarters.
D.H.Q.	Divisional Headquarters.
G.O.C.	General Officer Commanding.
C.O.	Commanding Officer.
C.M.F.	Commonwealth Military Forces.
A. & N.Z. T.C. & D.	Australian and New Zealand Training Centre and Details Camp.
O.R.	Other ranks.
Descorps	Desert Mounted Corps.
C. in C.	Commander-in-Chief.
B.G.C.	Brigadier-General Commanding
R.S.M.	Regimental Sergeant Major.
S.S.M.	Squadron Sergeant Major.
R.Q.M.S.	Regimental Quartermaster-Sergeant.
S.Q.M.S.	Squadron Quartermaster-Sergeant
R.H.A.	Royal Horse Artillery.
Tell or Tel	A mound artificially built—sometimes the remains of an old fortress or village.
Wadi	A watercourse usually dry during most of the year.
I.C.C.	Imperial Camel Corps

Colonel J. M. Arnott, C.M.G., V.D.,
C.O. 7th Light Horse, October, 1914, to August, 1915; temporarily commanded 10th L.H. in 1916; Commandant A. and N.Z. Forces at Tel-el-Kebir and Mouscar, 1916 to 1919.

Brig.-General G. M. Macarthur Onslow, C.M.G., D.S.O., V.D., Order of the Nile, 3rd Class, C.O. 7th Light Horse, August, 1915, to September, 1918.; Brig.-General commanding 5th Light Horse Brigade, September, 1918.

Foreword.

This history of the 7th Light Horse, A.I.F., has been written in accordance with instructions received before leaving Egypt—that every unit should endeavour to have its War History written up before returning to Australia. The first draft of this MS. was completed before Sydney was reached, but as this had been very hastily written it was revised, and a great deal was completely re-written. The MS. was then submitted to whatever officers were available, and these were asked to comment upon it. As a result many valuable corrections and suggestions have been made, and I sincerely believe that this little volume now gives a thoroughly accurate account of the operations of the 7th Light Horse Regiment during the Great War.

It should be explained that the data from which this History was compiled was extremely meagre as far as written records were concerned, for the war diaries of the Regiment gave practically no detailed stories of events, and could only be relied upon for dates. The memories of those who took part in the various operations were therefore taxed to clothe the skeleton history with more substantial matter, and in this the wisdom of having the History written as soon as possible, was shown. Many circumstances have affected the delay as regards publication, but the author makes no apologies for this, and feels convinced that if publication had been left to the critics, that the volume would never have been published at all.

It has been suggested that nominal rolls of original members of the Regiment, and also complete nominal rolls for the whole period of service should have been added as appendices, but, unfortunately, the cost was found to be prohibitive.

The author is well aware of, and sincerely regrets, the fact that many gallant deeds are not recorded. It was inevitable that many of these should escape notice in the turmoil of active operations, whilst others remembered for a while, were not entered in the war diaries or official records, and are therefore lost as far as this History is concerned.

It has also been found to be quite impossible to state just for what act of gallantry or piece of good work decorations were awarded, in many cases. That they were fully deserved in all cases can be taken as a matter of course, just as the fact that perhaps many equally deserving cases for some reason or another escaped notice.

As regards the cost of publication of this History, it must be borne in mind that volumes such as these, of a purely Regimental nature, can have no great appeal to any save ex-members of the Regiment or their next of kin. Consequently, sales must be limited, and therefore the cost of the volume is correspondingly greatly increased. It must be understood, therefore, that no profit can be hoped for in this direction, and, in fact, some loss is expected, which will be met, if necessary, from a private Trust Fund belonging to the Regiment.

As regards maps and photographs, the author has again had to consider the cost, and many excellent ones have had to be excluded. The maps have been simplified as much as possible, and in these, as in the book generally, technicalities have as far as possible been eliminated.

Only passing reference has been made to the splendid work of the Red Cross and of Dame Alice Chisholm and Miss Macphillamy at Kantara, but the author has been assured that adequate prominence is being given to this in the official history—prominence which could not be attempted in a purely Regimental History. But the Regiment does not forget.

In conclusion, I wish to express my thanks to those who have helped in any way to make the publication of this volume possible, either by suggestions, comments, photographs or maps, and especially Brigadier-General G. M. Macarthur Onslow, Colonel Arnott, Majors Windeyer, Bird, Barton, Willsallen, Easterbrook, Davies and Wikner, and Lieuts. Chapman, Donkin and Gibbs. Also to Lieutenant-General Sir Harry Chauvel and Mr. Harry Gullett for their practical interest and appreciation.

J. D. RICHARDSON, Lieut.-Colonel,
Lately Commanding 7th Light Horse, A.I.F.

"Leigh,"
Raymond Terrace,
1/11/23.

Contents.

PART I.

		Page
Chapter I.—Early Days		1
,, II.—Egypt		4
,, III.—Anzac		7
,, IV.—Anzac Settling Down		10
,, V.—Ryrie's Post		13
,, VI.—Anzac, Last Phase		16

PART II.

		Page
Sinai		19
Chapter I.—Mounted Work		20
,, II.—The Desert of Sinai		23
,, III.—Patrols and Reconnaissances		25
,, IV.—Romani, Katia and Bir El Abd		29
,, V.—Last Days in Sinai		35

PART III.

		Page
Palestine: The Philistine Plain		38
Chapter I.—The Advance Towards Gaza		39
,, II.—First Battle of Gaza		41
,, III.—Between Battles		44
,, IV.—The Second Battle of Gaza		47
,, V.—On The Beersheba Flank		49
,, VI.—The Beersheba Flank		53
,, VII.—Battle of Beersheba		56
,, VIII.—Breaking Through		60
,, IX.—The Pursuit		63
,, X.—The Pursuit Continued		65
,, XI.—Operations Near Jaffa		68
,, XII.—Esdud, Wadi Hanein and Nalin		72

PART IV.

		Page
The Trans-Jordan Campaign		75
Chapter I.—New Country		76
,, II.—Jerusalem		78
,, III.—The Jordan		80
,, IV.—The First Battle of Amman		83
,, V.—The Jordan Valley		88
,, VI.—The End In Sight		98
,, VII.—The Old Battlefields		107
,, VIII.—The Egyptian Rebellion And Embarkation for Home.		114
Conclusion		117
Decorations and Awards		118
Casualties		120
Map		123
,,		124

List of Illustrations.

Colonel J. M. Arnott, C.M.G., V.D. .... *Facing Abbreviations*

Brig. General G. M. Macarthur Onslow, C.M.G., D.S.O., V.D., Order of the Nile, 3rd Class .... *Facing Prologue.*

Lieut. Colonel J. D. Richardson, D.S.O., Order of the Nile, 3rd Class ..... *Facing Page 4*

Watering Horses, Hebron Road Camp ....
No. 3 Gun, 7th Battery, at Anzac ....
Watering Horses at Ancient Wells at Katia, Captain Easterbrook supervising } *Between Pages 4 and 5*
"Orangie, beeg ones—veery good, veery nice!" Ma'adi, December, 1915 ..
Friendly (!) Arabs east of Jordan ....

Crossing Wadi on way back from a day's Swimming to Wadi Hanein ....
Camels Unloading Berseen in the Horses' Lines at Ma'adi, 1915 .... } *Facing Page 5*
"B" Squadron Horses. Halt at Romani en route Nabit to Hill 70, October, 1916

Etmaler, looking North .... *Facing Page 12*

Watering from Wells in Katia Hod .... *Facing Page 13*

Greek Monastery on Jebel Kuruntal .... *Facing Page 44*

Nabit. The Bivouac is under the Palm Trees ....
Poppy Valley four days after the snow fell. Anzac, 1915 .... } *Facing Page 45*
Brigade Transport Camels on lines near 5th Regiment ....

Brigade Camp at Romani .... *Facing Page 60*

Boundary Posts between Sinai and Palestine .... *Facing Page 61*

The dimly-seen figures in foreground are washing near the spring at the base of Tel el Fara .... *Facing No. 68*

Troop of Turks captured by "A" Squadron on Beersheba Plain ....)
Es Salt Road ....) *Between Pages*
Camp at Kilo 7, Kantara ....) *68 and 69*
Talaat ed Dumm ....)

Mosque of Omar, Jerusalem .... *Facing Page 69*

Mount of Olives, Russian Church with Gilded Domes, Garden of Gethsemane .. *Facing Page 76*

Jericho, from South-West .... *Facing Page 77*

Sig. Sgt. Laugier and Sig. Harper in Trench, Wadi Mellahar .... *Facing Page 92*

Turkish Trenches at Shellac, Wadi Ghuzze ....
Regimental Officers' Cook and his "offsiders" at Hebron Road Camp .... } *Facing Page 93*
Camp at Kilid Bahr, Gallipoli, in 1918 ....

Christian Refugees at Jericho after 1st Amman Stunt .... *Facing Page 116*

7th Regt. Camp at Salhia, from the air.
Samakeen Markets, near Salhia. } *Between Pages 116-117*

"B" Squadron Patrol returning from Samakeen Markets to Salhia Camp .. *Facing Page 117*

CHAPTER I.

EARLY DAYS.

IT was with almost stupified astonishment that the average Australian citizen received the announcement of England's declaration of war on Germany, but only the enemy was astonished when the Great Dominions rallied to the support of the Motherland.

One recalls the Military measures adopted in those early days against the first possible menace to our shores since the days of the Crimea; the secret orders for quick mobilisation, and the partial calling up also of certain forces, the opening of recruiting offices, the rush of eager volunteers, and the formation of big training camps. Flashing of searchlights from the forts at Sydney and Newcastle, and the firing of a shot across the bows of a German liner endeavouring to escape from Port Phillip Heads, helped people to realise that the War clouds had burst.

By September one Infantry Division with one Brigade of Light Horse had been organised, and the training of these troops was proceeding rapidly. A force of the strength approximately of an Infantry Brigade had also been sent to German New Guinea. But thousands of recruits were still pouring in; men who had, for different reasons, been unable to offer their services before. It was, therefore, decided to form another Light Horse and another Infantry Brigade.

The 2nd Light Horse Brigade, composed of the 5th, 6th and 7th Regiments, with attached units, was placed under the command of Colonel (now Major-General) Sir Granville Ryrie, K.C.M.G., C.B., V.D. Recruits were drafted into training camps for the 6th and 7th Regiments, first at Liverpool and later at Holdsworthy. The 5th, a Queensland Regiment, joined up with the Brigade just before embarkation.

The 7th Regiment was brought into being during October and November, 1914. Lieut.-Colonel J. M. Arnott, of the 11th Light Horse (C.M.F.), was appointed to command, and was given discretionary power in the selection of his officers. These, however, were not finally appointed until about a fortnight before sailing, and officers were probationally selected to carry on the administration and training. There were many applicants for Commissions, either from Regiments or Battalions of the C.M.F. or from men who had seen service in South Africa. It was well that this was so, for the Light Horse Depôt soon became crowded with men who were anxious to serve, but whose ideas of discipline and the routine of Army life were vague. They were men of splendid physique, too big, in fact, for mounted troops, and imbued with the spirit of venture and patriotism.

After the move from Liverpool to Holdsworthy, camp was made on a semi-permanent basis. The famous clock, afterwards so well known at Moascar, in Egypt, was placed in position, and the strictest punctuality was insisted upon by Lieut.-Colonel Arnott. A large design was painted with the maxim: "The best way to kill time is to work it to death," to emphasise the fact that no slackers would be permitted to remain in the camp, either as officers or other ranks. This maxim was recalled in the strenuous days at Anzac when the situation demanded the utmost exertion from even sick and weak men, in digging and tunnelling. In the ranks the maxim was altered to: "The best way to kill men is to work them to death."

While the Regiment was being gradually built up to War Establishment, the camp was also used as a depôt for officers and other ranks who were to form the nuclei of fresh units. Men selected for the 7th Regiment were put through their riding test over jumps; some of the results of this method were not quite satisfactory. It was not until about three weeks before embarkation that rifles or bayonets could be obtained, and horses were not drawn until four days prior to date of sailing. In the last week in November a number of officers attended a Light Horse School at Moore Park, under Major Holman, but those selected to go with the Regiment were recalled before the School closed. A fortnight before sailing, the officers were finally appointed and posted to Commands and Squadrons, and the final selection of N.C.O.s and men for these was also made. The officers were posted as under, and their ranks confirmed before leaving Australia:—

Headquarters C.O. ...	Lieut.-Colonel J. M. Arnott, 11th L.H. Regt.
Second in Command ...	Major G. M. Macarthur Onslow, V.D., 9th L.H. Regt. (who had been prevented from obtaining the Command of the 1st L.H. Regiment owing to an operation for appendicitis).
Adjutant	Lieutenant P. J. Higgins (Imperial Service).
Quartermaster	Lieutenant G. H. M. A. Hession (34th Infantry C.M.F.).
Machine Gun Officer ..	Lieutenant A. Thorne (R.M.C., Duntroon).
M.O.	Captain Flecker.
Chaplain-Captain	Chaplain Captain K. Miller.
Veterinary Officer	Captain Gilbert.
"A" Squadron O.C. ...	Major E. Windeyer (6th L.H., C.M.F.).
Second in Command ...	Captain J. D. Richardson (6th L.H., C.M.F.).
	Lieutenant Gilchrist (Reserve of Officers).
	Lieutenant T. H. Bird (6th L.H., C.M.F.).
	2nd Lieutenant McLean (no previous commission).
	2nd Lieutenant Maney Lake (no previous commission).
"B" Squadron O.C. ...	Major T. Rutledge (11th L.H., C.M.F.).
Second in Command ...	Captain A. Hyman (9th L.H., C.M.F.).
	Lieutenant Elliott (R.M.C., Duntroon).
	Lieutenant L. Bice (Reserve of Officers).
	Lieutenant G. Board (13th Infantry Battalion, C.M.F.).
	Lieutenant Maddrell (11th L.H., C.M.F.).
"C" Squadron O.C. ...	Major H. B. Suttor (Reserve of Officers).
Second in Command ...	Captain H. C. de Low (A.F.A., C.M.F.).
	Lieutenant Fulton (R.M.C., Duntroon).
	Lieutenant Stevenson (9th L.H., C.M.F.).
	Lieutenant N. D. Barton (34th Infantry).
	Lieutenant Weston (no previous commission).
	S.S.M. C. C. Easterbrook (Instructional Staff, Machine Gun Sergeant, later R.S.M.).
	S.S.M. C. C. Edwards (Instructional Staff, R.Q.M.S.).

During the second week in December it became known that embarkation would take place before Christmas. Officers at the School of Instruction were hastily recalled, and every effort was made to get the Squadrons into shape at once. This was effected under difficulties, as officers, N.C.Os. and men were new to one another. Difficulty was experienced in obtaining clothing and equipment, and much of it had to be distributed on board the transport. Four days before sailing, orders were given to draw horses from the Remount Depôt. Of necessity, some mounts that were not suitable had to be taken.

On embarkation, the Regiment was split into parties, one going on the "Ayrshire," under Lieut.-Colonel Arnott, and the other on the "Ajana," under Major Onslow. Major Windeyer and Captain de Low were appointed O.C.'s Troops on other ships.

On December 17th, 1914, "C" Squadron and the Machine Gun Section—the whole party under Major Onslow—moved off from Holdsworthy and bivouacked for the night in the grounds of Lieut.-Colonel Arnott's residence at Homebush. They moved out early next morning and embarked on H.M.T. "Ajana," lying at Woolloomooloo Wharf. On the 18th, the remainder of the Regiment moved out, bivouacked at Homebush, and embarked on the 19th on H.M.T. "Ayrshire," being inspected on board by Colonel Wallack, Commandant 2nd Military District. The "Ayrshire" pulled out into the stream as soon as embarkation was completed and anchored until the following morning. On the "Borda" Major Windeyer, 10 O.R.s and 33 horses belonging to the Regiment embarked, and on H.M.T. "Berrima" Lieutenant Jackson was placed in charge of 52 1st Reinforcements. The "Ajana" sailed on the 19th and the "Ayrshire," "Berrima" and "Borda" on the 20th.

During the voyage from Sydney to Albany and Fremantle (where the "Ajana" called) various shortcomings which the hurried departure had made almost inevitable were remedied. No rough weather was experienced either on the first or latter part of the voyage, and although all light had to be shielded at night, owing to the danger of raiding cruisers (the "Karlsruhe" and "Konigsberg" had not yet been destroyed) no great discomfort was caused, and the ships were not overcrowded. The "Ayrshire" was a slow boat and was often from 50 to 150 miles in rear of the rest of the fleet, whose only escort was Submarine A.E.2, afterwards lost in the Dardanelles. The routine on board consisted chiefly of "Stables" and exercising horses round the decks, which had been covered with ashes, sand, etc. Some musketry and rifle exercises were also given, officers' classes were held, and there was instruction in sword exercises.

Colombo was a port of call, but no shore leave was granted, though a few men broke ship. Aden was reached towards the end of January, 1915, and a good passage was made up the Red Sea and Suez Canal towards Port Said. The fleet passed through the Canal, which was then being subjected to the first Turkish attack. The chart and wheel houses on all the ships were heavily sand-bagged. The defences of the Canal could be very plainly seen; they were manned to a great extent by Indian Troops. On one or two occasions cavalry were observed galloping forward, evidently to meet the Turkish attack. Port Said was reached on the 30th, and the day was spent there coaling. No general shore leave was granted, though again a few men broke ship. On the following day the voyage to Alexandria was resumed. This port was made on the morning of February 1st, and without delay disembarkation commenced.

CHAPTER II.

EGYPT.

THE first train left Alexandria Docks at 5 p.m. in charge of Captain Richardson. Detraining of the men and horses was quickly effected at Cairo Railway Station, and guides were provided to lead the parties to the camp site at Maadi, eight miles distant. Owing to the state of the horses' legs after the long sea voyage, all men were compelled to walk. They, like the horses, were not in condition for strenuous work, and the march was exhausting. Maadi was reached about 3 a.m. on February 2nd, and after watering the horses and picqueting them, the men lay down and slept where they were. The other Squadrons followed on succeeding days, and had practically the same experience.

The camp at Maadi, that pleasant little English suburb of Cairo, had just been vacated by the 1st Light Horse Brigade, so that horse troughs and other fixtures of a permanent camp were there. No time was lost in settling down, and training was commenced, though for a fortnight no mounted work was done owing to the risk of serious leg breakdowns among the horses. Instruction in musketry, rifle exercises, marching, troop and squadron drill dismounted was constantly given, and a proper syllabus of training was adhered to every week. Later on this training was carried out under the direction of Indian Army officers, under orders of the General Staff of the Australian and New Zealand Army Corps, superintended by Major-Generals Walker and Spens.

Lieut.-General Sir W. Birdwood, commanding A. and N.Z.A.C., inspected the camp and horses on February 6th, and all officers were introduced to him. At Church Parade on Sunday, February 14th, General Maxwell (C.-in-C. in Egypt) and General Birdwood were present and inspected the Brigade at a March past. Mounted training was commenced on the 15th, and Lieut.-Colonel Arnott personally supervised it. He insisted upon all movements being carried out with dash and smartness, and a good foundation was laid for the cavalry work required in the future.

Of the lighter side of Egypt something may be said. Cairo of 1914-15 was a very different city from the Cairo of the later years of the war, after British Military regulations had purged it. It is always a city of light and colour, with a charm and fascination hard to describe. Outside the European quarter of the great hotels and business houses it is meanly built with narrow streets and bazaars that are often unspeakably dirty.

These bazaars are rich in beautiful things, from inlaid brass to wonderful old Persian rugs; there is also plenty of shoddy stuff, possibly made in Birmingham and Manchester to entrap the unwary tourist.

So-called music and dance halls abounded, and contributed greatly to the unhealthy and feverish gaiety of the city. There were numerous places and objects of the utmost interest to be visited, but, from a social point of view, as far as the average trooper was concerned, there were few possibilities, and it cannot be denied that, owing to the lack of these, men sought pleasure in undesirable quarters.

Although the training and camp work were hard and constant, leave was easy to obtain, and the streets of the city, especially on Saturday nights, were crowded with soldiers, mostly Australians, though Lancashire Territorials were also numerous. Almost at once it was found necessary to limit the spending powers of the Australian soldier, and a special Egyptian drawing allowance was authorised; this prevented extravagance and also, perhaps, the purchasing of many presents for the people at home.

Lieut.-Colonel J. D. Richardson, D.S.O., Order of the Nile, 3rd Class.
Temporarily commanded 7th Light Horse, August, 1916, to November, 1916;
Brigade Major, 2nd Light Horse Brigade, June, 1917, to September, 1918;
C.O. 7th Light Horse, September, 1918.

(Top)—Watering Horses, Hebron Road Camp.
(Middle)—No. 3 Gun, 7th Battery, at Anzac. Members of the 7th L.H. who occupied the trenches right under this gun will remember it!
(Bottom)—Watering Horses at Ancient Wells at Katia. Capt. Easterbrook supervising.

(Top)—"Orangie, beeg ones—veery good, veery nice!" Ma'adi, December, 1915.
(Bottom)—Friendly (!) Arabs east of Jordan, 1st Amman Stunt.

(Top)—Crossing Wadi on way back from a day's swimming to Wadi Hanein.
(Middle)—Camels Unloading Berseen in the Horses' Lines at Ma'adi, 1915.
(Bottom)—"B" Sqdn. Horses. Halt at Romani en route Nabit to Hill 70, October, 1916.

General conduct and discipline, when allowance is made for the environment and new conditions, were excellent, and when the men were handled by their own officers there were very few really serious breaches of discipline.

Many persons have been ready to criticise the behaviour of the Australian troops in Egypt. These good souls have never even tried to understand the men or their home life, so different from that of manufacturing cities in England and peaceful farming villages of the Shires. Do the critics forget that these high-spirited men made "The Landing" a glory forever, and carried forlorn hopes to victory on many other fields when other troops might reasonably have failed? There were, certainly, a few undesirables, but they were soon sent back to Australia. After the first flush of excitement men settled down to their work, and the wheels of the great Army machine began to run smoothly.

On March 8th the whole Brigade, in marching order, was inspected by Generals Birdwood and Walker. A small tactical scheme was given, but was not particularly well carried out. From this date more attention was given to Squadron and Regimental schemes in training. Many of these proved interesting, and gave excellent opportunities for officers to gain experience in handling their men and making dispositions for attack or defence. The country worked over was generally close to Napoleon's Old Fort, east of Tura, and gave firm going for the horses, while the broken and undulating nature of the country made it almost ideal as a training ground for mounted troops. There was no lack of good horsemanship in the Regiment, but many of the horses soon proved unsuitable, and had to be cast and replaced by others of a more serviceable type.

Manœuvres with the 1st Light Horse Brigade were participated in on the 23rd. The 1st Light Horse Brigade made an attack on our camp area, from the direction of the Mokattam Hills, and in the action that followed the Regiment which was guarding the right flank carried out the duty required in a satisfactory manner. The training was continued, and soon a great improvement in efficiency was noticeable, though, as in all operations in which rifle or shell-fire is lacking, there was a tendency to do things which would not be considered for a moment in the actual presence of the enemy.

Early in April General Birdwood was present at a Regimental scheme which failed in its objective, and he was critical as regards some of the leading. From the beginning of this month great attention was given to the work of bringing the equipment, clothing and interior economy of the Regiment generally up to the highest standard, as it was felt that ere long orders would be received for active service.

The health of the men in general was good. Some undesirables were shipped back to Australia for discharge; but, on the whole, the discipline and morale were excellent. Lieutenant Maclean, who had been ill on the voyage over, was evacuated to hospital at Heliopolis, and from there was eventually sent to England. Lieutenant Jackson, in charge of the 1st Reinforcement, took his place. During the stay at Maadi, 2nd Lieutenants Howard and Straker arrived with reinforcements, but the former was almost immediately evacuated to hospital, and from there was invalided back to Australia.

Towards the end of April news of the heroic landing at Anzac and Cape Helles was received, and the Brigadier called a conference of C.O.s on May 1st, with a view to offering the services of the Brigade, dismounted. There was a natural disinclination to leaving the horses, but as the situation at Anzac was believed to be serious, the Brigadier forwarded a written request that the Brigade should proceed as a dismounted unit to the assistance of the 1st Infantry Division, whose casualties had been severe.

Several Brigade route marches to Helouan had tested the men and horses. During one of these marches on May 7th orders were received to return at once and prepare for immediate embarkation for the front. All haste was made with preparations. Equipment for dismounted service was issued, and all men were re-examined medically.

The first units of the Brigade to move were the Machine Gun Sections, which were brigaded, and Captain Hyman, of "B" Squadron, was placed in command, Lieutenant Thorne having the Section belonging to our Regiment. They left Maadi on the 9th and reached Anzac in time to help beat off the great Turkish attack on the 19th.

On May 10th orders were received that the Brigade would move out, dismounted, on the 15th, leaving a small percentage of men to take charge of the horses, which were now housed in open stables, the summer heat being severe. Captain de Low was detailed to take charge of the men and horses of the 7th Regiment. On May 15th, at 7 p.m., entrainment took place from Maadi, and the Brigade marched from Bab El Louk to Cairo main station. Alexandria was reached after an uneventful journey, and the Brigade embarked on H.M.T. "Lutzow," a captured German ship. The Regiment embarked with a strength of 20 officers, including attached, and 433 other ranks.

CHAPTER III.

ANZAC.

THE "Lutzow" sailed at 4 p.m. The voyage was uneventful up to the night of the 17th, when flashes from the guns at Cape Helles could be plainly seen. On the following day we anchored in the open roadstead at Helles. Submarines had not hitherto appeared in the Mediterranean, but destroyers, circling round the battleships and transports at anchor, kept a careful lookout. The shelling of the beaches by enemy guns was plainly visible, and this and the flights of our aeroplanes coming from Tenedos were watched with great interest. Some excitement was caused by the "Lutzow" dragging her anchor, sidling down on a French ship close by, and raking off a good deal of deck hamper.

On May 19th the ship was ordered to disembark the Brigade at Anzac Cove. Leaving Cape Helles at 5 p.m., she reached her distination at 6.30 p.m. News of the wounding of Major-General Bridges, G.O.C., 1st Infantry Division, was received, and it soon became evident that the Turks had been making a determined attack, as the gun and rifle fire was intense. The ship anchored for the night, and after midday on the 20th disembarkation commenced. First we boarded the fleet-sweepers "Clacton" and "Reindeer," then barges which were towed by naval picket boats, about half a mile from the shore. The operation was shelled by the enemy guns, particularly from the direction of Anafarta, and the guns of the "Clacton" opened in reply. There were, however, no casualties in the Regiment. After landing, sites for dug-outs were allotted, those given to the 7th Regiment being behind a low hill entering into "Shrapnel Gully"—the name of this place was Death Gully.

A rear party was left on the beach under Major Onslow, to take charge of regimental baggage. The remainder of the Regiment, burdened with packs and equipment, marched in single file along a track, afterwards known to be most dangerous, without sustaining a casualty, or indeed, without a shot being fired at them, and commenced to dig in without delay. After we had been there for about half an hour, the enemy commenced to shell the place and one or two men were hit. Gun and rifle fire on both sides was sustained during the whole night, and made sleep almost impossible. Batteries were located on either side of our position, and the flashes and reports of their guns drew the fire of many enemy guns; a number of shells burst close to our dug-outs. During the night orders were received to be ready to support the Infantry, as an enemy attack was considered imminent, and our place of assembly was given as "the hill in front." It was well that we were not required, as only the vaguest ideas were held as to front-line positions, and any attempt to support on our part might have caused us to blunder into a very ugly place.

The Regiment remained in this place until the 22nd, when the squadrons were divided up among units of the 3rd Infantry Brigade on the right flank in order to give the men of that Brigade a better opportunity for rest. "A" Squadron went to the extreme right position and was placed under the command of C.O., 9th Infantry Battalion, "B" Squadron to the 10th and "C" to the 11th.

A short description of Anzac, particularly of the right flank, which eventually became our home until the evacuation, will be fitting here. Anzac Cove, the original landing place, is a pleasant little sandy beach from which the hill system of Sari Bair rises very steeply in scrub-covered slopes intersected by many valleys and gullies. This system culminates about three miles north-east in the height of Chunuk Bair, or 971, as it was more generally known, which commands a most extensive view of the Dardanelles and of the roads leading to Maidos, Gallipoli and Cape Helles. This hill was one of the main objectives of the Suvla Bay landing in August, and some New Zealanders are believed to have almost reached its summit and to have seen the blue waters of the Straits and the stream of traffic on the military roads along which the Turk was hurrying up his reinforcements.

The intervening country between 971 and the beach, especially on the left flank in the vicinity of what is marked on the map as Fisherman's Hut, is distorted and rugged. One feature, known as the Sphinx, is a high clay pinnacle falling sheer almost to the beach level; water-torn ravines of great depth cut into its sides, while the western slope of nearly all the heights close by are precipitous and most difficult to climb. Further north, however, the hills recede and the Suvla Bay Plain commences. On the edge of this was the extreme left flank of Anzac, in the lower hills known as No. 1, 2 and 3 Outposts.

From 971 to the right flank the terrain is less uneven, though valleys and ravines are numerous and difficult. The ground, however, falls without interruption until practically the beach level is reached in the vicinity of the bluff headland of Gaba Tepe. To the south and south-west undulating country opens up and a plain, which extends on a narrowing frontage round the northern slopes of the Kilid Bahr Plateau, reaches Maidos, on the Straits. The great hill mass of this plateau, with its highest point of 703, makes a great rampart, which shields the forts on its eastern side from attack from almost any direction; it loomed in front of us on the right flank in rugged grandeur at a distance of about three miles. The undulating country to the south is covered with low scrub and dwarf oak trees (the famous Olive Grove and the lair of "Beachy Bill," afterwards found to be at least a battery, and not one gun), which extends right down to Cape Helles. The gently rising hill of Achi Baba, about a mile east of the village of Krithia, alone rises to any great extent above the surrounding country.

Following the beach from Anzac Cove to the southward for about 500 yards, one meets the opening to the famous Shrapnel Valley, fairly wide here, but narrowing and forking often as it runs north-east to its watershed at the equally famous Pope's Hill and Quinn's Post. Walker's Ridge is a high plateau to the north of this valley. Continuing south along the beach for 400 yards, one comes to a spot where it is narrowed by almost sheer low cliffs; this is Casualty Corner, and a water-torn ravine cutting deeply into the hillsides runs for some distance north-east. The ground rises steeply from this ravine to the south and south-east. Upon the crown of the ridge were situated the first front-line trenches on the right flank. A small and more level piece of ground just in rear of these which had been recently cultivated was known as Shell Green. From the site of the trenches on the heights the ground falls steeply to the beach, which was here held by a sandbag barricade with wire entanglements. The spot, known as Beach Post, is a little more than 2,000 yards from Gaba Tepe.

The trenches above Shell Green followed practically the same ridge north-west by Lone Pine, Courtney's Post, Johnson's Jolly Bloody Angle and others, until Pope's Hill, at the head of Shrapnel Valley, was reached. The Turkish Line opposite us, on the extreme right flank, was thrown far back to the solid bulwark of Gaba Tepe, as the fire of the warships prevented the occupation of the intervening and more level ground. From Gaba Tepe their positions ran north-east to meet our line, following the left bank of the deep wadi or watercourse just to the north of Gaba Tepe. Their trenches turned sharply northward to within long bombing range of ours in the vicinity of Lone Pine; but in the early days the nearest enemy position on the right sector was at least 300 yards away.

Out at sea lay the hospital ships and transports, with battleships in false security at anchor, and the ever-active patrol of destroyers circling round. Picket boats, horse boats, barges and trawlers constantly plying between hospital ships or transports and the shore made a scene of great activity. And further out were Imbros and Samo-Thrace rising from the beautiful blue Ægean in imposing grandeur. In front of all our trenches in "No Man's Land" lay thousands of Turkish dead. Most of these men had been killed during the great Turkish attack of May 19th, when the desperate effort to drive us into the sea failed. The gruesome sight undoubtedly affected the morale of the enemy.

CHAPTER IV.

ANZAC.—SETTLING DOWN.

THE sandwiching of the squadrons among the tried battalions of the Infantry was a sound procedure and soon enabled our men to learn everything that was known of trench warfare without paying too dearly. It also permitted a large number of men of the Infantry to rest. The digging of new trenches, especially on the right flank, running down to the sea where "A" Squadron was situated, and the strengthening and improvement of the old ones, went on unceasingly. The rifle fire was almost continuous, occasionally swelling into a roar, and the enemy snipers were very dangerous; all the trenches were heavily shelled at intervals. In spite of the excellent protection, which most of the trenches afforded, and the care taken to avoid enemy sniping, a few casualties occurred almost daily.

It was perhaps more dangerous in rear and toward the beach than actually in the trenches, as the notorious "Beachy Bill" (enemy field guns firing from the Olive Grove) levied a heavy toll from Casualty Corner, just below our positions to well beyond the landing piers. What was probably a single-shot machine gun, firing at long range, was very accurate at sniping any men bathing near our Beach Post, and even as far as Hell Spit; many of our ration and water carrying parties suffered from this. Great care had to be taken in looking over the top of the trenches; indeed, the only safe way was to use the periscopes, and these often had bullets put through them. Fortunately, the enemy seldom fired his guns at night, though on one occasion, after a night raid by the 9th Battalion on the Twin Trenches, he savagely bombarded the lines on the extreme right held by "A" Squadron. The shelling began before day-break and continued for about an hour; only one of our men was wounded, though the 9th Battalion had about a dozen casualties.

Rations, as a rule, were brought up by mules of the Indian Transport Service; but water parties had to be detailed from the units themselves and had to seize their opportunity of getting water from whatever well seemed to have a supply. Long hours had often to be waited to obtain it, and though water was brought in barges and fresh wells were sunk, the supply was inadequate right up to the time of the evacuation.

On May 24th an armistice, to enable the dead to be buried, was arranged. From 7 a.m. until 4 p.m. hostilities ceased, and the silence was a great relief. A number of men from the Regiment were employed in gathering up arms and burying our dead in "No Man's Land"; dead Turks were carried to a dividing line and handed over to their comrades, while the enemy brought our dead to us in the same manner. Any rifles found were handed over to their owners minus the bolts. The slaughter among the Turks during their great attack on May 19th was even more clearly seen, and there is no doubt that the failure greatly disheartened them and prevented a similar attack on the same scale taking place again at Anzac. Shortly after 4 p.m. gun and rifle fire began again from both sides.

We witnessed on the 25th the sinking of the battleship "Triumph" by a German submarine; the destroyers racing to her assistance from every quarter, smothered in smoke and foam, made a picture that will not be forgotten. Next day news was received that the "Majestic" also had been torpedoed near Cape Helles. Henceforward battleships appeared only at intervals, and well escorted; they did not lie anchored off the roadstead as hitherto, and the task of guarding our flanks on the beaches was entrusted to destroyers, which most efficiently performed their duty. The black mass of the destroyer on the right flank on a dark night, with her searchlights flashing every now and then towards the Twin Trenches or Balkan Gun Pits, and her guns throwing high-explosive into enemy back areas, was always a most comforting sight.

On the 30th the Turks mined Quinn's Post, and after the explosion captured some trenches, which were immediately recaptured by an infantry bayonet charge. Up to the end of the month the Regiment had sustained 45 casualties.

The 5th Regiment relieved the 7th on May 31st, and we withdrew to dug-outs in Rest (White's) Gully. This was not a good place, as a gun from the direction of 971 fired shrapnel into it at intervals during the day, and numerous casualties resulted. A period of "rest" at Anzac always meant that the unit supplied large working parties for trench digging and road making, so that really conditions were better in the front line. An unfortunate accident, the fall of a dug-out wall, resulted in the death of three men of "B" Squadron who were asleep in it at the time. Lieutenant A. K. Maney-Lake was severely wounded in the foot at night by a rifle bullet fired at long range.

On June 18th a return was made to the line on the right flank, as the sector from the sea to what became known as Tasmania Post exclusive, and the positions in rear was handed over permanently to the 2nd Light Horse Brigade. The 5th Regiment held from the Beach Post to where the new sap ran out to Chatham's Post (inclusive), the 6th Regiment from the new sap to within about 50 yards of the Gun Road, and the 7th Regiment from that place to just in rear of Tasmania Post. The Regimental Machine Gun Section, which had been split up among other units, now rejoined. The trenches taken over were the old ones belonging to the 3rd Infantry Brigade. They were deep and well provided with loopholes, but were apt to crumble and fall in badly, if shelled, or if the two field guns of Brown's Battery, which had positions in them, opened fire. The sub-sector held by the Regiment was divided between the Squadrons, "C" being on the right, then "B" and "A" linking up with the Infantry, who were just then building Tasmania Post on Holly Spur, a low ridge about 300 yards in front. In addition to the front-line trenches, a line, carefully screened, was tunnelled about 20 yards in front, to hold riflemen and bombers to surprise an enemy attack. In rear, under the steep ridge, were R.H.Q., Reserve dug-outs, kitchens, latrines, etc.; but this area could be easily searched by the enemy's guns, and many casualties occurred there. It was also a dangerous spot for rifle bullet "overs" fired from Lone Pine. Patrols were sent out from the front line at night to watch for any enemy movement; but, as a rule, the Turk displayed very little patrol activity on our immediate front.

Casualties for the week ending June 20th were one O.R. killed, 11 O.R.s wounded The effective strength was now 19 Officers and 478 O.R.s, as some reinforcements had arrived. Many of these were, however, employed on well-sinking duties, and strong parties had constantly to be detailed for new trench work. The water-fatigue work became increasingly wearisome and disappointing. One water bottle was the allowance for each man for 24 hours, so that all bathing and washing of clothes had to be done off the beach, a very dangerous place, as "Beachy Bill" had all ranges exactly.

On June 25th General Birdwood and Admiral de Robeck visited the trenches, and on the 27th Sir Ian Hamilton, Commander-in-Chief, made an inspection. Next day—the well-remembered June 28th—the Regiment had its first big operation. Seventy men under Captain Richardson, with Lieutenants Gilchrist and Bird as Troop Leaders, were ordered to move down Poppy Valley beyond the Ruined Hut and to engage the Echelon Trenches, getting in touch with the 5th Regiment on the right and the 9th Battalion on the left, who were making a similar demonstration. No attempt was to be made to storm the trenches, and the whole operation was simply to prevent the enemy taking troops from Anzac to reinforce Cape Helles, where a big attack was proceeding. As much firing as possible was to take place, and everything to be done to make the enemy think that a serious movement against his left flank was developing.

No time was lost in assembling the party, though the notice given was short. Moving out at 12.30 p.m. through the Infantry trenches and their sap in rear of Tasmania Post, the men filed quietly down Holly Gully into Poppy Valley without a shot being fired against them, though they came into plain enemy view from both the Echelon and Boomerang Trenches, after passing the Ruined Hut. Possibly the enemy sentries were drowsy, or taking their afternoon siesta, for the target offered was unavoidably a good one. Lieutenant Gilchrist, with his troop, was detailed to watch the left flank of the party, on what was afterwards Ryrie's Post, and the remainder moved forward to within about 200 yards of the Echelon Trenches, which were on the opposite side of the valley. No further progress towards these could be made without being greatly exposed or without coming under enfilade fire from Pine Ridge and partly from Boomerang Trench, so the men were directed to take cover in some shallow watercourses, which provided rough trenches. The 5th Regiment was observed shortly afterwards moving along the spine of the ridge from Chatham's Post towards the Balkan Gun Pits, led by an officer in white breeches. The enemy had now awakened, and the volume of fire gradually swelled to a continuous roar as the afternoon progressed.

As the 9th Battalion, on our left, had got into position, as well as the 5th Regiment, our men commenced to fire, making Echelon Trenches their target, and also some of the Turkish works on Pine Ridge. Casualties soon occurred, and it was seen that the 5th Regiment was suffering severely, and any of their men who appeared on our side of the ridge were instantly struck down by bullets from machine guns firing from the direction of Sniper's Ridge or perhaps from a spur of Pine Ridge. The shrapnel fire became very severe, and many of the shells burst just over the heads of our party in Poppy Valley, to spray the 5th Regiment further on. On the other hand, our fire easily dominated the Echelon Trenches and caused the Turks to reinforce heavily. These reinforcements, in coming up, were brought under our rifle fire, while machine guns and the field guns in the trenches also harried them considerably.

Early in the afternoon Lieutenant Gilchrist was slightly wounded, but carried on directing the fire of his troop. Shortly afterwards he was wounded again badly, and was with difficulty carried out of action. He died on board a hospital ship next day, and the Regiment lost a very gallant officer. Four men had been killed, including two stretcher-bearers (Campbell and Dobbie), and towards the end of the afternoon there were more than 20 wounded. The more serious cases were carried out of the firing line, not without considerable difficuty, and the dead, with one exception, were eventually brought in.

The object of the demonstration (making the Turks retain their troops at Anzac) had been attained. They became afraid, too, of a blow on their left flank, as large bodies were observed massing behind Lone Pine. The 5th Regiment was ordered to withdraw at 4.30 p.m., and shortly aftrwards Lieut.-Colonel Arnott ordered the party of the 7th Regiment in Poppy Valley to return to the trenches. The casualties for this action were heavy to all the troops engaged, and ours would undoubtedly have been even more severe but for the watercourses in which cover was taken.

On the following day a gallant effort was made by Sergeant Teschner and Trooper Kelly to recover the one body which it had been found impossible to bring in. These two men made their way quietly through the scrub, and actually reached the body in full view close to the Turkish trenches. They recovered the dead man's identity disc and personal effects, but were unable to do more, as a machine gun was turned on them.

Etmaler looking North.

Watering from Wells in Katia Hod. (General Onslow sitting on stump.)

CHAPTER V.

RYRIE'S POST.

IT was decided, towards the end of June, to obtain more ground, and a clean area, by occupying the ridge in front, known as Holly Spur. Tunnels and saps were commenced, and a base line (afterwards the support line) for working saps forward to a new front line, was laid out. Work was started on July 2nd, parties lying in the scrub in front to protect the men who were working. These covering parties were often shelled, and machine guns were turned on them at the slightest movement. Fortunately, few casualties were sustained. The strain was greatest at night, when the enemy fired almost incessantly. Bullets "zipped" over the heads of men lying in small depressions of the ground, and the sound of the enemy's rifle bolts was plainly heard. At any moment a charge or raid might come, and few men slept at night when on this duty.

The tunnelling and digging work was very exhausting for the men, whose health was becoming bad. The rations of bully beef and biscuit were unappetising in the hot weather, and as many men were unable to eat properly, they soon became very weak and unfitted for heavy work. Dysentery was prevalent. It was vital, however, that the work should be proceeded with, and gradually a firing line (later support line) was built up, well traversed, with good, roomy firing "possies," and connected to the old lines with a sap and tunnel.

Water carrying from the beach and the wells was at this time and later a great tax on the health and rest of the men, as mostly they had to go away at night, and sometimes would not return until fairly late on the next day. One remembers a typical mid-day meal at Anzac with feelings of disgust. The menu would consist of bully beef (dripping out of the tin on account of the heat), hard biscuits with plum or apricot jam, and tea without milk, brewed in a dixie in which a bully beef stew had been made. Over all hovered big green flies. There was little or no change in the food in those early days, though later it improved somewhat.

The enemy, on our front, showed little activity during the early part of the month, though spasmodic shelling of our new and old positions was occasionally very heavy and produced casualties, mostly with the first two or three shells, before the men had entered their trenches or dug-outs. Various demonstrations on our part, such as bursts of fire, sending up flares at night, cheering, etc., in order to make him expend ammunition, although at first successful, eventually drew hardly any response from the enemy. Towards the middle of the month our sappers commenced to push three saps to the forward slope of Holly Spur, and rather more forward than Tasmania Post, the Infantry position on our left. These were gradually linked up into a good firing line, having roomy firing bays with deep communication trenches in rear, and dug-outs tunnelled in these, for men not on duty. The new support line had been occupied on the 10th. This fact appeared to make the enemy very jumpy, for in the early part of the night he would fire almost continuously, making things very awkward for covering parties and sappers. The new forward line, with supports and dug-outs on Holly Spur, now known as Ryrie's Post, was occupied on the 19th. This increased the enemy nervousness, and he commenced feverishly to strengthen his trenches on Pine Ridge and secretly to make a firing line low on Holly Spur, about 30 yards from our front, which afterwards became known as the Turkish Despair Trench.

Bomb-throwing by both sides increased greatly, and the casualties in proportion.

The true importance and strength of the new enemy trench was discovered by a patrol under Sergeant Walker, which, just after "Standown" one morning, jumped over our trenches and ran down to the enemy line. Many shots were exchanged, but the Turks were very rattled, and failed to hit any member of the patrol, which returned, after observing that the enemy trench was about half dug, and seemed to be full of men.

Great preparations for enemy raids were now made in our line and plentiful supplies of jam-tin bombs were stored in the firing "possies," with slow matches burning in a socket all night. Wire-netting screens were also put up in the most dangerous places to prevent bombs from falling in the trenches, and efforts were made to have barbed wire run out in front. These were not very successful at first, as at night almost a continuous fire was kept up, and no movement was possible in the day. However, loose wire was thrown over and tangled in the scrub, forming a fair obstacle; later, again, cheveaux de frise or "knife-rests," as they were known, were pushed over.

A demonstration on July 12th to prevent the enemy reinforcing Cape Helles against an attack, took the form of parties of men jumping over the back trenches and shouting and running forward as if to storm the enemy's position. Parties from the front trenches were also well pushed forward, especially by the 6th Regiment on Holly Spur. Lieutenant Bird and Warrant-Officer Easterbrook led the party from the 7th Regiment, which was fortunate in suffering only five casualties (one man killed and four wounded), as the enemy's machine guns soon swept the whole of our front and his shell fire became intense. The manœuvre was successful. The whole of our sub-sector was very heavily shelled for about two hours and the demonstration undoubtedly prevented the sending away of any troops.

Towards the end of the month, the strength of the Regiment had been seriously reduced by casualties and sickness, and it was difficult for two squadrons to hold the front line position; men often had to be in the firing bays, keeping watch for two and three nights in succession. The casualties among the officers had become serious. Lieut.-Colonel Arnott was slightly wounded; Captain Richardson, Lieutenants Board, Bice, Hession and Barton were wounded and evacuated to hospital, and Major Onslow was evacuated, sick. On the 27th, just before daylight, Lieutenant Thorne was shot through the forehead and killed instantly. This officer was a Duntroon graduate with every promise of a brilliant career.

The enemy's shelling greatly increased towards the end of the month, and trenches and dugouts had to be deepened further to minimise casualties. On the 31st, the 3rd Infantry Brigade captured the trench immediately in front of Tasmania Post, and consolidated and retained it under heavy fire. This was afterwards known as Leane's Trench, and was joined up with our front line. The Regiment and the other units of the Brigade co-operated in making a demonstration to help this operation.

On July 28th the 4th Light Horse Regiment was attached to the 2nd Light Horse Brigade, and the working parties supplied by this Regiment helped greatly to give our men some badly needed rest. With the use of the periscope rifle, and by careful observation and sniping, practically all the enemy snipers had now been cleared from our front line, and their rifle fire was, as a rule, badly aimed and lacking in control.

On July 30th and 31st enemy aeroplanes dropped bombs, which did no damage in our sector. On the 31st Lieut.-Colonel Harris, commanding 5th Light Horse Regiment, was killed during another demonstration, made to prevent enemy reinforcements being sent to Cape Helles. A heavy shelling of our line resulted from this demonstration, and henceforth the enemy artillery showed greatly increased activity against our front.

The positions held by the Regiment and the Brigade, now that Ryrie's Post (as the new works of Holly Spur were named) had been completed and manned, were as follows:

5th Light Horse Regiment, from Beach Post to just beyond where the sap running from Chatham's Post joined the old front line trenches, and with the forward redoubt on Chatham's Post, and later the advance work of Wilson's Lookout.

6th Light Horse Regiment, from Chatham's Post, exclusive, across Poppy Valley, along the new trenches on Holly Spur, to No. 6 Sap, exclusive.

7th Light Horse Regiment, from No. 6 Sap to Tasmania Post, exclusive.

The front line trenches, with numerous saps running back to the strong support line, had now their reserve dugouts, R.H.Q., kitchens, &c., just in rear in Holly Gully, but were linked up with the former front line by saps and tunnels; and this old front line was considered as the reserve position. Work was continually pushed forward, in deepening and improving the trenches in every way, and as it was believed that the enemy had commenced mining, counter measures were taken. Special parties of tunnellers and sappers were detailed, and did excellent work blowing in enemy tunnels on several occasions. An effort was also made to obtain water in Holly Gully by sinking a deep well, and thus to obviate the great fatigue experienced by the water parties; but this attempt, unfortunately, met with no success.

On August 8th Lieut.-Colonel Arnott was evacuated to hospital sick; Lieutenant Stevenson and Capt.-Chaplain Miller were sent away very ill about the same time. Major Windeyer assumed temporary command of the Regiment. The Regiment was now very weak and most of the remaining officers and men were greatly reduced in strength; many who should have been in hospital, had to remain, otherwise we could not have held our position. At the end of July, however, the Regiment was taken out of the trenches and placed in rest dug-outs on the steep slope running down to the beach, just west of B.H.Q. To replace casualties and evacuations to hospital, the following N.C.O.'s had been granted commissions:—Warrant-Officer Easterbrook, Squadron Sergeant-Major Bailey, Squadron Sergeant-Major Broadly, Sergeants Jarman, Suttor and Ducker. Officers and men in great numbers had been evacuated to hospital sick or wounded, and those remaining were often in a most wretched condition with diarrhœa or dysentery. Some were so weak that they could hardly stagger to their places in the firing line, and men fainted where they stood at "Stand to" in the morning, after a long night of watching. The sappers and tunnellers were given special conditions, otherwise their work could not have been performed. These men, however, did magnificiently, often upon a scanty ration and insufficient water.

Evening at Anzac was, as a rule, a period of peace and quiet. Except for the occasional chatter of a machine gun, or a stray rifle shot from the direction of Lone Pine, all was still. The sun went down in a blaze of glory behind Imbros and Samothrace. For a brief period there were no fatigues. Men crawled from their dug-outs and looked longingly towards the lights of the hospital ships, which meant comfort and good food, and, above all, real rest, such as they had not experienced since landing. The stars, with the Great Bear showing instead of the Cross, appeared in a sky of the same intense blue as the sea; all was quiet and beautiful. To break the spell a destroyer's searchlight would flash towards the Twin Trenches, and with a shattering roar her guns would open upon some Turkish back area—and the evening calm would be gone—one peaceful hour alone in all the twenty-four.

CHAPTER VI.

ANZAC. LAST PHASE.

THE Suvla Bay landing and our attack from Anzac on Lone Pine and Walker's Ridge took place at the end of the first week in August. The 1st Infantry Brigade, by a magnificent charge, took the strongly held trenches at the former place, but sustained heavy casualties, and had to be relieved almost at once by the 2nd Infantry Brigade, which was subjected to a constant succession of counter attacks and bombing raids.

Although our Brigade did not actually participate in these attacks, we had everything in readiness had a break through occurred. Our final objective was to be Gaba Tepe, but orders were received at the last moment not to move. On August 9th, six officers and 150 men (a mixed party of "A" and "B" Squadrons) were sent up to Lone Pine to reinforce the infantry, whose casualties were very severe. Portion of the firing line was given over to our men and parties were engaged in burying the dead of both sides in the old trenches. The enemy bombarded the whole position, savagely and incessantly, and as the trenches in some places were only 10 yards or less away, bombing was also constant on both sides.

Men were detailed to be ready with old blankets or partly filled sandbags to smother the bombs before they burst. There was no rest, and enemy bayonet charges were momentarily expected. After remaining in this place for two days, the Squadron was relieved. However, until September 9th, turn had to be taken with other units of the Brigade in finding a squadron to help garrison Lone Pine, the term generally coming every fourth day. The enemy's sniping at close ranges was very good here, and a periscope put up on a thin stick would often be cut in two by a bullet. Nearly all our casualties at this time occurred at Lone Pine. For conspicuous gallantry as a bomber, from August 6th to September 1st, Lance-Corporal F. P. Curran received the D.C.M. On one occasion he stopped a Turkish bombing attack single-handed. From September 4th to 6th he displayed the greatest bravery and skill, fully exposing himself regardless of all danger.

Major Onslow returned from hospital on the 20th and took over the command of the Regiment. The general health now was deplorable; each day from 30 to 50 men would be marked unfit for duty, but they could not be spared to be sent away. During the month Major Windeyer, Lieutenants Maddrell, Ducker and Suttor were evacuated to hospital. Lieutenant Bice returned from hospital on the 25th. In the last week of August, the 4th Light Horse Brigade landed, and the 12th Light Horse Regiment was sent to reinforce our Brigade; "B" Squadron of this Regiment was posted to the 7th Regiment for duty. This reinforcement helped greatly; it is difficult to imagine how the unavoidable regimental duties could have been carried on without this assistance.

From August 29th detachments of nearly squadron strength had to be sent to the Holly Spur trenches, coming under the orders of the C.O., 4th Light Horse Regiment, and being relieved daily by similar detachments. The Squadron to Lone Pine still had to be found every fourth day, and this place had become no more desirable, though our bombers and snipers were getting the upper hand of the Turk. From the beginning of September, however, this Squadron was made a composite one, by including a party from the 5th Regiment; but the men for this had now to be found daily.

The health had not improved and dysentery and jaundice were very common.

On September 10th, the old trenches on Holly Spur were again taken over, the 4th Regiment being relieved at 9.15 a.m. "A" and "B" Squadrons were put in the front line, with "C" Squadron in reserve. Captain Richardson returned from hospital early on the morning of the 10th, and was placed in command of "A" Squadron; Captain Hyman, who had been in charge, had been evacuated sick two days previously.

No time was lost in establishing marked superiority over the Turkish snipers, and we suffered few casualties now, except from shell-fire, which became more frequent and severe. General Walker made two inspections of the Holly Spur trenches, one on the 13th and the other on the 15th. The trenches on Ryrie's Post were now the show ones of Anzac, and parties of officers from other sections of the line were frequently taken over them.

On the 16th a new 5.9-inch howitzer, established somewhere in the Olive Grove, commenced to shell our positions. Four men of the 4th Light Horse Regiment, on our left, were killed by one shell, but there were no casualties in the 7th. On the following day the intermittent bombardment was continued, with more severity. In the afternoon Captain Richardson was again severely wounded, and a trooper was so badly hit by the same shell that he died later on the hospital ship. That night Captain Rupert Richardson and Lieutenant Buskin, of the 6th Light Horse Regiment, and three men, were killed by one shell from a 75 bursting on their parapet.

By the end of the month barbed wire in some form or other had been placed in front of all the trenches on Holly Spur. Nothing of much incident occurred during this period, though the enemy shelling increased a good deal. Great difficulty was now experienced in finding sufficient men to garrison the trenches and for ration and water fatigues, owing to the very heavy evacuations of sick to hospital. On the 23rd, Captain Fulton was evacuated sick, and Lieutenant Easterbrook and Captain Evans (M.O.) shortly afterwards. A steady drain of casualties of killed and wounded also greatly reduced the strength of the Regiment. Fortunately, on October 2nd Lieutenants Roberts and Brunton arrived from Maadi with 104 reinforcements. During October, the routine of trench warfare was almost without special incidents. Many minor demonstrations were made by sending up flares, by bursts of fire and sudden shelling to make the enemy uneasy, to cause him to keep his trenches fully manned, and to give him little rest. He responded by artillery bombardments of increasing severity, and it was evident that he was obtaining more guns and ammunition.

Days of perhaps more interest were those when the battleships "Agammemnon" and "Lord Nelson" came up, surrounded by destroyers, and shelled the Olive Grove and the enemy redoubts on the Kilid Bahr Plateau. "Beachy Bill's" shrapnel against the fighting tops of the warships was a very feeble response to the roar and burst of the great shells of the 12-inch guns. All efforts to exterminate "Beachy Bill" were, however, unsuccessful.

The weather, generally, was good, but preparations were made for the winter by improving and building extensive dug-outs. Canteen goods could now be obtained, with a good deal of difficulty, from Imbros. During the greater part of November, nothing unusual occurred, though parties were sent to help garrison Chatham's Post and Wilson's Lookout, where some lively bombing from both sides often took place. The enemy's "broomstick" bombs now became too familiar to us. Although quiet days came occasionally, as a rule the enemy fiercely bombarded some portion of our front. In one of these shellings Lieutenant Holdon, of the squadron of 12th Regiment attached, was killed. Our guns also were now very active, and fired a good deal in retaliation; more ammunition was available. During the month the operation known as "The Silent Stunt" took place. For several days not a shot was fired from a rifle along the whole line, no matter how fierce the enemy's fire became. This made him very uneasy, and in order to try and clear up the situation, a raiding party was sent against our trenches on the night of November 27th. The alarm was given in time, although the night was dark, and in spite of the attack being made in some strength, it was repulsed entirely by rifle fire. In the morning about 20 dead Turks lay in front of our trenches. Next day a great rain storm and blizzard took place, and although, owing to the high situation of the trenches, our men did not suffer so severely as the troops in the Suvla Bay area, the hardship was considerable. The snow gently covered the bodies in front of the trenches.

The weather now became very unsettled and remained so until the evacuation. For two or three days it would be beautifully fine, but cold at night; and then perhaps for a week a violent storm would rage, making conditions miserable beyond belief. Rations had to be husbanded, for the Anzac piers had been destroyed and it was impossible to land supplies. Firewood was scarce, barely sufficient for cooking purposes was available, and none for warming dug-outs. Old newspapers were considered valuable as fuel. The water supply became worse when the water lighters could not get to the pier. The expedient of collecting snow had to be adopted, but the quantity of water obtained in this way was almost negligible. The greater part of December was thus passed, and although nothing official was known, the general impression gained ground that it would not be long before the last of Anzac would be seen. Everything was done to deceive the Turk, and our shelling and rifle fire increased. The number and calibre of his guns had also greatly increased, and a few days before our departure the shells from the great Austrian Howitzers, specially sent to Gallipoli for our benefit, began to fall. Great secrecy was maintained until the last, but when the orders for evacuation were issued, the greatest care was taken to explain them to all ranks, so that no hitch would occur.

The evacuation commenced on December 18th. The Regiment was divided into three parties. "A" left at 6.30 p.m., "B" at 9 p.m. on the 19th, and "C," which was again sub-divided into three parties, "C1" (one officer and 9 other ranks) under Captain Willsallen (who had been transferred from the 12th Light Horse Regiment and appointed Adjutant), "C2" (one officer and 9 other ranks) under Captain Bice, and "C3" (one officer and 7 other ranks) under Lieutenant Easterbrook, at 2 a.m., 2.15 a.m. and 2.30 a.m., respectively, on the 20th. All these parties silently filed down to the beach, over tracks on which rice had been spread, to prevent the possibility of mistaking the way. Rifles and bombs timed to explode mechanically, as well as mines under Walker's Ridge and Quinn's Post, had been left to make the Turk think the trenches were occupied long after the parties had withdrawn. These ruses were most successful. No hitch occurred, and embarking quietly in trawlers, all the men, without a single casualty, were evacuated and shipped on transports, sailing at night time for Alexandria. It was most fortunate that the weather had been fine or it would have been impossible to carry out the evacuation as planned.

Alexandria was reached early on December 25th, and we disembarked in the afternoon. Trains commenced at 5 p.m. to move the Regiment to Cairo. A temporary camp site was allotted at Heliopolis. On the 28th the Regiment again moved to Maadi and took over the details camp and horses there. In spite of all the hardships endured and the need for proper rest, the situation did not permit of anything but rapid re-organisation.

Mounted drill was commenced on the 29th, and every effort was made quickly to restore the Regiment to efficiency as a mounted unit.

THE 7th LIGHT HORSE, 1914-1919.

PART II.

SINAI.

CHAPTER I.

MOUNTED WORK.

THE New Year, 1916, found the Regiment again back at Maadi, re-fitting and training, so that the exhaustion due to the Gallipoli Campaign might, as soon as possible, be overcome. There were, fortunately, plenty of reinforcements of a very good type available, and with these the strength of the Regiment was practically double that of the establishment. Physical exercises, mounted and dismounted drill, route marches to Helouan and back, and the ordinary regimental duties made up the routine for the month. On the 11th, 26 other ranks, who for various reasons had been left at Mudros, rejoined. Major Onslow, who had been promoted Lieut.-Colonel, was in command, as Lieut.-Colonel Arnott had not yet returned, and Captain Willsallen was Adjutant.

During February the training and equipping were intensified, and it was felt that the Brigade would not long be left outside the sphere of active operations. Outpost schemes were practised, special attention was paid to the manœuvring of led horses, and another route march was held. One remembers these route marches to Helouan as great events.

On February 25th, "A" and "B" Squadrons and the Machine-Gun Section were entrained, and left for Serapeum just north of the Bitter Lakes. "C" Squadron followed on the 26th. Officers and men, surplus to the establishment, and various details, were left under Lieutenant Maddrell at Maadi; these, later on, were moved to Tel El Kebir. Later still, they were shifted to Moascar to the "A" and "N.Z.T.C." and "D" Camp, formed there under Colonel Arnott, our former C.O. As soon as camp at Serapeum was made, the training was continued as at Maadi, more regimental work being carried out.

On April 4th a move to Salhia, on the edge of the Delta country, west of the Suez Canal, was commenced. This was our first long trek, and the first stage of the journey was to Ismailia, where bivouac was made for the night. Next day Salhia was reached and camp was pitched on the sandy desert, just outside the Palm Belt. The whole Mounted Division was now concentrated at Salhia, and training was continued, Brigade schemes often taking the places of the regimental and squadron operations hitherto carried out.

Salhia is a small native village, among palm groves and fertile fields, on the very edge of the desert of Sinai. It is the terminus of a branch line of the Egyptian State Railways, and is important as a base for any operations eastwards of the Suez Canal, from which it is separated by twenty-five miles of moderately firm desert sand. Napoleon used it as his base for the attack on Syria, and followed practically the same track across Sinai that we did 120 years later.

Twenty miles to the north of Salhia is San El Hagar, the ancient Tanis of the later Pharoahs, and possibly the Rameses of the Old Testament, one of the Cities of Bondage from which the Israelities took their departure. The fertile Delta country provides good supplies of forage for horses, and also camels, which now became essential for our transport. The limber and G.S. waggons had to be left out of any movement across the desert, and were eventually parked at Kantara, on the Canal, until the desert had been crossed.

The Anzac Mounted Division had now been formed. It consisted of the 1st, 2nd and 3rd Light Horse Brigades and the New Zealand Mounted Rifle Brigade, with the Royal Horse Artillery Brigade of the Inverness, Ayrshire and Somerset Batteries. Its composition was changed considerably later on; Major-General H. G. Chauvel was placed in command. On April 22nd, news of the Turkish advance against the Yeomanry at Quatia and Oghrantina having been received, the whole Division was ordered to move to Kantara with all speed. On the 23rd, the eventful march of the 2nd L.H. Brigade to Kantara, Dueidar and Romani was commenced. This march was a forced one, as it was considered probable that the enemy might follow up his blow, or failing that, that an opportunity might occur to strike him one in return. A difficult canal was passed just before reaching Kantara, with a few minor accidents. The narrow pontoon bridge over the Suez Canal was crossed, and after the long desert march a halt of two hours was made, the advance being then continued to Hill 70, eight miles from the Canal, which was reached at about 3 a.m. on the 24th. A rest of a few hours was allowed, and the column again moved on, reaching the railhead, since known as Anzac Siding, before night, and bivouacking there. All ranks were greatly tired, as were the horses, owing to the march across the heavy sand, but the stream of fugitives from the Yeomanry disaster at Quatia showed that the position was serious, and raised every man to his highest effort.

Early next morning the march to Romani was resumed, and the late Yeomanry camp, a scene of great confusion, was entered at 10 a.m. A strong outpost line was carefully placed that night, and strengthened later on by the erection of sangars and the digging of trenches. The water difficulty was rather acute, as there was barely enough for the animals of the Brigade; but new wells were sunk and soon yielded a sufficient supply. All desert water is, to an extent, saline. Fresh water for the men, later on, was brought on camels from Anzac Siding. On the 26th, a patrol under Lieutenant Snow was sent to Quatia, six miles east of Romani, to reconnoitre. Upon the battlefield they collected five wounded Yeomen and buried a number of dead. On the 27th, a strong patrol of the 6th L.H. Regiment was sent to Oghratina, four miles east of Quatia, where 32 men killed in the fight there were buried; some wounded were brought in.

From this time forward turn was taken with the 6th Regiment, which, with ourselves, formed the garrison of Romani, to send out patrols to Hill 110, Quatia, Hamisah, Errabah, Mahamadiya, and, occasionally, to Hod El Enna, towards Dueidar. The patrol to Quatia was usually of a squadron in strength, and one troop was then sent to the south to Hamisah. The 5th L.H. Regiment was stationed at Dueidar to watch the southern flank. The days were hot, but the water at Quatia and Hamisah was of a fair quality, and there was plenty of shade under the palm trees. At Hill 110 and Mahamadiya, a patrol meant a day in the sun without water, though the sea bathing at Mahamadiya compensated a good deal. No signs of the enemy were seen by these patrols, though a few Bedouins, who were perhaps spies on our movements, were brought in. As the days passed, efforts were made to strengthen the position at Romani and improve the camp site. On the 28th, Captain Richardson, who had been evacuated wounded from Anzac to England, rejoined and was placed in command of "B" Squadron.

The days passed uneventfully, though the strain of patrols, outposts and heat without abundance of water, was severe, but more strenuous days were ahead. The regimental roll of officers and the posting to squadrons at this time were as under.—

Headquarters.—C.O., Lieut.-Colonel G. M. Macarthur Onslow; 2nd in command, Major E. Windeyer; Adjutant, Captain T. L. Willsallen; Quartermaster, Captain Roberts; Machine Gun Officer, Lieutenant E. L. Zouch; R.M.O., Captain O'Hara; Chaplain, Lieutenant-Colonel Maitland Woods.

"A" Squadron.—Major L. Bice, Captain T. H. Bird, Lieutenants L. L. Williams, L. W. Davies (reinforcement), K. Suttor and A. Broadley.

"B" Squadron.—Captain J. D. Richardson, Captain C. C. Easterbrook, Lieutenants H. I. Wikner (reinforcement), H. O. C. Maddrell, P. V. Ryan (reinforcement), and D. R. Waddell (reinforcement).

"C" Squadron.—Major H. Suttor, Captain N. D. Barton, Lieutenants J. Dalton (reinforcement), G. Snow, T. Humphries and H. I. Johnson. Warrant-Officer Keene was R.S.M., and C. E. Holland R.Q.M.S.

Sergeants-Majors Newton, Spencer and Mitton were the S.S.M. of "A," "B" and "C" Squadrons respectively. Lieutenant Chapman was R.T.O. at Salhia, and when the railhead reached Romani he was transferred to that place. Later on he rejoined and was succeeded by Lieutenant Finlay, a reinforcement officer, who had been a N.C.O. in the 2nd Australian Field Artillery Brigade at Cape Helles, where he had received the D.C.M. for an act of extreme gallantry.

CHAPTER II.

THE DESERT OF SINAI.

THE desert of Sinai extends to the eastward from Kantara almost to the Egyptian frontier station of Rafa, where the soil is scantily grassed and firmer. A great deal of the sand is not as heavy to travel through, as might be supposed, though in drifts a horse would sink to the shoulder. It is of a whitish-yellow colour and very clean; stunted shrubs and rough herbage grow fairly plentifully from the coast to about fifteen miles inland, when the country takes on a more desolate and forbidding aspect, the sand dunes also increasing in size. The coastal area is undulating for the most part, with occasional giant sandhills, like our old friend Katib Gannit at Romani, standing up as land marks for many miles. The north-eastern sides of many of these are often almost precipitous, and frequently in the depression at the base, one finds a pleasant grove of date palms with a Bedouin well and palm branch huts. These oases are known as hôds; they extend almost in a straight line, at irregular intervals, between Kantara and El Arish, but are not found any distance inland, except in isolated cases. These are most numerous in the vicinity of Quatia or Katia, which is a large hôd running roughly from north to south for two miles with an average depth of a quarter of a mile. It is here that perhaps the best water in Sinai is found, with the exception of that obtainable on the beach at El Arish; one well of great antiquity was a God-send to man and beast in those days of thirst and heat.

At Romani plenty of water is to be found, but of inferior quality, and only suitable for watering horses. Along the greater length of the Sinai seaboard runs the Sabket Bardawil, a great shallow salt lake, for the most part dry in summer with many treacherous salt pans. Winding in and out among the oases is the old Darb es Sultan or King's Highroad, which for thousands of years has carried the armies of Asia and Africa to conflict against each other. It was along this way that the Egyptian Thotmes III., the greatest soldier of ancient days, led his armies in many campaigns to victory as far as the Euphrates, though it is true also that many of his attacks were made by sea through Phœnicia; he was possibly the first to realise the importance of sea power. In turn, Assyrian and Persian marched along the King's Highroad, against Egypt; Napoleon followed it, and in the earlier years of last century, Ibrahim Pasha, whose statue stands in Opera Square, Cairo, led his Egyptians again upon it to drive the Turk from beyond Aleppo. The Israelites in the Exodus from Egypt formed the one great exception to the general use of this highway by great hosts; in their migration the tracks through the rough mountain country of Southern Sinai, and the great depressions south of the Dead Sea were used. They then turned east, skirted Edom and when north-east of the Dead Sea turned west again, and passing through Moab, crossed the Jordan not far from Jericho.

The Turk had used Katia or Quatia as a base for his first attack upon the Canal in 1915, and it was of the utmost importance that this water area should be denied to him for future operations. To this end a brigade of Yeomanry had been stationed from Romani to Oghratina, being dispersed in squadrons or regiments over a considerable distance. A criticism of their dispositions, which led to defeat in detail is here unnecessary, but there is no doubt they were surprised at dawn on April 23rd, during a heavy fog, and the two posts at Oghratina and Katia were wiped out.

Romani, where Brigade Headquarters were, was not attacked, and an attack upon the post at Dueidar, ten miles south-west of Romani, garrisoned by infantry of the

52nd (Lowland) Division, was beaten off with loss. As the Yeomanry Brigade (5th Mounted) had been practically cut in two by this disaster, and their flank and rear had been menaced by the attack on Dueidar, a withdrawal was made by the Brigade to the Canal. The Anzac Mounted Division was now hurried forward from Salhia to restore the situation, but the enemy had gone as quickly as he had come, and only a few footsore prisoners were taken by the 5th L.H., the leading regiment.

The most forward Turkish posts were now at Bir El Abd and Salmana, twenty-five to thirty miles east of Romani, with stronger garrisons at Bir El Mazar and El Arish. Bir El Bayoud, eight miles to the south of Bir El Abd, among heavy sand dune country, was also held by the enemy as a flank outpost. His forward troops were practically all camel corps men, and in this recent raid, it is believed, his extreme mobility was due to the camels each carrying two men.

CHAPTER III.

PATROLS AND RECONNAISSANCES.

ON May 7th the first long reconnaissance was made, to Bir El Abd, the object being to discover any enemy movement, or concentration there. Quatia was the point of assembly for the Brigade, and at 8 p.m., in column of route, a move was made from there, "A" Squadron providing the advance guard. It was a dark night, and the march had to be made on compass bearings, aided by occasional telegraph poles.

Oghratina was reached at 11 p.m., and a halt was made till daybreak, as the country beyond was unknown. The Brigade was concentrated, and outposts were put out. At dawn the advance was resumed, "B" Squadron being now in the lead with wide flank guards, and moving in line with a similar advance guard of the 6th Regiment. Bir El Abd, reached at 7.30 a.m. on May 8th, was unoccupied, though it was clear that enemy troops had recently been there. At 11.30 a.m. the retirement commenced, the advance guard being now the rear guard.

Aftr a hot and thirsty march, with short halts at Oghratina and Quatia, Romani was reached again at 6 p.m. After a hurried meal outposts had to be found as usual. On the 10th a squadron was sent to Mahamadiya (whose ancient ruins of Roman or Greek occupation can still be seen) to assist in digging a canal from the sea to portion of the Sabkket Bardawil, so that the latter might be flooded, and the defences of Romani made less approachable from this flank. The project, however, was not successful owing to the high level of the Sabket. On the 11th, the troops at Romani were reinforced by the arrival of the N.Z.M.R. Brigade at Bir Et Maler oasis adjoining Romani. On the night of the 15th, the 6th Regiment, with some troops of the N.Z.M.R. Brigade, commenced a reconnaissance to Hod El Bayoud. The next two days were probably the hottest that most men in the Brigade had ever experienced. At railhead one day the thermometer in the Engineers' tent registered 125 degrees, and there were over 30 cases of sun-stroke in the 6th Regiment, returning from Bayoud.

The Brigade, less the 5th Regiment, on the 22nd moved out on another reconnaissance to Bir El Abd and Gedieda, where buried arms were reported. Bir El Abd was reached about daybreak next morning, and an enemy camel patrol was surprised and one prisoner taken. "B" Squadron was sent to Gedeida and made an unsuccessful search for buried arms or ammunition. Shots were exchanged with Turkish camelmen towards Salmana, which was reported by our prisoner to be occupied by 200 enemy and some guns. The long hot retirement was commenced at 9.30 a.m. on the 23rd; Romani was reached at 5 p.m.

The 1st Light Horse Brigade had now arrived from the Egyptian western frontier. It took over the patrolling, and enabled us to go back for a badly-needed rest. On the 26th the 6th Regiment moved to Hill 70, and next day we followed them. The period was supposed to be one of rest, though we were to be in readiness to support Dueidar (where the 5th Regiment was) if called upon. A good deal of work was also required, including the building of shelter stables, which were almost completed during the stay.

On June 25th, the march back to Romani was commenced, the Brigade now being under the command of Colonel Royston, an old South African veteran, in the absence of Brigadier-General Ryrie on leave to England. Camp was made at Bir Et Maler, about a mile in rear of our old camp at Romani, which was now occupied by the 1st

Light Horse Brigade. The Wellington Mounted Rifles were also brigaded with us, whilst the 5th Regiment, still at Dueidar, came under the command of the N.Z.M.R. Brigade, which had returned to Hill 70. This arrangement continued until after the battle of Bir El Abd. Outposts were found to the south and south-west of our camp, but these were now more in the nature of standing patrols, as redoubts for main defence were being dug and manned by troops of the 52nd (Lowland) Division, which had been recently pushed forward to Romani. The railway line had made progress, and railhead with numerous sidings was formed at Romani. A branch line to Mahamadiyia had also been completed.

The camp at Et Maler gave a fair amount of shade, and a certain number of tents were available. The health of the men was fairly good, but all ranks suffered from what was known as "Barcoo"; this took the form of nausea and vomiting, possibly caused by fly-infected food; sand colic, from which we were to lose so many horses later, also began to make its appearance.

On the 29th, another long reconnaissance to Bir El Abd, similar in all respects to former ones, was made. Owing to the advance of summer, the heat, thirst and hardship generally increased with each one of these. Patrols to Oghratina, Quatia, Hamisah and Hill 110 were taken in turn with other regiments of the Brigade. The night standing patrols in the vicinity of the camp area received much personal supervision from the Brigadier, as it was felt, as indeed really happened, that the enemy might make an attempt to force the back door of the Romani defences.

On July 5th General Chauvel inspected the camp area.

On the 8th another of the Bir El Abd-Salmana reconnaissances were undertaken; it differed somewhat from the others in the actual scheme and its carrying out. It was known that there was a certain number of the enemy at Salmana, and the 6th Regiment was directed to move from Oghratina in a wide circling movement to the south on that place and the 7th Regiment to act similiarly, from the north. Romani was left early in the morning, and Oghratina was made by 10 a.m., where the Brigade camped for the day. The encircling movement commenced after dark from Afein, about four miles further east, but unfortunately, the track to be taken by the 7th Regiment was beset with difficulties. The steep sand dunes run roughly north-east and south-west, and a succession of these had to be crossed or skirted, and in places the horses climbed almost perpendicular hills of sand, which would never have been attempted in daylight. This caused great delay and a very long and straggling column; somehow "C" Squadron and the Machine Gun Section, whose pack horses found the track especially difficult, became detached, and did not join up again until next morning. After the sand dunes had been passed, a belt of bad salt-pan country on the edge of the Sabkhet Bardawil was entered, and many of these pans had to be skirted owing to their boggy nature. Finally, when daylight broke, the Regiment was a mile short of Salmana, which the 6th Regiment, whose going had been good, had attacked, capturing a Turk and some camels. "C" Squadron was hurried forward, and exchanged shots with a Turkish rear guard, but the encircling movement had failed. An amusing incident of this reconnaissance was the effort made by Colonel Royston to round up, with his A.D.C., a flock of Bedouin goats; they proved too difficult to drive, however, and had to be abandoned.

Retirement commenced at 6 a.m. on the 9th, and after lunching and resting until 3 p.m. at Oghratina, where water was very scarce, Romani was reached at 5.30 p.m., all ranks and horses being wearied.

The Brigade left camp on July 19th under orders to make a reconnaissance of Bir El Abd, and then to return with a line extended from the Caravan route to the sea. Just after the Brigade left, an aeroplane dropped a message to the effect that Oghratina and Sagia were occupied by about 8,000 enemy with transport and guns.

The Brigade then moved forward and occupied Katia, "B" Squadron being on outpost. A patrol was also sent to Hamisah. Colonel Royston laid out this outpost line almost at the gallop. The 6th Regiment, and the W.M.R. got in touch with the enemy next morning at Oghratina, and later in the day a combined demonstration with guns, was made against him. It was discovered that he had already dug himself in, and seemed to be in considerable force. The outpost line outside Qatia was held until 2 a.m. on the 22nd, when a withdrawal to within $1\frac{1}{2}$ miles north of Katib Gannit, the great sand dune observation post of Romani, was made to obtain rations. After bivouacking there for an hour, a return was made to the camp at Et Maler. The 1st Light Horse Brigade now took over the day outpost line, east of Qatia, and after a day's rest, we (i.e., the 2nd Brigade) moved out of camp, at 1 a.m. on the 24th, again to take over this line. Patrols were sent to get in touch with the enemy at Oghratina, Hill 245, Hamisah and Sagia, and although the enemy was found in strength and subjected our forward troops to heavy machine-gun and rifle fire he did not move out of his entrenched positions. A return was made to camp at Et Maler at 6 p.m.: the eastern entrance into the Romani fortified lines had now to be taken, both in going out and in returning, as the northern one was almost completely blocked with wire, and there was a great possibility of moving troops, especially at night, being fired upon by infantry garrisons of the redoubts guarding the entrance. This caused a considerable detour, and some difficulty was always experienced in picking up the entrance, as it was situated at the foot of one of three almost similar large sandhills, and could be easily missed in the darkness.

After another day's rest, the outpost line beyond Quatia was again taken up by daylight on the 26th, the 7th Regiment being in Brigade Reserve on this day. In the afternoon, however, upon receipt of orders from Division to define the enemy's positions between Oghratina and Sagia, "B" Squadron, under Major Richardson, was sent forward to get as close up to the enemy's line as possible. The Squadron moved off in four successive lines, widely extended, and steadily advanced practically up to the south-western slope of the hill of Oghratina, with flanking patrols to the east towards Sagia. The enemy was silent until there was danger of his positions being galloped, and then the nerves of some of his men gave way; they opened fire, and soon the machine guns and rifles were spluttering from along the whole Turkish line. Some Turks concealed in a hod actually snatched at the bridles of our screen. Upon the retire whistle being blown, the Squadron wheeled files about, and concentrating into troops at the gallop, dismounted and took up a position about 400 yards further back. The men were excellently handled by their troop leaders. The Turkish fire was severe, and this position also had soon to be evacuated; another, 500 yards in rear, was taken up, two badly wounded men being gallantly brought into safety by Troopers Manley, Byrne and Harrington. This position was held until the wounded could be got away; one man had to be carried in a blanket for about a mile, over the heavy sand. The object of the reconnaissance had been achieved and the Turkish line located. The Squadron was congratulated, on behalf of the Brigadier, by the C.O. on the excellent way in which the work had been carried out. Two men were killed and two wounded in this small operation.

On the 28th, again moving out early in the morning, the patrols were pushed through Quatia, and discovered that the enemy had moved forward about a mile, and was digging in. We "drew fire," "A" Squadron being on the left and "B" on the right, with orders to feel the enemy's position towards Hill 245. "A" Squadron was quickly held up, but "B" was able to advance some distance before being checked; the screen, under Lieut. Maddrell, being well handled. The Turks then attempted to outflank this squadron, and a pleasant morning was spent in out-manœuvring them. The enemy would advance on foot over the heavy sand, against our fire, sending bodies of men down flanking gullies in the hope that they would not be noticed. These were allowed to advance fairly close up, and then our horses would be quickly mounted, and the squadron would retire by troops by a covered way already selected, to another position a few hundred yards in rear. The Turk, however, quickly became tired of this game, which must have been most exhausting for his men. The excellent morale of our troops was evinced by the calm manner in which the men boiled their billies and had breakfast, whilst the enemy was advancing against the position. Our guns did good work on this day shelling the enemy's lines. Major Richardson was slightly wounded, this being the third occasion.

When we moved out on the 30th, it was found that the enemy had again advanced about a mile. The line was inspected by Major-Generals Lawrence and Chauvel. On the 31st whilst we were resting, the camp area at Romani was bombed by enemy planes; but largely owing to the heavy sand, no damage was done. The duties of day outposts in great heat, with very little water, and the lack of sleep were telling severely on all ranks. In addition to other duties, officers' patrols were now left out at night time, a most exhausting and nerve-racking experience. Sandflies and mosquitoes were numerous and the horses could not be kept quiet. It was found on August 3rd., that the enemy had occupied Quatia and Errabah during the night. Our guns heavily shelled these places, and an attempt at galloping some positions was contemplated, but news was received of other large forces of the enemy moving up from the south-east. A withdrawal was commenced at 7.10 p.m.; the 1st Light Horse Brigade found the night standing patrols in the vicinity of Mount Meredith, and to the west and south of the Romani lines. Our officers' patrols were left out near Hamisah as usual, but were compelled to withdraw early in the night owing to the enemy advance; heavy firing at mid-night indicated that the 1st. Brigade Posts had been attacked near Mount Meredith.

CHAPTER IV.

ROMANI, KATIA AND BIR EL ABD.

AT 1 a.m. on August 4th., orders were received to be ready to move, and at 3.30 a.m. the Brigade moved out to Wellington Ridge, half a mile to the S.W. of our camp, to support the 1st Brigade, whose posts were being slowly driven in, whilst making a most gallant fight in the darkness.

Under shelter of Wellington Ridge, the 7th. Regiment dismounted and moved forward under severe fire to support the 3rd. Regiment, heavily engaged with the enemy on a long low spur, running north-east from Mount Meredith. This advance took place over nearly a mile of heavy sand and many men were greatly exhausted before the ridge was reached. Here it was found that the enemy was in strength. The machine gun and rifle fire were severe, and enemy mountain batteries sprayed the whole line with shrapnel; an effort was being made to encircle both our flanks.

The 3rd. Regiment now commenced to retire, having their horses with them; as the position was clearly untenable, Lieut.-Colonel Onslow also gave the order for the 7th. Regiment to fall back on Wellington Ridge and the horses. There had already been over twenty casualties, including Major Windeyer and Lieutenant Ryan, both severely wounded. During the long retirement to Wellington Ridge, the Regiment came under heavy shell, machine gun and rifle fire, and only the very exhausted state of the enemy, owing to his long advance over the sand, prevented him from profiting more by this withdrawal. He was, undoubtedly, slow in following up his advantage.

Many gallant acts were performed in getting our wounded away, the behaviour of Corporal Harrington being especially notable.

At Wellington Ridge, orders were received to take up a position on a low sand dune, about half a mile due west of our camp at Et Maler, and to cover it. The 6th. Regiment had been sent well out on to the right flank, and the Wellington Regiment was in reserve behind our position. This was an excellent one, as, later, when troops of the 1st Light Horse Brigade moved to some high ridges on the north, it could not well be enfiladed, and had to be approached across a long flat. Here the men scooped rough cover in the sand, and our machine guns and two Lewis guns, only that morning obtained, were set up, and any enemy movement brought forth a burst of fire. Turkish snipers pushed forward among the bushes on the flat in front of us, but, excepting some intermittent fire from the direction of Wellington Ridge, there was little movement for some time. The enemy bombardment of the redoubts to the west and north of Katib Gannit was now intense, the 5.9. shells making an appalling explosion with clouds of sand and smoke everywhere; but the damage done was not great. Enemy planes hovered overhead, bombing any targets that presented themselves; among others our led horses; but without great results. Our field guns commenced to open at 8 a.m., and did some good shelling of enemy troops that were moving at some distance, on our front.

The day became intensely hot, and difficulty was experienced in keeping up the water supply to the men. After dark, hot tea was sent up by the quartermaster under difficult conditions, as the camp area and the kitchens were riddled with bullets, and it was close to these, that Corporal Curran, who had gained a decoration at Gallipoli, was killed after most gallantly bringing to safety a number of wounded men. By mid-day it was evident that the Turkish advance had been help up, and Colonel Royston galloped along the line directing that every effort be made to harrass and pin the enemy down. Later in the day, news came that 500 Turks had surrendered on the right flank, after being cut off, and orders were received that a continuous fire was to be kept up on those in front. This was done, with due regard to the expenditure of ammunition, and produced the almost inevitable result—heavy shelling of our position by the enemy's mountain guns. This bombardment lasted for half an hour, most of the shells falling just behind us. A signaller was killed, and half a dozen other men were slightly wounded. The shelling, however, had the effect of making the men dig in deeper, and by night fair trenches had been constructed. The horses were watered late in the day with some difficulty, as the watering area was constantly under the enemy's fire. As night approached the position was consolidated and reinforced by 50 men of the 52nd Division, and we linked up on the left with other troops of this Division, and on the right with the 1st. Light Horse Brigade.

The enemy became nervous as soon as darkness set in; there were frequent bursts of rifle fire and a "display" of Verey lights. At intervals also, his 5.9. shells burst with a deafening roar, but as a rule, they did not fall close to the defences. Little sleep was obtained. Orders were received that at 4 o'clock next morning, the whole line would advance.

Lieut.-Colonel Onslow left "B" Squadron with the led horses and the fifty men of the Infantry to act as reserve and to garrison the position; with "A" and "C" Squadrons, and, leading the advance, he commenced to move dismounted against Wellington Ridge. Some time was lost in permitting the Wellingtons and troops of the 1st Light Horse Brigade to get into position; then, in one thin line, the attack was begun. Enemy snipers among the bushes on the flat were soon disposed of, and when their front line was reached, only a feeble resistance was made, though unfortunately among our casualties was Lieut.-Colonel Onslow, who was severely wounded through the leg at point blank range. Major Suttor automatically took charge of the Regiment, and the advance proceeded. The enemy now commenced to surrender in a body, and it was evident that his demoralisation was complete. Many machine guns were captured with their crews standing round them without attempting to fire a shot, and a large proportion of these were Germans. The long heavy march through the sand, with the shortage of water and the great heat, had exhausted even the Anatolian troops, the Flower of the Turkish Army. Many were almost in a state of collapse. Altogether 700 enemy were captured by the Regiment, with many machine guns, camels and booty of all kinds.

The led horses with "B" Squadron were brought up, and the Brigade moved on in pursuit under Lieut.-Colonel Meldrum (W.M.R.), Colonel Royston having been slightly wounded in the knee on the previous day. No check was experienced until near Katia, where at a small hod Bir Abu Gulud, south-west of that place and towards Hamisah, an ammunition column and Field ambulance were captured. Here we came under some shell fire, and the Wellingtons on our left ran into machine guns. The 6th. Regiment were still with the 1st Brigade in our rear, and as the enemy strength on our right and in the vicinity of Hamisah was unknown, Major Suttor decided to halt until the 1st. Light Horse Brigade came up. The opportunity was taken to water the horses at rather a poor well, and to pile up the captured ammunition ready for destruction in the event of the Turks making another attack.

About 10 a.m. the 1st. Light Horse Brigade, under Colonel Meredith, came up and orders were received to be ready to make a combined assault by the whole mounted Division on Katia, in the afternoon. In this attack, the 2nd. Light Horse Brigade was placed in the centre position against Katia itself, with the Yeomanry Brigade on the left and the 1st. Light Horse Brigade on the right, the N.Z.M.R. Brigade being on their right, and the 3rd Light Horse Brigade, directed against Hamisah, were to move against enemy's left flank and rear. The 7th. Regiment was in Brigade reserve. The advance commenced mounted, the 6th. Regiment leading, and no check was experienced until the scrubby flat just to the west of the palm groves of Katia was reached, when the enemy's field and heavy guns opened, and shortly afterwards his machine guns began to splutter. The impression had been that the whole Division was to go in mounted, but apparently this idea was abandoned later, though it is possible, that if it had been carried out resolutely, it would have meant the annihilation of the Turkish Force. In a small palm grove and behind a low ridge, the Brigade dismounted for action, and the 6th. Regiment and the Wellingtons moved forward extended, the 7th. Regiment being still in reserve. The horses were now moved up behind the low ridge on the edge of the scrubby flat. It was fortunate that this was done, as the palm groves, in which cover at first had been taken, were soon heavily bombarded by 5.9. and mountain guns.

The battle had now become general. The 6th. Regiment and Wellingtons made some progress at first under heavy fire, but soon sustained a number of casualities, and their advance was finally checked by machine guns, sweeping an open flat, on which no cover could be obtained. The 1st. Light Horse Brigade on the right, was heavily shelled. It was soon seen that the Yeomanry, on the left, had run into some machine guns; they commenced to go right out of the action, which left the flank of our Brigade in the air. The 5th. Light Horse Regiment, which was still attached to the N.Z.M.R. Brigade charged Bir El Maraieh mounted, with bayonets fixed. A few prisoners were taken, but a cross fire from machine guns was met, and so many casualties were sustained, that a short withdrawal had to be made.

The enemy's shell fire increased as the afternoon wore on, and he did his utmost to locate the horses sheltering in rear of the low ridges; but though many shells fell within a few yards, and the shrapnel was like rain just behind, there were only two or three casualties. It seemed as if the muzzles of his guns could not be depressed sufficiently, firing as they were at very close range. The palm groves close by were well searched and his heavies reached for our field guns, which had opened from the high ground, about a mile in our rear.

As the whole line had been checked, and there seemed no further hope of an advance with our greatly exhausted troops, orders were received to be ready to retire at 7 p.m.; about a quarter of an hour before this, the firing ceased on both sides. It was afterwards discovered that the enemy had also made simultaneous withdrawal.

The 7th. Regiment was now ordered to form the rear guard, and "B" Squadron was given the post of honor as rear troops. The main body of the Brigade quickly got away, but much time was occupied getting the wounded into sand carts; this operation had to be covered, though there was no trouble from the enemy. Finally, all were got away, and after a troop had been detailed as escort to the sand carts, the Squadron moved back in rear of the Regiment, both men and horses being exhausted. The casualties for the Regiment for the battle of Romani were 9 O.R's. killed, and 3 officers and 42 O.R's. wounded. The Regiment suffered only one casualty at Katia. The 6th. suffered fairly heavily here, Lieut.-Colonel Fuller, the C.O. being severely wounded.

The next two days were spent in resting, and, in the meantime, Major Richardson was placed in command of the Regiment; he continued in this capacity for three months, until the return of Lieut.-Colonel Onslow, holding also the rank of Temporary Lieut.-Colonel for two months.

Orders were received to move out on the 8th., and hang on the flanks and rear of the slowly retiring enemy. He had now withdrawn to Bir El Abd, being followed up by the Yeomanry, N.Z.M.R., and 3rd. Light Horse Brigades, who were comparatively fresh troops. It was thought that no great opposition would be encountered and permission was given to leave a number of the more exhausted men and animals in camp. Consequently, the Regiment moved out with a total strength of only 214. After a long night march the two brigades (1st. and 2nd.) at dawn on August 9th, were moving among melon patches on the sand dunes to the north-west of Bir El Abd. Suddenly a 5.9 burst close to the centre of the column and others followed. Cover was found under the steep banks of the sand ridges close by, and the Wellingtons were sent forward dismounted, to occupy the high sandhills to the west of, and overlooking Bir El Abd; their advance was quickly checked. A consultation between the Brigadier and Regimental Commanders was held as to the advisability of a dash across the low ground to the north-west of Bir El Abd, but a personal reconnaissance showed this to be strongly held and the idea was abandoned.

At 11 p.m., orders were received that the Regiment would move, dismounted, on the left flank of the Wellingtons, and make a demonstration against the enemy, in which the whole Division would co-operate. The 1st. Light Horse Brigade was on our left. The horses were placed under good cover and a march on foot through the sand was made for about a mile, until the enemy was found occupying a high steep sand ridge running like a whale back into the plain of Bir El Abd, and distant from it about 2,000 yards.

Under our covering fire, which quickly wore down that of the enemy, the Wellingtons advanced and drove him off the ridge with the bayonet; our advance was then continued. Half the Regiment occupied the captured position with the Wellingtons, who were in close touch. The other half of the Regiment, under Captains Willsallen and Easterbrook (Major Bice had collapsed under the heat and the long march in the sand), pushed down the valley round the north-eastern slope, but were quickly held up, and forced to retire back to the position first advanced from, by heavy enemy fire and a determined counter attack, which also stopped the 1st Light Horse Brigade. Captain Easterbrook was tossed into the air by a heavy shell, and Lieutenant Waddell was badly wounded in the face; Lieutenant Humphries had sustained a severe wound in the hand during the first advance.

Meanwhile, the captured ridge was undergoing a severe bombardment by 5.9's and mountain guns, and a great strain was imposed on the men holding it, lying, as they were, quite in the open, without shelter of any sort. The enemy machine guns and rifles also opened, and his infantry could be seen advancing about 800 yards distant. Our field guns now commenced to fire, and helped to check this advance, but were presently themselves subjected to a searching fire from the 5.9's, which killed many of the gun horses, and later made it difficult for the men to get guns and limbers away. The enemy advance was finally checked about 500 yards from the ridge and an afternoon of great heat wore on under incessant rifle fire, with heavy intermittent shelling. Fortunately, the effect of a 5.9 burst in the sand is very local. In many cases, these shells burst within six feet of men and horses, without doing any damage.

Great difficulty was experienced in getting the wounded away, as owing to the steep ridges, the sand carts could not be brought within a mile of the front line. The horses were brought up closer, and many wounded men were placed upon them and brought out, suffering agony as they went. For gallant work as stretcher bearers, Troopers McFarland and Gould, later on, received Military Medals and the Serbian Star.

Touch could only be obtained with Brigade Headquarters by dismounted orderly, as the Brigade helio stations were heavily shelled, and found it impossible to carry on.

About 4 p.m. it was decided to make a simultaneous withdrawal from the forward position, in conjunction with the Wellingtons to ridges about half a mile in rear, where proper touch could be obtained with B.H.Q. and orders received. This was done gradually, the retirement being heavily shelled and the enemy machine guns becoming particularly active. On reaching the first firing line position of the day, the remainder of the Regiment was linked up with; the 6th. Regiment was also found in position there. Orders were then received to retire to a position in rear, and cover the withdrawal of the field ambulance and the wounded from a hod close by. The horses were mounted under heavy shell fire and the Regiment moved back, the 6th. Regiment covering our withdrawal, and retiring also shortly afterwards. The enemy quickly followed up to the positions vacated but did not attempt any attack on the new line, which was held until all the wounded had been safely taken away.

Abu El Afein, four miles in rear, was the point of concentration given, and after resting there some hours, further orders were received to retire to Oghratina, as there were indications of an enemy counter attack; Oghratina was reached after mid-night and bivouac was made, all ranks being greatly exhausted. Our casualties for the day were 5 O.R.'s killed, and 3 officers and 14 O.R.'s wounded—marvellously light considering the severity of the fire. To those who endured the shelling on the ridge all that hot afternoon at Bir El Abd, it will always be a memory of great mental and physical strain.

Next morning the Brigade moved to Khirba, eight miles west of Bir El Abd, and patrols were sent out to observe the enemy movements in the vicinity. Turkish ambulance waggons were busy, indicating that the enemy also had suffered severely. It was evident that he was still holding the line in strength. At Khirba, much Turkish grain and stores of various kinds were found, including rolls of dried apricots; without these, the rations for men and horses would have been scanty.

On the 11th, a reconnaissance by the Wellingtons, still showed the enemy to be in strength; but on the following day, when our turn came, it was discovered that he had slipped away during the night, and his column could be seen retiring beyond Salmana, now his centre of resistance. The Regiment on this day, came temporarily under the orders of the G.O.C., 5th. Mounted Brigade (Yeomanry) and moved to within shell fire of Salmana; but beyond observing the enemy nothing eventful occurred, and at 4 p.m. retirement was made to Bir El Abd, and later to Khirba. There, orders were received to move back to Katia on which the remainder of the Brigade had already commenced to retire. Katia was reached late that night, and Infantry of the 42nd. Division were found there. Bivouac was made among the palm trees to escape observation by the enemy aeroplanes, and on the following morning we returned to camp at Et Maler, both men and horses being badly in need of rest.

The Brigade remainded at Et Maler until September 10th. This period was spent in refitting and recuperating in every way. The condition of the horses was not good and many cases of sand colic occurred. Remounts were obtained to replace the battle casualties. Brigadier-General Ryrie rejoined and took command, Colonel Royston being appointed to command the 3rd Light Horse Brigade. The following N.C.O's were granted commissions to replace officers wounded in the recent fighting:—R.Q.M.S. Holland, S.S.M. Spencer, S.Q.M.S. Carter, Sergeant Stanley, and Corporal Richards. Lieutenants Chapman and Findlay reported back from detached duties. Captains Bird, Barton, and Willsallen received their promotion to Major after Bir El Abd.

At 5 a.m. on September 11, the move forward again commenced and Hassaniyia, eight miles south-west of Bir El Abd, was reached at 1 p.m., B.H.Q. being established there. The 6th Regiment camped on the hill to the north close by the 5th at Hod El Fatir, and the 7th. at Nabit taking over the camp of the 10th Regiment. This was a fairly comfortable place, giving plenty of shade to both horses and men, and no time was lost in placing it in a state of defence by digging trenches on the ridges around.

In the period between the first occupation of Romani by the Brigade until after the battle of Bir El Abd, endurance was so severely tested as finally to eliminate from active service any men whose physical conditions were not near perfection. Officers and men who survived the hardships became so seasoned, that the rough conditions experienced later in Palestine, seemed to have little effect upon them. Utter and constant discomfort was the rule in those days. Even in camp and when resting there was nothing to make life worth living.

Canteens were not established until later, and the army ration was the only food for all ranks. This is good and sufficient to support life, though it often leaves men hungry. In hot weather, however, it is unappetising. The water brought in fantasses (small copper or tin tanks) on camels under the direct rays of the sun, was almost boiling at times and was only endurable when made into tea. Water obtained from the desert wells was cold, but so brackish or saline, as to be only drinkable by very thirsty men. When made into tea it would often curdle like sour milk.

The reconnaissances to Bir El Abd or Salmana, meant a sleepless night march of intense weariness across the heavy sand followed by a day of torture with empty water bottles in the fierce heat until we returned to Romani. The ordinary patrols, such as those to Katia or Oghratina, were not so bad, though the observation posts put out by these, suffered greatly through being out on a bare sand hill. We were fortunate to miss the Bayoud operation, in which the 6th. Regiment suffered so severely from sunstroke and heat exhaustion.

Most trying of all were the days of the Turkish advance on Oghratina, Katia, and Romani. Reveille at midnight was followed by a tedious march through the baffling eastern gate of the Romani defences, to Katia reached just at dawn; then came the pleasant operation known as drawing fire and defining the enemy's line in which the squadrons pushed slowly forward, and rode back very rapidly, followed by a hail of bullets. Next came the forming of the day outposts line to watch the enemy movements and prevent his advance upon Katia. Those who have lain out on the bare sand dunes round Katia with an utter lack of shade and the hot desert sand reflecting back the blazing heat of the mid-summer sun, know well what a purgatory it was. Men endeavoured to sit or lie in the small flakes of shadow cast by their horses which were also suffering greatly and would not remain still for long. The enemy was quiet, as a rule, during the mid-day heat. Darkness alone brought a cooler atmosphere; but camp often was not reached until 10 o'clock. A hasty meal and the sleep of exhaustion compensated to some small extent for the hardships of the day.

The decorations awarded to the Regiment for the Romani operations were:—
D.S.O.: Lieut.-Colonel G. M. Macarthur Onslow.
D.C.M.: Corporal Harrington and Sig.-Corporal Kilpatrick.
Military Medals: Troopers McFarland, Gould.
Servian Gold Medal: R.Q.M.S. Holland.
Other Servian Decorations: Troopers McFarland, Gould.

During this period our machine-gun section was taken away to form with other units, the Brigade machine gun Squadron. Two Lewis Guns to some extent replaced the loss of the machine guns, which, however, were mostly attached to us again during an action.

CHAPTER V.

LAST DAYS IN SINAI.

THE enemy had now retreated to Bir El Mazar, on the caravan route to El Arish, and it was decided, during September, to make a divisional reconnaissance of that place, 30 miles away. At 2.30 a.m. on the 16th, the Brigade moved out of Hassaniyia reaching Ge Eila, a luxuriant palm grove, shortly after daybreak. Here we remained during the day, in order that our advance should not be disclosed to enemy aeroplanes. At 6 p.m., the march was resumed, the 7th. Regiment following the 5th. Regiment, which was advance guard. After a wearisome night march, the wide salt pan about two miles west of Mazar, which was the place of deployment, was reached at 4 a.m. on the 17th.

After receiving orders, the Regiment, less "C" Squadron (in Brigade reserve) moved with two machine guns, under Lieutenant Zouch, to attack Mazar from the south-west, the left flank being on the caravan route and in touch with the 5th. Regiment there. "A" Squadron, under Major Bird, formed the advance guard, and, moving rapidly, a troop, under Lieutenant Stanley, surprised and captured a camel out-post of six men. No check was experienced until we were close to the ruins of Mazar, where the enemy was strongly entrenched on bare sand ridges, which commanded all ways of approach. His guns commenced firing on our aeroplanes.

Major Bird's squadron pushed forward, dismounted, but was quickly held up by machine gun and rifle fire. It still seemed possible that, by means of covering fire, an assault could be made, and preparations were in progress, when a message was received that the 3rd. Light Horse Brigade, on our right, had been held up and was withdrawing. Some of their troops crossed our frontage, and being in close formation, received concentrated fire from the enemy, sustaining a number of casualties. Our field guns had opened fire but, although the enemy guns were firing in plain view from our positions, and messages were sent to that effect, no attempt was made to shell them. Possibly the messages were not received until after the withdrawal had been ordered.

All troops were now ordered to retire to the position of deployment, but it was some time before our front line could be drawn back, owing to the necessity of getting a man, badly wounded in the abdomen, away in a sand cart. Before this was effected three more men had been wounded and our casualties for this ineffective little action were, 1 killed and 5 wounded: two men subsequently died of wounds. The enemy shelled us without result, as the withdrawal was continued. We followed the Northern or Bardawil Road, thus, as we learned later, avoiding congestion and disorder at the water rendezvous. As no bivouac had been indicated, it was presumed that Ge'Eila would be the place; but we arrived there only to find it deserted. Much trouble was experienced in watering the horses from buckets, and at 8 p.m., it was decided to return to Salmana, where B.H.Q. was found. The 6th. Regiment had just arrived. After a quiet night, at 3.15 a.m. on the 18th., the march back to Hassainyia was resumed.

The greatest difficulty, in these little actions, was getting the wounded away; carried over long distances, in a sand cart or on a camel cacolet, they must have suffered greatly. The Mazar stunt was most strenuous, and tested the endurance of men, whose vitality had been greatly decreased by the fighting, fatigue and heat of the last few months.

Towards the end of the month, the Brigade was ordered back to Romani and Hill 70, to recuperate. We remained at Romani from September 29th, until October 10th., when the Brigade, less 5th Regiment (to Duiedar), marched to Hill 70. No great progress had been made with the stables since our departure. Patrols, one troop for each place, were taken alternately by the two Regiments, to Hod Al Arras and Bally Bunion. Otherwise, the period was devoted to rest and training. Much attention was devoted to the horses, which were very debilitated; some of the forage was very bad. Parties were sent to Rest Camps at Port Said and Alexandria. Winter clothing was issued, and everything was done to bring the Regiment up to its former state of efficiency.

The cavalry school for officers was opened during October and practically all the officers of the Regiment attended, sooner or later. Lieut.-Colonel Onslow now returned from hospital and assumed command, Major Richardson becoming second-in-command.

On the 23rd, the move forward commenced again. We bivouacked at Romani, moving next day to Hod El Khirba, and on the 25th., to Hassaniyia, where the camp of the Warwickshire Yeomanry, the former camp of the 6th. Regiment, was taken over. The role of the Brigade now was to watch the right flank of the army line of communications and prevent any enemy raid from the Maghara Hills. The 6th Regiment was based upon Bayoud and Mageibra, and the 7th and 5th Regiments took it in turns to find certain minor patrols, also out-posts for their own camp and B.H.Q. Training was continued and classes were constantly held to instruct additional crews in the use of the Lewis Guns. Football matches, athletic events and race meetings were held. November and December passed uneventfully. It was felt that the Brigade was losing opportunities through being left out of the front line; but the efficiency of the Regiments was greatly increased. The weather became very cold, and driving sand-storms were frequent. One occurred on Christmas Day, and rather spoilt a Regimental Sports Meeting. The rain would drive through the men's palm leaf bivouacs as no tents were permitted; perhaps none were available. A day of rain and wind was usually followed by a period of clear, bright weather, which compensated for hardships. After the blinding heat of the summer months these semi-arctic conditions were severe. Plenty of warm clothing had been issued however, and many cases and parcels of comforts had been received from Australia. Every effort was made to celebrate the Christmas season, and our lot was certainly more pleasant than it had been since we crossed the Canal. Reinforcements in men and horses brought the Regiment well up to strength; it was not until later that the falling off of recruiting in Australia had its effect in thinning the ranks. Apart from the battle casualties, which had been severe, the toll taken by sickness and exhaustion during the Sinai campaign caused many new faces to be seen in the Squadrons. The new-comers were sandwiched with the old campaigners, and soon learned most of what was known of mounted warfare. Numerous promotions were made to fill vacancies caused by casualties or sickness.

Although a state of extreme quiet prevailed with us, early in the New Year the other Troops of the Desert Column (as the Anzac Mounted Division, and 52nd. and 42nd. Infantry Divisions were now known) had pushed as far as El Arish and to Rafa, on the Egyptian Frontier, battles having been successfully fought at the latter place and at Magdaba.

The New Year was ushered in by boisterous weather, which later developed into a driving sand-storm, with rain at intervals. It became bitterly cold. In spite of these drawbacks a Brigade Sports and Race Meeting was held, and our competitors won the majority of events. During this month training was pushed forward, much field firing was done, certain schemes being given to Squadron Leaders with hidden targets of men and machine guns, against whom they were to come into action in the best possible manner. On the whole, the results were good. The training with the Lewis Guns was made an important matter, and good results were achieved later.

Towards the end of the month, word was at last received of an early move northward, and at 8 a.m. on February 2nd, as part of the Brigade, we moved out of Hassaniyia, which has been our home for a long time. At Moseifig, on the caravan route, we bivouacked for the night, proceeding next day to Mazar. The camp site allotted just inside the wire entanglements of this post was a confined space, but on the following day a move was made to a better place, about a mile away and not far from the position reached by the Regiment during the battle in September, 1916. From here "A" Squadron, under Major Bird, was detached to Gererat, and "B" Squadron, under Major Willsallen, to Malha, to watch for any Turkish movements from the Maghara Hills.

Patrols were sent out, and one reported supposed enemy cavalry moving on the hills in the far distance. Efforts were made to confirm this report, but without success, and it was later believed that the "cavalry" was a large flock of goats. This report however caused an alarm from El Arish to Kantara. Troops stood to arms, and patrols were sent out to reconnoitre in all directions. On the 8th., the Brigade moved off at 8 a.m. and reached Bardawil at 3 p.m., the Squadrons joining up on the march. Bivouac was made here for the night and the march was resumed next day. The last part of this march was along the sands close to the sea, and it was a fine sight to see the Brigade moving troop after troop stretched over nearly two miles across the level beach until the palm trees at Masaid near El Arish were reached. Here the 3rd. A.L.H. Brigade was found to be in occupation.

Railhead had been pushed forward with wonderful speed by strong gangs of the Egyptian Labour Corps, and was now at El Arish, the centre of a considerable area of palm oases. The country here grows figs and other trees, as well as crops of vegetables, melons, etc. From 8th to 21st training was proceeded with, special formations being practised and adopted to meet cavalry attacks. These were of different types, but the one most in favour was a hollow square with horses in centre and men on the outside, the front being especially strengthened and Lewis Guns posted at corners.

The bathing at Masaid was much appreciated, and as the bivouac was among the palm trees, the camp was pleasant. Enemy 'planes often passed over us, endeavouring to locate troops, but their task must have been difficult. Major-General Chetwode, Desert Column Commander, inspected the Brigade during our stay. On the 22nd, a move was again made and after leaving the sand dunes of El Arish behind, gradually improving country was met until finally, near Sheikh Zoweid, our horses were marching on practically firm ground. A bivouac was formed to the south of the village.

THE 7th LIGHT HORSE, 1914-1919.

PART III.

PALESTINE
THE PHILISTINE PLAIN.

CHAPTER 1.

THE ADVANCE TOWARDS GAZA.

AT 1 a.m. on February 23rd., the Brigade moved out, with the N.Z.M.R Brigade, on a reconnaissance to "Khan Yunus", the first Turkish village across the Egyptian border. The 7th Regiment formed the rear-guard. No casualties occurred as the Brigade was not actually engaged, though the N.Z. Brigade, the advance troops, encountered fairly severe opposition; no attempt was made to force the enemy's position. We returned to camp about 4 p.m. and moved to another site, near the beach.

On the 24th, the Regiment rested, but on the 25th. another reconnaissance was made along the beach towards Khan Yunus. Only small bodies of enemy Troops were seen. On the 25th "C" Squadron was sent on patrol of Hill 250, three miles south of Rafa where numerous tracks meet. No signs of enemy were seen. The country here is partly cultivated and grassed, carrying a scattered Bedouin population and a fair number of cattle and sheep. On the 26th the Regiment again rested, but on the 27th. moved out with the Brigade on a country and road reconnaissance. The Regiment was advance guard. A halt was made just north of El Abreisa, six miles south-east of Rafa, "B" Squadron going towards Hill 410, N.W. of E., in El Ghabi, "C" Squadron moved towards Hill 380, about four miles S.E. of U., in Khibu. Both these hills were occupied by the enemy, but no attack was made as the squadrons were acting as screens for surveying parties.

About 40 shots were exchanged, and during the day five of the enemy gave themselves up. The Regiment rested again on the 28th. This reconnaissance was typical of many that followed, a day's rest coming after each. The main object was to get an accurate idea of the country in the vicinity of Khan Yunus, and to the north and east of that place, and to find covered approaches for large bodies of troops to advance against the enemy's positions at Weli Sheikh Nuran.

By the end of the month, Khan Yunus was evacuated by the enemy and this was the first town on Turkish soil to be entered by our troops. It is a typical Syrian village, surrounded by orchards and gardens, with a fine old ruined Crusaders' Church. Enemy patrols were not active, and he contented himself with shelling at long ranges, sitting down behind entrenched positions at Weli Sheikh Nuran.

We moved, on March 7th, to another camp site on the beach, more conveniently situated for patrolling. Bir Abu Shunnar is close to Rafa, and the long marches hitherto necessary before reaching the patrol area were obviated. The enemy now evacuated the lines of Weli Sheikh Nuran, and on the 9th a reconnaissance was pushed out beyond Deir El Belah, and from the heights to the north-east of this place the white domes and roofs of Gaza could be plainly seen, with the solid rampart of the hill of Ali Muntar, soon to be so well-known, standing clear against the sky. Deir El Belah is a rather pretty mud village, as seen from a little distance, with a shallow sheet of water, dry in summer, close by. A broad level plain, fertile and well grassed, extends from Khan Yunus past Belah to Gaza. Many flocks were seen. The inhabitants—Syrian Arabs — displayed no hostility. The Regiment returned to camp at 6 p.m.

On the 17th, in conjunction with the 6th Regiment, a move was made to Khan

Yunus as covering party to surveyors. We returned to camp in the afternoon. The health and spirits of the Regiment were now perhaps better than they had ever been before, and the keenness and smartness displayed upon patrols and reconnaissances had never been equalled. It was well that this was so, for the tests of endurance and of sound training were to be very severe.

The country between Rafa, the little Egyptian frontier police post, and Gaza, twelve miles to the north-east, is, for the most part, of a gently undulating nature, occasionally rising into higher ridges, from the summits of which wide views of the surrounding country are obtained. At Weli Sheikh Nuran, with the knoll as an observation post, the Turks had dug a very elaborate trench system, capable of holding ten thousand men. Weli Sheikh Nuran was the apex of this system and the flanks were thrown back to the Wadi Ghuzze, in the vicinity of Abu El Hisiea, to the north, and Tel El Fara, to the south. It came as a surprise that the enemy should have evacuated these works, constructed with so much labour; but if the map is studied it will be seen that the country south of Tel El Fara is practically all plain and gives excellent opportunity for a strong force of cavalry to turn the flank of the position and cut off all communication from Beersheba. Direct communication with Gaza could also be cut, without much difficulty, from the north. It was said, also, that the lines were really too elaborate, and that the enemy had insufficient troops to man them properly. These works now passed into our possession and were later used as reserve and flanking positions to our posts on the Wadi Ghuzze.

The enemy had retired to a fairly strong position at Gaza, having also entrenched lines and a garrison at Beersheba, twenty miles to the south-east. The attacking and capture of Gaza by the troops of the Desert Column, isolated as it was almost in the manner as at Rafa and Maghdaba, became the next objective, and all our reconnaissances were for the purpose of getting to know the intervening country as thoroughly as possible. The infantry of the 53rd Division were to make a frontal attack, supported by the 52nd Division, whilst the Anzac Mounted Division, in a wide sweep to the north and west, reaching the sea north of Gaza, were to cut off all possible lines of retirement. The Imperial Mounted Division was to watch for, and fend off, any movement from Beersheba.

CHAPTER II.

FIRST BATTLE OF GAZA.

THE Brigade and Division moved out at 2.30 a.m. on the 25th, on what was to end with the first battle of Gaza. A divisional reconnaissance was made on the line of Wadi Ghuzze, from Tel El Jerai to the sea. Later, a concentration of cavalry and infantry was made at Deir El Belah, and bivouac was established until 2 a.m. next day. During the afternoon, Captain Maddrell, with Captain Tooth of the 6th Regiment, made a reconnaissance of a track leading across the hills, near In Seirat, to the Wadi Ghuzze at Um Jerar, with a view to leading the division by night.

At 2 a.m. on the 26th, with the 7th Regiment leading as advance guard to both Anzac and Imperial Mounted Divisions, a start was made. The track proved to be very rough, and our Maltese medical cart, which, with two ammunition limbers, was the only wheeled transport we had, was frequently tipped right over, the drivers being fortunate to escape injury. The track was not well defined, and in the darkness was lost several times. After a tiring march, during the latter part of which a fog came up to add to our difficulties, the Wadi Ghuzze at Um Jerar was reached at about 4 a.m. The fog now became thick and a halt was made; but as the air did not clear, and time was of vital importance, we moved again, bearing at first toward El Mendur and then north-westward to the Sheikh Abbas Ridge.

The advance guard squadron, under Major Bird, was splendidly handled, also the flank guard troops, and Lieutenants Williams, Carter and Holland did particularly good work in not losing touch or direction over country intersected with wadis and covered in dense fog. No sign of the enemy was seen until Sheikh Abbas was reached, when a few shots were fired by an outpost, which bolted immediately, but, unfortunately, gave warning to two German aeroplanes on the ground on the reverse slope of the ridge. Before our galloping horsemen could reach them the 'planes managed to rise and commenced machine-gunning the column, though without getting a hit. From this on, the fog having lifted, the Regiment moved with great dash and speed, capturing a party of German mechanics or engineers close by, and chasing down transport waggons.

After reaching the Beersheba Road, the whole column swung to the left in the direction of Abu Zeid, and, moving rapidly, soon reached the main north road. Here Lieutenant Holland's troop chased down and, after a smart gallop, captured the G.O.C. Turkish 53rd Division and his staff, who were coming into Gaza. No sound had been heard from Gaza hitherto, but now fire was opened from heavy guns, the shells bursting close to B.H.Q., in our rear. The town could be plainly seen, about three miles to the west. After passing the main north road, the ridges running parallel to it, which afforded magnificent positions for defence, were galloped by a troop under Lieutenant Johnson, and were found to be unoccupied.

The country beyond and towards the sea, to which the Regiment was now swinging, consists largely of sand dunes, with small villages and orchards gradually being overwhelmed by the encroaching drift. The Regiment moved steadily on through Jebalie and finally reached the sea, taking up a line from the village to 181, Sheikh Redwan, and the beach to the west. Brigade Headquarters were located on a commanding hill close to the main north road, and since known as Australia Hill. Shots and sniping were exchanged, but on our front it was fairly quiet, though the shell bursts over Gaza and the trenches in front of it, especially in front of Ali Muntar, and the rattle of machine guns and musketry, marked the progress of the infantry battle. The squadrons were now pushed forward, "A" being close to the beach, "B" in the centre, and "C" on the left, about a half a mile from B.H.Q. As our objective had been secured and all the exits from Gaza blocked, the Regiment awaited further orders and commenced to have breakfast and lunch.

At about 3.30 p.m. word was received that the Brigade, in co-operation with the other units of the Division, would attack Gaza from the rear with the bayonet. Some of our batteries had been brought up and did a certain amount of shelling. Refugees were pouring out of the town, and it is remarkable that many of them did not fall victims to machine-gun fire, which was, at times, intense.

"B" and "C" Squadrons, under Major Richardson, commenced at about 4 p.m. to move, dismounted, into the cactus hedges of Gaza; "A" Squadron being kept in reserve and to hold the beach road on our right. The 5th Regiment was on our left, and one of its squadrons, under Major Newton, lost touch with it and joined with us. Progress was very slow owing to the thick cactus hedges, through which paths had to be chopped with the bayonet. The whole operation had to be carried out by bounds to lines of hedges, short distances in front, otherwise touch would certainly have been lost.

A good deal of fire was encountered from a redoubt in the sand on our right; but this was disregarded and there was no other organised resistance. Snipers among the trees were disposed of quickly. Isolated parties of Turks, very demoralised, were met; they quickly surrendered; 23 in one party gave themselves up to Lieutenant Wikner, who was, for the moment, almost alone. By pushing on resolutely, if slowly, most of the cactus hedges and gardens were passed through, but darkness had come on during the advance, and the only light was that of a half moon. The buildings and streets of Gaza were now within a few hundred yards of us, but an ominous silence had fallen, broken only by the occasional stutter of a machine gun, well in front. A mountain battery, which had opened against our led horses, had also ceased firing. The prisoners taken had been sent back, and an officer was sent to Lieut.-Colonel Onslow for orders.

In the meantime a long narrow lane, with high cactus hedges on either side, had been reached. It was an excellent position for defence, so it was decided to remain there until something definite was known. We had lost touch with our horses, which had kept well up and had been smartly handled by Captain Madrell. Apparently there was no one on our right or left, no one behind, and it was not known what was in front. After waiting for about half an hour, it was decided to pull out on to the sand to the west and try to regain touch with "A" Squadron and R.H.Q., as well as the horses. This was difficult, as a way had again to be cut through the thick hedges, and nearly three-quarters of an hour must have elapsed before the sand was reached.

It was now nearly 9 o'clock and nothing could be seen of the horses, though the place where they were to have been was close by. It was learned afterwards that the horse-holders also had been fighting small battles, and had captured some Turks and killed others. As they had lost touch with their squadrons, they were concentrated by Lieut.-Colonel Onslow with "A" Squadron.

Meanwhile Major Bruxner, from B.H.Q., had fallen in with the dismounted party, shortly after it issued from the hedges, bringing the astounding news that a withdrawal of the whole force was in progress. He urged the necessity of haste, but without the horses little could be done. Soon afterwards a party, bringing the others of our prisoners, came along, and those with the dismounted party were handed over to this escort.

After about half an hour's delay, Lieutenant Zouch, with the only horse available, located the remainder of the Regiment and guided it to where the dismounted men were waiting. The delay had been caused by the necessity of recalling the troop, under Lieutenant Carter, on the beach, which was nearly a mile from "A" Squadron's position. This Squadron had moved forward earlier in the day well up to Sheikh Redwan, but had met such a concentrated machine gun and rifle fire, that further movement was impossible. One troop of "C" Squadron, on our left, which had become detached early in the advance, joined with the Wellington Mounted Rifles, and assisted a troop of that Regiment to capture two field guns. Lieutenant Snow, who was in command, did gallant work, using a Hotchkiss rifle with great effect; later on this officer received the M.C. This troop afterwards rejoined the Regiment at the Brigade concentration point.

As soon as the Regiment was mounted, a move was commenced through the heavy sand to B.H.Q., signal lamps being flashed to guide us. The enemy did not interfere with the withdrawal though there was plenty of noise to indicate our position; this in itself probably was the reason, as the confident tone of the troops, and the apparent indifference as to their whereabouts being known, seemed to the enemy the prelude of forming up for another attack. Whistling, the regimental call, was found to be a useful means of locating parties of men at night.

The Squadron of the 5th. Regiment had to be helped with mounts to B.H.Q., as their horses had been left on the other side. It was a strange night, which might have ended for many in a Turkish prison but for the confidence and calm behaviour of all ranks; in any case, the determination was there, if horses had not been forthcoming, to march on foot round Gaza, and this most probably would have been successful.

The Brigade concentration was at last made and the withdrawal commenced. The darkness was intense, and if touch with the column had been lost, it would have been regained only by a miracle. The Regiment was in the centre of the Brigade column, with the 6th. Regiment in rear; but such was the confused state of mind of almost everyone through want of sleep, that at times it appeared as if many other units were marching parallel or in touch with us also. The extraordinary number of lights, possibly some of them for guidance, added to the bewilderment; but to this day many things have never been clearly explained.

It must be remembered that this was the third successive night without sleep, and that it had been practically impossible to rest in the daytime; under such conditions a curious state of mind is developed. Imaginary objects become focussed upon the brain, and real ones assume gigantic proportions. The march was continued, the leading troops following the telephone line, which had been laid during the day. The Wadi Ghuzze, at Um Jerar, was at last reached about daybreak after what seemed to be an eternity of marching; shortly afterwards two enemy planes passed high over us, fortunately without bombing. It must have been strange for them to see the troops returning from Gaza, which was practically won, as later stories from the enemy led us to believe.

Bivouac was made at Deir El Belah, and then the Brigade moved to just west of In Seirat, where a few hours' rest was allowed the exhausted men and horses. The Regiment in this first battle of Gaza did well in taking about 150 prisoners, including a divisional commander and his staff. Our own casualties were, one man killed and two wounded.

It may be well to relate briefly the events generally, which led to this check and retirement from Gaza. The infantry were in position in the Wadi Ghuzze at the appointed time, but the fog, which delayed our advance and should have been a godsend to their movement held it up completely. Some officer of high rank evidently considered it dangerous to move, and perhaps lose direction, until the fog had lifted. When this did occur it laid the advance bare to the eyes of the enemy over three miles of country almost destitute of cover. If the advance had been made resolutely under cover of the fog, it could have been maintained without loss up to the very redoubts of the town; whereas, heavy casualties were sustained before the attacking force was within striking distance of the enemy. Even then, although tired, with a long march under a hot sun, and thirsty owing to scanty supply of water, the 53rd. Division most gallantly went to the assault and Ali Muntar itself was taken and retaken several times; but night fell without any decisive advantage. In the meantime, reports of strong enemy forces moving from the north and from Beersheba, to relieve Gaza, made it appear that some of our mounted troops might be cut off. Hence a retirement was ordered.

CHAPTER III.

BETWEEN BATTLES.

THE Regiment watered at the shallow lagoon close to Deir El Belah. An officer's horse went down in a boggy place and rolled right over him. With mud plastered over hair, face, and uniform, he was a sight for the gods, and there was no opportunity for a change of raiment, as the regimental baggage had been left at Rafa. The victim had to remain in a state of nature at a well until his clothes had been washed, and dried in the sun.

As it was believed that the enemy would make a counter attack, a line of observation outposts was taken up east of In Seirat during the morning of the 28th. The Regiment was relieved at 4 p.m. by troops of the N.Z.M.R. Brigade. On the 29th., a camp site near the beach was allotted to us, but at 4 p.m. we moved to the former outpost line, relieving the troops on duty there, our relief taking place at 6 a.m. next day. There was no sign of the enemy.

During the ensuing fortnight the same routine of outposts and relief was followed and covering parties were provided for Royal Engineers. However, swimming in the sea close by compensated for much, and helped to keep all ranks in good condition.

One night an outpost was rather out of the usual order, since it was reported that bodies of Turks had been seen in the vicinity of Weli Sheikh Nuran in the afternoon. The 7th. Regiment accordingly hurried to Abasan, five miles east of Khan Yunis and the outpost line of one squadron already there was strengthened. The night passed quietly, save for the barking of dogs and howling of jackals. On April 13th., the enemy attempted to shell our horse line with long range guns, and some troops were obliged to move temporarily.

On April 16th., commenced the operations which led up to the second Battle of Gaza. At 7.45 p.m., the Regiment, in column of route, following the other units of the Brigade, left Belah and passing through the Infantry camps (where the numerous lights would have caused confusion as to direction, unless great care had been taken), and moving across the In Seirat ridges reached Shellal on the Wadi Ghuzze at 6 a.m. on the 17th. Excellent march discipline had been maintained, and it was commented upon by the Divisional Staff.

Bivouac was made in the Wadi, where the troops soon became congested. Two enemy aeroplanes observed this, but fortunately they were without bombs. One plane shortly afterwards, returned with a supply, but most of the units had moved to the north bank. B. H. Q. and the Field Ambulance however, were bombed, and numerous casualties in men and horses were sustained. Captain Easterbrook, of the 7th Regiment, who was doing duty as staff-captain, was dangerously wounded by a splinter in the neck.

A demonstration was now made mainly by the 22nd. Mounted Brigade (Yeomanry) against Abu Hareira, a strong Turkish position half-way between Gaza and Beersheba, in order to draw attention from the infantry attack against Mansoura Ridge, near Gaza. The 2nd. L.H. Brigade was in reserve. The Division was again bombed, but no casualties occurred in the 7th. Regiment. The worst feature of the day, so far as the Regiment was concerned, was the scarcity of water, though later, a plentiful supply was discovered in a cistern. We returned to Shellal the same night, and next morning another demonstration was made against Abu Hareira; while special patrols were pushed out to Hill 410, Bir Ifteis, and also along the Gaza-Beersheba road, where

Greek Monastery on Jebel Kuruntal. (Mount of Temptation.)

(Top)—*Nabit. The Bivouac is under the Palm Trees.*
(Middle)—*Poppy Valley four days after the snow fell. Anzac, 1915.*
(Bottom)—*Brigade Transport Camels on lines near 5th Regt. Camp when 7th was at Nabit and Bde. Hqrs. at Hassamifeh.*

three wounded men of the Staffordshire Yeomanry were picked up. They had, through some mistake, been left out all night, and had been attacked by Bedouins. At 11 p.m., the Brigade again moved out, and concentrated, by daylight, with the remainder of the Division, on a flat, east of the Wadi Hareira, about two miles south-east of Elmendur.

The country to the south and west of Gaza, in the vicinity of the Wadis Ghuzze and Imlieh, and to the west and south of Beersheba, may now be described.

Gaza, itself, the ancient Philistine city, a town in pre-war days with 40,000 inhabitants, lies on the very edge of the sand dune country, which runs, on an average, about two miles inland from the sea from Rafa and Jaffa. It is surrounded by luxuriant plantations of figs, almonds, lemons, etc., upon which the sand is gradually encroaching. The hill of Alimuntar, to the south-east of the town, which had been converted into a most formidable redoubt, is supposed to be the place to which Samson carried the gates of the city when the Philistines attempted to shut him in.

Six miles south-west of Gaza, on the sea coast near Tel Nujeid, is the mouth of the Wadi Ghuzze, a huge torrent bed, with water-torn sides, often precipitous for fifty feet or more; this is practically dry for the greater part of the year, save for clear springs which rise from its bed in certain places. Whilst the country, for the most part, falls gently to this Wadi on either side, as at Shellal, there are places where it has been distorted into fantastic hillocks sometimes for half a mile on either bank. Two mounds, where nature has been helped by man, are prominent landmarks. These are Tel El Jemmi and Tel El Fara, and are supposed to have been fortresses erected by Thotmes III, the Egyptian Conqueror of Syria. These mounds fulfilled many of the requirements of modern redoubts and were used both by the Turks and ourselves, and Tel El Fara made a particularly good observation post. In the days of Thotmes, however, there was no heavy artillery, which would quickly have made these too prominent fortresses untenable. In the vicinity of El Shellal, and Tel el Fara are possibly the best springs of water in the whole length of the Wadi, and these places later on, became our bases for all operations against the Turkish lines at Abu Hareira and Beersheba. The steep banks of the Wadi and the intersection of its numerous water torn ravines, made excellent cover for men and horses from enemy shell fire.

From this weird and fantastic Wadi, Gustave Dore is believed to have obtained his inspiration for the illustration of Dante's Inferno; its unearthly appearance, is particularly marked in midsummer, when the ground is almost bare of grass and herbage. About half a mile to the north of Tel El Jemmi another Wadi breaks off, running a little south of east. This forks again at Erk, and the Wadi Imlieh commences with high and narrower banks in the direction of Beersheba.

While the country to the immediate south of Gaza consists of fairly steep ridges, near Shellal it opens out into gently undulating plains, which, as between Shellal and Erk, are often level for miles. East of Tel El Fara and towards Beersheba, the country rises again, but with such gentle slopes that the going is very easy. The Wadi Shanag is a southern continuation of the Wadi Ghuzze. At Bir El Esani, ten miles west of Beersheba, there is another good spring, and large pools of water. In the vicinity of this place, the desert begins to appear, and as one goes further south towards Khalasa and Asluj, fifteen miles south of Beersheba, the good country almost entirely disappears giving place to forbidding limestone hills, often very steep, and heavy patches of sandy soil upon which only poor herbage grows and where the flocks and herds of numerous Bedouins exist. In the actual vicinity of Beersheba, the soil is better and some crops of barley and wheat are grown, though the rainfall is apparently insufficient, and desert conditions prevail. Beersheba, which was formerly a miserable Arab village, has been transformed by a railhead and the energy of German engineers, to something approximating a modern Syrian town. A continuation of the line had also been built to Asluj for the invasion of Egypt and substantial buildings erected there. As this project had failed after two attempts, the wells supplying this base had been blown in and the place abandoned. Water difficulties are always acute in Sinai and Southern Palestine, and doubtless, have been so for centuries. Man has found it necessary to conserve water and to dig wells wherever possible, and those at Beersheba are supposed to date from the time of the patriach, Abraham. Scattered over the land also, are huge cisterns cut in the limestone rock by people more progressive than the present inhabitants of Palestine; surface drains led the rain water to these during the wet season. But for these cisterns (which are very numerous on the Beersheba plain, particularly near El Buggar) and the springs in the Wadi Ghuzze, operations on a large scale on this flank would have been impossible. The country between the Wadis Imlieh and Ghuzze and almost to Beersheba itself, is ideal for cavalry purposes, whilst even the rough going near Asluj is not such as greatly to hinder mounted movements.

In the Spring, when our troops first arrived before Gaza, the fields, especially to the Wadi Ghuzze, were bright with flowers and green with wheat and barley, which afforded welcome grazing for our horses, which had not seen any green forage since crossing the canal. These crops, and the sparse grass, gradually were eaten off, or were burnt up by the summer heat. Later, the country, which is of a loose sandy nature, with stiffer soils in places, was cut up by traffic, and the dust became a great affliction.

The plan of operations for the 2nd. Battle of Gaza, consisted briefly of an Infantry frontal attack on the main defences of the city, aided by tanks, whilst cavalry and the Imperial Camel Corps attempted to break through between Gaza and Hareira, and to thus isolate the former place. Any advance of the Beersheba garrison, which contained among other troops, a cavalry division, was to be watched for and held up.

CHAPTER IV.

THE SECOND BATTLE OF GAZA.

ON April 19th., commenced the second battle of Gaza. The 7th. Regiment was ordered well out to the right flank toward El Dammath, to protect that flank of the Division from an attack from the south and south-east. Whilst moving to this position, "B" Squadron was bombed by an enemy plane, and lost a few horses. Observation posts were put out north and south of the road Abu Shawish, getting in touch with the 1st. A.L.H. Brigade, on the north and the 22nd. Mounted Brigade on the south.

One troop under Lieutenant Zouch, was sent up the Wadi Imlieh to point 410, to observe enemy action in the direction of Hareira. This troop was heavily shelled, but adopting shell formation, escaped casualties. Another troop moved well down the Gaza-Khalasa road, to watch for movements from Beersheba.

At 9 a.m., the Wadi Imlieh patrol reported enemy guns firing on the 1st. L.H. Brigade from Abu Hareira, also that the enemy appeared to be numerous and was entrenched. At the same hour an observation post on Hill 510, on the Abu Shawish road, reported touch with Turkish Cavalry, some of whom they had driven from this hill, also that clouds of dust to the east indicated further enemy movements. At 10.55 a.m., orders were received from Brigade to leave strong observation posts on Hills 410 and 510 and concentrate the remainder of the Regiment at El Dammath. This was done and at 12.45 p.m., "A" Squadron was sent to the 5th. L.H. Regiment in rear to help in forming an outpost line. At 2.25 p.m., the presence of the enemy cavalry division moving up from Beersheba, began to make itself felt, and the observation posts were driven from Hill 510 and later from Hill 410, the latter post having a few casualties. Among others, Sergeant Hunter was dangerously wounded; he was brought out of action with great difficulty on horseback. Hill 510 was occupied by about 500 enemy cavalry and about 2000 of the enemy were reported to be moving along the Sheria-Beersheba railroad, at a point three miles north of Abu Irgeig.

At about 3 p.m. a very large body of enemy cavalry was facing our rear-guard of "B" Squadron and one section of the Machine Gun Squadron, under Major Richardson, at Dammath. Orders to withdraw had been received, but it was felt that there was no hurry and it was hoped that the enemy cavalry would come within range of our machine guns. They advanced, however, very cautiously, and the screen would not even attempt to encircle our small force. When it was seen that they would come no further (the advance scouts being about 1,600 yards distant and main body about 1500 yards further off) our machine guns fired a few bursts. The effect was instantaneous; scouts and screen galloped furiously for the ridges in rear for cover, although probably very few bullets went near them. This checked their whole advance, and upon any movement at all being made within distant range, a burst of fire was given, which instantly caused the enemy to stop. Men mounted on camels and donkeys, with apparently some on mares with foals at foot, caused this force to have a very motley appearance. Bedouins both mounted and dismounted could be seen. Something, which, through our field-glasses looked like wheeled transport, was now brought up. Soon shells from mountain guns began to scream over our heads, bursting close to the horses in the rear. The position was now clearly untenable, as there was no cover on the flat-topped hill, even for men. Lieutenant Cunningham got his machine gun section away smartly, and then the Squadron retired by troops in good order with the shells bursting very close. The machine guns were rushed into the outpost lines, half a mile in rear, which the 5th. Regiment had been preparing, and "B" Squadron was concentrated behind these.

The Regimental Chaplain was seen in a new light during this withdrawal, when he gallantly rescued a full case of ammunition and galloped away with it in company with our limbers, which, with horses extended, were followed by a hail of shells for a considerable distance.

As the enemy noticed the withdrawal, in a dramatic manner they drew swords and galloped in pursuit, to be quickly halted and driven back faster than they had advanced by our machine guns and those of two light armoured cars, which had come up. The rifle and shell fire was now severe and a move was made to join the remainder of the regiment in position on the left of the 5th. Regiment and extending to the Wadi Imlieh, near Erk. The enemy's guns continued to shell heavily, but no further advance was attempted and upon a battery of ours hidden in the Wadi on our left opening, his became silent.

Darkness had now fallen, and it was necessary to link up the outpost lines as speedily as possible. Our left rested on the Wadi Imlieh at Erk, where the right of the 5th Mounted Brigade was supposed to be, but no touch was obtained with them, and next morning they were found to be a mile in rear. To safeguard the flank, the troops had to be well swung back on the northern bank of the Wadi, "C" Squadron, under Major Barton, being in position there. On our right was the 5th. Light Horse Regiment, with its flank also well in the air. A start was made to dig in, but owing to the exposed position of the 5th. Regiment, the line had to be swung back, this was done under great difficulties, on a dark night, all ranks being exhausted.

Next morning the position was consolidated and our left was brought back to link up with the 5th. Mounted Brigade. Good work was done in digging trenches. Patrols were pushed out well towards 410; much enemy activity was reported in the vicinity of Abu Hareira, but no advance was made against our positions, possibly owing to the breaking up of a large concentration by the vigorous bombing of our aeroplanes.

This ended the second Battle of Gaza, a battle which, for the numbers engaged, produced possibly as many British casualties as some of the bloodiest actions in France. As far as the Regiment was concerned, the day was full of interest and the work was ideal for mounted troops. Few will forget the excitement of hanging on to positions as long as possible in order to hold up the enemy's cavalry division. The Regiment's casualties were not heavy, for moving troops in shell formation present poor targets for either field or machine guns, except at close range.

With other units the position had been far different. In addition to the Infantry frontal attack on Gaza, an effort was made to break through Turkish lines between Gaza and the large redoubt system at Atawineh and Hareira. Practically all the troops making these attacks had been severely handled without obtaining any decisive advantage. The Imperial Camel Brigade, in common with the British Infantry, suffered extremely heavy casualties, as also did the 3rd and 4th Light Horse Brigades. The 1st Light Horse Brigade and our own, being more on the flank and not being thrown so much into the gap, escaped lightly. The general positions of the opposing armies were not greatly changed, except that now our troops occupied trenches as close to the enemy as possible, especially in the vicinity of Gaza, and warfare of fixed positions, as in France, had begun. On the right flank, however, a huge area of "No Man's Land" existed; our right flank was placed at Gamli and Tel El Fara with the enemy's left at Beersheba. The intervening country, roughly between continuations of the Wadi Ghuzze and Imlieh and then in gradually narrowing lines north-westward along these Wadis themselves, to the vicinity of El Mendur, became a great zone of patrols and reconnaissances for our mounted troops, from which finally the Turk was practically excluded both by day and by night.

CHAPTER V.

ON THE BEERSHEBA FLANK.

THE Brigade was relieved at 6 p.m. on April 20th., by the 1st. Light Horse Brigade, and after a night march in confusing country, bivouac was made at Weli Sheikh Nuran. On the 21st. the Regiment relieved troops of the N.Z.M.R. Brigade, half a mile north-east of Weli Sheikh Nuran.

The work now consisted of outpost duties, with a patrol squadron pushed across the Wadi Ghuzze, in the direction of the northern 510 on the Abu Shawish road. On the 25th., "A" Squadron, on this duty, brilliantly effected the capture of a Turkish officer and 17 O.R.'s, all cavalry, and armed with lances, swords and carbines. Major Bird, who was in command of "A" Squadron, noticed this Turkish troop against the centre of his line, and by withdrawing his centre troop and at the same time sending two flanking troops forward, through some covered ground, enticed the enemy into ambush.

As soon as the Turks saw that they had been trapped, their officer endeavoured to form them up for a charge, in which, if they had shown determination, they probably would have done well against our men, who were armed only with rifles and bayonets. But the Turk's resolution failed; they broke and galloped wildly for home. And then commenced a two miles gallop, in which the speed and endurance of the Waler gradually wore down the Arab, and the entire troop was finally captured. Turks showing any resistance were clubbed off their horses with rifles. The two troops effecting this capture, were dashingly led by Lieutenants Holland and Carter. A supporting enemy troop, after firing a few shots also bolted, but had too much of a start for our people to capture them. A special congratulatory message was received from the G.O.C, Desert Column, upon this brilliant little action. This performance was almost repeated the following day, but complete success was missed by one troop inopportunely moving over the sky-line. Two prisoners, however, were galloped down.

Patrols and covering parties for R.E's now came as a regular thing, these being always of Squadron strength. The objectives aimed for as observation points were, as a rule, northern 510 on the Abu Shawish road and point 450 Goz El Basal.

May 9th. was rather a special day, as the Brigade moved out to cover an inspection by the army commander, General Allenby, who had lately taken over command; he made a reconnaissance from Goz El Basal and Goz El Gelieb. Two days later, the Brigade made a demonstration against Wadi Imlieh, near Bir Ifteis, with a battery of 60 pounders. The advance troops usually came in for some ineffective shelling from the enemy's guns during these operations; otherwise, there was nothing much to report. The days were intensely hot and water was scarce. The return to camp was usually commenced about 4 p.m.

On the 16th., a special patrol of two squadrons went out, crossing the Wadi Ghuzze at Um Urgan, now a very dusty place. One troop of "A" Squadron was sent to El Dammath, and another towards El Magam, and one troop of "C" Squadron towards 410, one to 510 on Abu Shawish road and another to Goz El Basal; headquarters, with three troops, being 2,000 yards north-east of El Dammath. The Magam Patrol under Lieutenant Holland, commenced to cross the Wadi Sheria, just north of Point 340, when fire, which was held, was opened and two men of the screen were killed. The patrol retired and took up a position about half a mile south of point 340. The Patrol to 510 encountered heavy rifle fire, and had also to pull back a little distance.

An aeroplane duel between three of ours and a fast enemy machine ended in favour of the latter, one of our planes being forced to the ground. Later in the day, a fast monoplane come low over our lines, but received such a burst of fire, that it at once turned tail and made for home. It must have been hit somewhere, though possibly not in a vital spot. Other enemy planes dropped bombs in the vicinity of our fallen aeroplane, which had been taken over by troops of the 22nd. Mounted Brigade. We returned to camp at 4 p.m. As the strain of operations was producing its toll in sick, as well as in ordinary battle casualties, 25 reinforcements, who arrived that day, were very welcome.

On May 18th. orders having been received, the Regiment took posts "V", "X", "Y", "Z", of the Gharbi-Gamli line with headquarters at Jezariye, the 5th. Light Horse Regiment being on our left. These posts were formed by the throwing back of our right flank to meet a possible attack from due south. The worst feature of this position, was its distance from water, the extreme right post being five miles away. All the horses were, as a rule, sent to the Wadi Ghuzze, and remained there all day, returning just before dark. A party of five N.C.O's and five O.R's were at this time sent to the Royal Engineers for training in explosives; this party afterwards participated in the blowing up of the railway at Asluj.

On May 21st., Major Richardson was ordered to report to B.H.Q. to take over the duties of Brigade Major, this appointment being confirmed as from June 12th, Major Bird becoming second-in-command of the Regiment. On the 22nd, the Brigade moved out for the Khalasa-Asluj operations, in which large sections of railway line and some bridges were completely destroyed. Asluj was the enemy base already mentioned 15 miles south of Beersheba.

Fara was left at 7 p.m. on the 22nd. and the vicinity of Asluj was reached at 6 a.m. next day, the regiment taking up a line south-west of Goz Shelili, as far as El Erni, being in touch with the 1st L.H. Brigade, on the right. One of our outposts was sniped at by Bedouins, but two of these were killed and one taken prisoner. These Bedouins were often armed with old-fashioned rifles, which showed no great accuracy, but went off like small cannons, and whose bullets hummed in an appalling manner. A quiet day was spent. Retirement commenced at noon, Bedouin wheat and tibben (straw chaff) being destroyed as the withdrawal was made. Some fowls, which seemed to have no owners, were made "prisoners" and one squadron disdained bully beef stew for at least one meal. Camp was reached at 11 p.m.; it was found with some difficulty owing to the darkness and the camp-fires of many units of the Imperial Mounted Division, which had been brought up to assist in the operation. The usual outpost duties were continued. On the 28th. the whole Brigade was relieved by troops of a Yeomanry Brigade, and marched to Tel El Marakeb on the seashore near Khan Yunus, to rest and recuperate. The period from the first battle of Gaza had been strenuous and exhausting, and the now frequent evacuations to hospitals, showed that the strain was beginning to tell. However, 41 reinforcements arrived at the end of the month, and the rest, with surf bathing, did much to restore the physical condition of the Regiment. Whilst at Marakeb, the old rifles, many of which were the original ones brought from Australia in 1914, were exchanged for weapons of later pattern, and pointed bullet mark VII ammunition was henceforth issued, instead of that of conical shape, which had been used. Bomb throwing was practised and reserve crews were trained for the Hotchkiss rifle, which had now been issued, one to each troop.

On June 8th., the period of rest came to an end and together with the Brigade, the Regiment moved to a bivouac site, near El Fukhari, two miles south-east of Khan Yunus. Whilst at this place, training was continued, special attention being given to musketry to test the new rifles. These did not appear to be quite satisfactory at first, but after the men had become accustomed to them, were found to be thoroughly efficient. Bombing instructions and the training of Hotchkiss gunners were continued. On the 29th., a move was again made to Tel El Marakeb, for another week's rest, before returning to the front line. On July 6th., the Brigade marched to Umurgan on the Wadi Ghuzze, and took over the camp site of the 3rd Light Horse Brigade.

The camp allotted to the Regiment was close to Shellal, and was formed in the shape of a hollow square to obviate casualties from bombing by enemy planes. This spot was dusty beyond belief, and it was almost impossible for officers or men to keep clean, though the water supply at Shellal was plentiful and convenient. On the 8th., the Brigade moved out towards Irgeig and the Wadis Hanafish and Imlieh to cover a reconnaissance by the C. in C. The Regiment took up a position at point 630, El Girheir, with the 6th. Regiment on the right across the Wadi Hanafish on 730; a troop was sent to point 510, with strong patrols out in the direction of El Damath. The enemy shelled our lines heavily at intervals during the day, and opened machine-gun fire upon any advanced post; but beyond losing a few horses, we suffered no casualties; the 6th. Regiment was not so fortunate. We returned to camp at 8 p.m.

Now came a period of intense patrol activity, with constant minor operations at night; ambushes of all sorts were prepared so as to make it dangerous for enemy troops to venture into "No Man's Land" at any time.

The usual reconnaissances were pushed forward more actively than ever, and officers' patrols were sent right up to the enemy's lines to reconnoitre and make sketches of positions, particularly in the vicinity of Bir Abu Irgeig. The day patrol extended from Goz Mabruk to Kh Khasif, Goz El Basal and Northern 510. Night standing patrols had to be found in front of the Infantry barbed wire from Gamli to Hiseia, making five posts of one troop each. This night outpost line was connected with B.H.Q. by telephone. These night enterprises with day patrols, made exhausting demands upon the Regiment and other units of the Brigade, but brought the scouting, patrolling and reconnaissance work generally to the highest pitch and greatly raised the morale of men, whilst correspondingly decreasing that of the enemy. The night enterprises were, as a rule, made in from one troop to squadron strength, though once or twice the Regiment moved out. Perhaps no great blow was struck at the enemy, but many of his men were killed, wounded or captured, and towards the end of our period in the front line, these ventures were mostly abortive, simply because the enemy was afraid to push men forward into what he probably considered were skilfully set traps; in consequence "No Man's Land" became undisputably ours.

Only on one occasion did the Turk become aggressive, and this was probably to cover the reconnaissance of some officer of high rank. This occurred on the 19th July, when the patrols of the 5th. Regiment, on going out through dense fog, were heavily shelled, from the direction of Khasif and point 630. Some of the enemy guns were well pushed forward, for shells fell close to the Infantry wire, near Um Urgan.

The Brigade and the Division were hurried out at all speed, and the 7th. Regiment, was directed to move rapidly towards Goz El Basal and Karm. The Wadi was passed in a cloud of choking dust, and, galloping in shell formation, the Regiment, after passing through the wire quickly came into a barrage of high explosives. The pace was sustained and Goz El Basal was occupied. Instructions were then received to push forward and find the enemy line. This was done and Turkish Infantry, with some cavalry was found in strength, and digging in on a line from the ridge running from just south of Khasif northwards to point 630. His field guns were numerous and accurate, but after the Regiment had advanced well out into the plain he left it alone and devoted his attention to D.H.Q. and B.H.Q. on a small ridge to the north-east of Goz el Basal. The 5th. Regiment, moving up on the left to northern 510, also came in for heavy shelling, as also did two guns of the Ayrshire Battery, under Lieutenant Smith, which had been brought close up to Karm. These guns gallantly maintained an unequal duel all day, under a very heavy fire, and eventually, with the assistance of the Somerset Battery, brought up on the left, silenced the enemy's guns.

A line was now taken up by the Regiment, from some low ridges, just east of Karm to point 550, and the enemy's movements kept under observation. It was understood that the 1st. L.H. Brigade was attempting a turning movement of the enemy's left flank. but this did not prove successful. In the afternoon, it could be seen, that the Turkish forces were beginning to retire; but the withdrawal was made in good order and strong points were solidly held, until all their guns and waggons had got away. Darkness now fell, and orders were received for the Regiment to retire and concentrate in the vicinity of B.H.Q., about a mile east of Goz El Basal. This was done and an outpost line placed, but no more enemy activity was observed. At 3 a.m. on the 20th., this line was relieved by troops of the N.Z.M.R. Brigade, and a return was made to camp. After about two hours' rest and breakfast, the Brigade moved out again as Divisional Reserve, to the east bank of the Wadi Ghuzze, and after passing through the barbed wire, halted until mid-day, when all being quiet in the front line, orders were received to move back to camp.

CHAPTER VI.

THE BEERSHEBA FLANK.

NOTHING beyond the usual patrol and night operation incidents occurred up to the end of the month. Night enterprises now chiefly consisted in raiding parties towards detached posts known to be held by the Turk during the day, such as the hut near 410, on the Wadi Imlieh, Bir Ifteis and point 630, but as the enemy was taking no chances, these were always found empty at night. Practically, all junior officers and a number of seniors also took their turn with these operations, purposely designed to make the enemy nervous and to destroy his initiative. An effort was made, unsuccessfully, to ambush his dawn patrols at point 630. A daring reconnaissance by day, by Lieutenant Carter, of an enemy redoubt near Bir Abu Irgeig, and a night reconnaissance of the Gaza-Beersheba Road, near point 570, by Lieutenant Williams, were particularly good pieces of work, and later were rewarded with M.C.'s.

On the night of August 3-4, a Brigade operation against a supposed enemy camp at Kh El Sufi, four miles west of Beersheba, took place; the Regiment acted as left flank guard, and took up a position near Kh Imlieh to prevent any enemy movements from that direction. The 5th Regiment moved against Kh El Sufi, but no camp was found, though some members of an advanced troop actually got in touch with one of the Beersheba redoubts, near the railway line, and drew fire. The Brigade retired at 3 a.m. without incident.

Another night enterprise undertaken by the Brigade, was to cover a party placing a bomb on the railway line near Irgeig. The 7th. Regiment had to find this party, but the attempt was unsuccessful, as too much time was occupied in reaching the objective, through little known country. When the railway line was approached, it was nearly daylight and orders were received from Division to withdraw, owing to the danger of heavy shell fire. This enterprise, however, showed the possibility of moving a large force right up to the enemy's line without his knowing anything of it, so timid had his patrols become.

On August 14th, the Brigade helped to cover an important reconnaissance from the south-west of Beersheba by the C. in C. by extending the left of the N.Z.M.R. Brigade from point 810 between the Wadis Sufi and Hanafish and 630. The Regiment had a quiet day, but was ordered to remain out that night and make another attempt to place a bomb on the railway near Irgeig. The Brigade withdrew at 5 p.m., and the Regiment remained hidden in the orchards at Karm until after dark, and then moved as rapidly as possible for Kh Imlieh and point 770, which was reached shortly before midnight; "C" Squadron, under Major Barton, supported by "B," was sent forward dismounted. "B" Squadron remained hidden in the Wadi El Sufi, and "C" Squadron moved on. The railway was gained and the engineers set to work, placing the bomb in position. It was a task which took some time, and before it could be completed, a Turkish patrol appeared. Corporal Moore and some men charged gallantly with the bayonet, but the Turks fired and gave the alarm. Corporal Moore was killed, but the whole enemy patrol was accounted for, four being bayoneted, and two taken prisoner.

As any further attempt at destroying the railway in this place would have been useless, the two squadrons retired to point 770, and the Regiment then withdrew to camp. The whole operation was daring in the extreme, and great risks were taken in going isolated right into the enemy's country; but this again showed how much he was lacking in enterprise. Operations like these, although physically exhausting, owing to the long marches and sleepless nights, brought the morale of the men and their confidence in the outcome of any operations against the enemy to a very high pitch. This period of front line activity came to an end on August 18th, when the Brigade moved back to the beach at Marakeb to rest.

The usual routine of a rest camp, combined with training, was carried out at Marakeb, and musketry (with gas masks) was made a special thing. The Regiment, with the Brigade, was inspected by both the Divisional and Corps commanders. The time spent here had an invaluable effect upon the health of both men and horses, both of whom had been feeling the exhausting nature of the period in the front line.

On September 18th., the Brigade came into the support line and moved to Kazar—the Regiment having a camp between that place and El Fukhari. Here the training was intensified, and every effort made to get all transport and equipment as complete and efficient as possible, in anticipation of the big operations believed to be pending. The C. in C. made a brief inspection on one occasion and the Brigadier held several, in which the transport was especially looked over. All units were expected to be ready to move, at the shortest notice, to a rendezvous, three miles north-east of Kazar, and upon the Division making a practice alarm, the results of these thorough inspections and the systematic grouping of the echelons of transport were found to be most satisfactory. On August 26th, manœuvres were held by the Brigade in the vicinity of Gamli and El Abreisa, the 7th Regiment having the role of the force attacking from Beersheba. The work was well carried out by both sides. Several operations of this nature took place during the early part of September, and on all occasions good judgment and leadership was shown. Special attention was always given to the supporting fire in the attack by other units and machine guns.

A Brigade sports meeting was held at Kazar during this period. The Sports' Committee drew up an elaborate programme of events, and among other officers of high rank invited was the C. in C. Provision had been made only for the Brigade, but men from all units of the Division swarmed to the grounds. A tent, in which afternoon tea was to be served to the C. in C., was hurled over and well trodden under foot in an excited rush to get a closer view of the races, and hurdles constructed for one race shared the same fate. When the C. in C. arrived he was with difficulty escorted from place to place, so that he might witness the events; he took no umbrage at the unceremonious behaviour of the gathering, stating that, although things were certainly free and easy, no disrespect had been shown to him by any man.

On October 15th, a diversion was caused by two air fights. Two enemy 'planes were brought down, one in flames. On October 16th General Allenby presented decorations to members of the Regiment.

Late in the month orders were received to be ready for the "Big Push," and the post of honour as advanced troops was given to the 2nd Light Horse Brigade. On October 21st, at 5.30 p.m., the Brigade formed up across the railway east of Kazar, in full marching order, three days' rations, and two for his horse being carried by each trooper. With the 5th Regiment leading, the Brigade moved off for Esani, seven miles south-east of Shellal, which was reached at 2 a.m. on the 22nd, after a dusty march. It was heavy work for the transport carrying reserve rations, forage and ammunition, as the road had been badly cut up and the dust was nearly a foot deep. After placing an outpost line, the troops rested until daybreak. An Infantry Brigade had also marched in during the night. A camp site was then allotted to the Regiment, close to where the road to Khalasa crosses the Wadi Ghuzze, and large working parties were immediately detailed for improving the road crossings and water area. The latter was insufficient for the requirements of the troops already in the area (one Light Horse and one Infantry Brigade), and during the stay at Esani, it was with great difficulty that the horses obtained two small drinks a day. Much was done to develop the water and regulate the supply, but it was by no means satisfactory, when the Brigade moved off again on the 25th.

Nothing of much importance happened at Esani, beyond one or two slight brushes with enemy patrols, in the vicinity of Khasif and El Buggar. On the 25th, at 6.30 p.m., the move to Asluj was commenced, A squadron acting as left, flank guard. The road as far as Khalasa was much cut up, and close to the advanced A.S.C. Depôt, which had now been established east of the Wadi, the dust was blinding. The road proved so heavy for the transport that this was eventually placed in charge of the 5th Regiment, and the remainder of the Brigade, with the 6th Regiment leading, moved on. Khalasa was reached in good time. It was found that the wells had been restored by our engineers, working under escort of the Camel Brigade and one Squadron of the 5th Regiment. The road improved greatly after leaving Khalasa, and Asluj was reached at 1.30 a.m., on the 26th, without incident. Outposts were at once put out around the Brigade. The Brigade Transport arrived with the 5th Regiment, at 3 a.m.

When morning broke, practically the whole strength of the Brigade, with the exception of a few observation posts, was demanded by the C.R.E. for working parties to restore the water supply of the place, which had formerly been an important Turkish Cantonment, destined as a base for the invasion of Egypt. The men worked cheerfully, as it had been impressed upon them, that to a great extent the success of the forthcoming operations depended upon their efforts to produce a plentiful water supply. Later on, it was found better to have one constant working party, with its shifts of men who knew the work, in preference to men being detailed haphazard from the squadrons. This party was housed in some of the buildings close to the wells, and the Brigade went into bivouac among the ridges to the south of the water area. Strong outposts had to be found at night, and patrols were pushed well up the different roads leading to Asluj, but without meeting any enemy.

The Regiment, on the 29th, made a reconnaissance of the road leading to Bir Arara, and covered a party of Staff officers, in motor cars, who were making an inspection. This road was to be the one taken in the advance, and a point three miles south-east of Bir Arara was reached before any opposition was met. Here enemy cavalry and camel men, with nondescript Bedouins, were encountered in some strength, and a good many shots, at fairly long range, were exchanged. Orders had been received not to push on, so after obtaining a good idea of the road and country, we returned to camp shortly after dark. General Allenby visited Asluj, on the 28th, and expressed his pleasure at the work which had been done, and the spirit in which the men had entered into their task. In spite of all efforts, the water supply proved inadequate, and two days before the big move most of the horses had to be sent back to Khalasa, where water had been found in abundance. This gave the pumps at Asluj a chance to fill the reservoirs for the other troops coming in.

On the night of the 29th, the other two Brigades of the Division marched in, and our horses returned from Khalasa. The 30th was spent in resting and getting ready to move off that night, in the great sweeping movement which was to destroy the power of the Turk in Palestine, and to end in the capture of Jaffa and Jerusalem.

Briefly stated, the plan of operations consisted in the turning of the Beersheba position by practically all the Cavalry of the Desert Mounted Corps, whilst infantry, which had been gradually concentrated at Esani, made a night march, and attacked the redoubts west of the town, after a heavy artillery preparation. A violent bombardment of Gaza was to take place simultaneously, in preparation for an infantry assault there, after the Turkish line had been rolled back on Hareira and Atawineh, the centre positions of their line. Special endeavours had to be made to prevent the enemy, when once broken, from re-forming behind previously prepared positions in rear.

CHAPTER VII.

BATTLE OF BEERSHEBA.

THE moment long waited for was now at hand, and the value of our careful preparations and patient training under trying conditions was to be tested. The morale of the army was of the highest; it had completely recovered from the two set-backs at Gaza. Complete confidence was felt in the new Commander-in-Chief.

At 5 p.m. on October 31st, 1917, the regiment left its bivouac at Asluj, and moving as advance guard to the Brigade, passed Asluj Station at 6 p.m. The track led between barren, stony hills, and a thunderstorm had made a number of small watercourses boggy. The cross-roads, four miles south-west of Bir Arara, was the point where the 2nd L.H. Brigade severed connection with the remainder of the Division, which moved on Kashim Zanna. The Regiment from these cross-roads proceeded temporarily alone, the objective being Bir Arara, which was to be taken silently with the bayonet, if held.

Bir Arara was reached at 2 a.m., on November 1st. It was not held, and apparently never had been during the night, though Turkish mounted patrols were there in the daytime in some strength. A halt was made to allow the remainder of the Brigade to join up, and then the whole column moved on in the grand, wide encircling movement against Beersheba. The second objective was Bir El Hamam, a deep well, about six miles due east of the town; a mere watering-place for Bedouin flocks. This place was reached at 8 a.m., without opposition, though the N.Z.M.R. Brigade, on the high ridges about Kashim Zanna, could be seen driving in some outposts. From Bir El Hammam the dome and minaret of the great mosque in Beersheba were plainly visible, and also many troops, mostly cavalry, moving to the north of the town. A short halt was made for breakfast.

The going since we left Arara had been good, though shallow ravines caused some congestion at times. Although the altitude had greatly increased, the country was gently undulating, and gave the Brigade the utmost scope for wide movements. Not until the true foothills of the Judean Range, which lie west of the Hebran Road, and in the vicinity of Towal Abu Jerwal, are reached, does it become really difficult for mounted troops. These hills then gradually converge on the Hebron Road, and the boundary of hills and plain is there abruptly defined at Kurnet Ghazaleh. From this spot one may be said to enter the mountain country of Judea, which extends like a great rugged backbone through to Galilee, and almost to the foot of Mount Hermon and Damascus. It is true that the plain of Esdraelon interposes a barrier between the hill systems of Judea and Galilee, but for this they are one, and the geological formation is the same. These hills, at which we had so often gazed in the far distance, were now close at hand, and were to give us a taste of their rugged quality in a few days' time.

Hurried orders directed us to move with all speed to seize the third objective, Tel Es Sakaty, and get astride the Hebron Road. The Regiment moved off at a sharp canter, and almost immediately captured six transport waggons loaded with forage, and later a fatigue party of 49 men, who were at work on a culvert. These surrendered to a section of four men, in charge of Corporal Picton, who afterwards received the D.C.M. The gallop across a wide flat, which opens on to the Hebron Road, will long be remembered by those who took part in it. Turkish Cavalry and a battery had been seen moving to the west of the road, evidently with the intention of covering that highway as a possible means of retreat. The 7th Regiment, galloping forward with the Brigade in rear, menaced this force, which hurriedly withdrew to the high ground about half a mile west of the road, dragging their guns up the steep slopes. These guns were at length brought into action, and a hail of shells fell among the troops of the Regiment, but such is the immunity against shell-fire, of "shell, or artillery formation," especially in fast-moving bodies, that not a man was hit, though a number of the Bedouins, whose camp was in the line of fire, were knocked over. The gunners possibly were somewhat rattled by the quick work. As the road was approached, the Turkish machine guns opened fire, and Lieutenant-Colonel Onslow realised that the position was too strong and too steep to be galloped; he therefore smartly swung the whole Regiment at the gallop to the right, and crossing the road, found good cover for the horses in Wadi Aujan. Beyond this, however, it was impossible to advance, as the enemy possessed many machine guns, and any movement at once drew severe fire.

Our position was consolidated, and we linked up with the 5th A.L.H. Regiment, which came in from the right shortly afterwards. Intermittent sniping continued during the day, but as the objective had been gained, no further attempt to advance was made. Our role was to hold these positions against any enemy retirement from Beersheba.

It was a fine sight to see the Australian Mounted Division moving forward to close in on the town of Beersheba. Regiment after regiment, troop after troop, they moved forward until the whole wide plain east of the town seemed to be covered with mounted men. This movement was to culminate in the gallant charge of the 4th Light Horse Brigade, which, disregarding trenches, galloped with bayonets fixed right into Beersheba, and captured a number of guns and enemy who would otherwise have escaped, besides preventing the blowing in of an all-important well.

On our left, the N.Z.M.R. Brigade was having a hard fight for Tel el Saba, a high mound strongly trenched, at the junction of two deep wadis. With the support of the 1st L.H. Brigade in dealing with machine guns flanking this position, Tel el Saba was taken at about 4 p.m. The Horse Artillery Battery (Ayrshire) attached to our Brigade, had now come into action against the guns which had attempted to check our advance; very soon the enemy guns were silenced and were withdrawn out of action. An effort was made to dislodge the machine guns in front of us by shell fire, but without success. The wadi in which the Regiment, horses and all, was hidden afforded excellent protection, but any movement above these at once drew a hail of bullets, and any advance must have caused the heaviest casualties.

At night, the line was drawn back somewhat, so as to link up better with the Brigade. The explosions and fires in Beersheba indicated that the town had fallen. At 4.30 a.m., on November 1st, the Regiment moved forward again to re-occupy the line of the previous day. Troops were pushed forward to feel for the enemy, but he had retired during the night, and the ridges hitherto held were occupied without opposition. The Regiment was relieved at noon by the 6th A.L.H. Regiment, and withdrew to a bivouac close to D.H.Q., where a water supply, in pools caused by the thunderstorm on October 31st, had been found. Most of the horses had been without water for nearly 36 hours. Thus ended the Battle of Beersheba, the first blow of a series which quickly followed, and from which the enemy dragged the remnants of his army right back beyond Jaffa, where they were only able to re-form with the assistance of fresh troops. The Infantry, in attacking Beersheba from the west, had done their part well; quickly the barb-wire in front of redoubts was destroyed by concentrated Artillery fire, and the redoubts were themselves then stormed. It needed only the encircling Cavalry to batter at the back-door to cause its speedy downfall. The Turk had, however, made all arrangements for quickly evacuating the place and blowing in the wells; the dashing charge of the 4th L.H. Brigade alone prevented him from making a good withdrawal; even so, the greater part of his Garrison and guns did get away, retiring to reserve positions at Tel el Sharia before our Infantry, advancing through Bir Abu Irgeig, could cut their line.

Many booby traps, against which all had been warned, were found in the town and near the railway station. A quantity of rolling stock was mined in such a fashion that the opening of a carriage door would have caused a violent explosion. Our engineers detected most of these little tricks of the Hun, and withdrew the charges before any damage was done.

The day following the battle was quiet, and opportunity was taken to give the horses a much-needed rest, and as much water as a rather inadequate supply permitted.

On November 2nd, the Brigade was ordered to move against Dhareriyeh, 12 miles south of Hebron; the 6th Regiment taking the Hebron Road, with the 7th working wide on the right flank. The 6th was quickly held up near Makruneh, where the 5th Regiment had been also checked on the previous day. The 7th was then ordered to make a wide movement and threaten the enemy's flank near Dhaheriyeh.

The country now became extremely difficult, and movement away from the rough tracks was out of the question. High ridges protect the Hebron Road, and these were found to be strongly held. An attack was made about a mile south of the village of Dhareriyeh; even without the enemy holding them, the rough hills would have been difficult to climb, and the attempt had to be abandoned. All movement was of necessity very slow. Four men were hit at distant range by enemy snipers. The 5th Regiment came up on our right late in the afternoon, and made its headquarters on Point 2,110 Ed. Deir, a high hill, about 1,200 yards south-east of Dhaheriyeh.

When darkness had fallen, the line held by the Brigade was in the shape of an inverted L, being from the vicinity of Deir El Hawa, due east to the Hebron Road, thence along the old road running parallel to the Hebron Road, through Bir En Nettuf to Point 2,110 Ed. Deir. This line had to be linked up at night by a chain of piquets, on account of its great length: for Infantry this would have been unsafe, as it was without depth, and a wedge might easily have been driven into it anywhere by a resolute enemy and the force divided. But against Infantry and such Cavalry as the Turks possessed, our mounted troops had little to fear.

Our posts linked up that night with the 5th Regiment on the right and the 6th on the left, R.H.Q. being on a high hill, a mile south of El Dier. Next morning the Brigadier visited the line, and in the afternoon decided to push forward the 5th and 7th Regiments in a demonstration to the rear of Dhaheriyeh. Two guns of the Ayrshire Battery were brought up to the vicinity of El Dier, and engaged a battery of 77's, without success, during the whole day, having a hole blown through one of their limbers by an enemy shell.

The Regiment moved off, with the 5th on the right, and reached a point about 1,500 yards from the Hebron Road, a mile north of Dhaheriyeh. This movement alarmed the enemy, and he reinforced his line with troops in motor lorries from Hebron. A depôt battalion was hastily thrown into Dhaheriyeh. It was afterwards discovered that our move had also caused him to withdraw troops from the Khuweilfeh area, as he feared that an advance against Hebron and through to Jerusalem was contemplated.

A message was now received from Brigade, that the Corps-Commander did not desire the attack on Dhaheriyeh to be pressed. Orders were given for the return of the two regiments to the line held during the previous night. Until Novmber 5th it was a matter simply of holding this line, and making every endeavour to get sufficient water for men and horses, in order that the strain on the already overtaxed supply at Beersheba should not be increased. Rations had to be brought up at night, as the track by which they came was badly exposed to shell fire during the day. A good deal of intermittent shelling took place on both sides, the enemy's fire being often directed by aeroplanes; the steep hillsides and deep wadis gave good protection, though they were well "searched." Rougher country for mounted troops it would be difficult to imagine.

By November 4th the rain pools in the wadis close by, upon which the Brigade had been dependent for water, gave out, and orders were received to move back to Beersheba, at daylight, on the 5th. A few men were left to appear on the skyline at daybreak, and thus deceive the enemy as to our purpose; and the Regiment, joining up with the Brigade, marched to Makruneh, where a halt was made to draw rations.

"A" Squadron, under Major Easterbrook, was now ordered to report with our Brigade M.G. Squadron, less one section, to Headquarters of the Camel Brigade, in the vicinity of Khuweilfeh, where desperate fighting had been in progress. Two troops, under Captain Maddrell, with two troops of the 6th Regiment, were left at Makruneh to protect the right flank of the Camel Brigade from any enemy advance along the Hebron Road. Khuweilfeh is a well-watered area, with important road junctions, seven miles west of Dhaheriyeh. "A" Squadron proceeded to Ras El Nagb, from which place an assault on the Turkish lines at Khuweilfeh was being made by the Imperial Camel Brigade and 53rd Infantry Division. This attack was only partially successful, and a Turkish counter-attack which followed might have caused a serious reverse. With great dash, Major Easterbrook rushed his Squadron into a gap between the I.C. Brigade and 53rd Division, which was most seriously menaced, and with the assistance of the M.G. Squadron attached, held up the advance, though suffering severely from the enemy's fire.

The M.G. Squadron, and two troops of "A" Squadron, were hotly engaged all day on the 6th, and suffered numerous casualties, owing to the accuracy of enemy snipers and machine gunners: these troops were practically isolated, as machine guns completely dominated the approaches to their position. Towards evening the remaining troops of the Squadron managed to get up in support; the night passed quietly. As the casualties amounted to six killed (including one officer), and 17 wounded in the M.G. Squadron, and in "A" Squadron two killed and 15 wounded (including one officer), and the men and horses had been 36 hours without rations or water, Major Easterbrook asked permission to withdraw. Both Squadrons moved out without further casualties, at dawn, on the 7th, and proceeded to Beersheba, remaining there for the night. Next morning they pushed on, and rejoined the Regiment and Brigade at 6 p.m., at Tel El Negile. For conspicuous gallantry at Khuweilfeh, in rescuing Lieutenant Carter, who was badly wounded, under heavy fire, Sergeant A. E. James afterwards received the D.C.M.

The Regiment, less "A" Squadron and the two troops (on outpost) on the Hebron Road, moved on with the Brigade to a point $1\frac{1}{2}$ miles east of Beersheba, arriving there at 1 p.m.

CHAPTER VIII.

BREAKING THROUGH.

THE general position now was, roughly, as follows:—The heavy guns from our warships and our land batteries had nearly smashed the Gaza defences to pulp; all was ready for the Infantry assault as soon as the enemy's right flank, now turned back through Abu Hareira and Tel El Sharia to Khuweilfeh, should be broken or rolled up. At Khuweilfeh, in very rough country, the enemy was holding us well, with practically fresh troops; but near Tel El Sharia, the 60th (London) Division was gradually breaking a gap, and it was through this that the two Mounted Divisions were to be pushed. Other Infantry Divisions were hammering at enemy trenches at Hareira and Atawineh, and although a stubborn resistance was being made, the end was in sight.

The 1st L.H. Brigade and the N.Z.M. Rifle Brigade, which had been fighting round Khuweilfeh, had fared far worse than our Brigade, as regards water for both horses and men; the latter Brigade was so exhausted that it was unable to march with the Division when it moved out, and did not join up till some days afterwards.

Our horses were sent into Beersheba for water, an excellent pumping plant and good supply of fresh water being available. At 4.30 p.m. the march was hurriedly resumed, owing to the receipt of urgent orders; a halt was eventually made two miles south of the Wadi Ghuzaleh for the night, after some rough going in stony Wadis. There were no further casualties on this day, but 17 men were evacuated sick, showing that the strain was beginning to tell.

Next morning, moving with the Brigade, the Regiment came under some long-range shell fire, but passing down a deep Wadi to Kh Um El Bakr, sustained no casualties.

Headquarters of 1st L.H. Brigade, with some of the Divisional Staff, were found at Kh Um El Bakr, where there were evidences of recent enemy occupation in abandoned ammunition dumps and baggage; Sharia is two miles to the west. This place was being subjected to long-range fire of 5.9's, which, as the troops of the 1st L.H. Brigade moved forward on Ameidat railway station, was switched on to them. Our Brigade was in reserve, and, in artillery formation, advanced widely extended, following the 1st, and coming also under the same long-range fire, without, however, suffering casualties. Ameidat railway station, four miles north of Kh Um El Bakr, was taken by the 1st Brigade, the booty including a great quantity of ammunition. The rolling downs country hereabouts was ideal for our purposes, and enabled us to keep enemy infantry and guns at long distances, and on the move for fear of being outflanked.

Some shell fire (light guns) from the rougher country east of Ameidat, and from the vicinity of Tel Abu Dilakh, was met later in the afternoon; the troops, however, dispersed widely and found shelter in railway cuttings and behind banks. When our horse batteries opened, the enemy fire ceased. Just before dark the 5th Regiment was sent forward to occupy Tel Abu Dilakh, a mile to the north of Ameidat. This Regiment was heavily shelled, and suffered a number of casualties, including two officers killed, but remained in possession of the Tel and the rough ground close by, during the night.

The Division had now called a halt, to enable the Australian Mounted Division, which was moving up on our left, to link up with us; during the night, our outposts and theirs came in touch. Our horses had had no water during that day, nor since leaving Beersheba, and it was imperative that they should get it on the morrow. A quiet night was spent.

At dawn, the 7th Regiment was pushed forward to support the 5th on Tel Abu Dilakh, and the two Regiments moved north into more rugged country, near to Wadi

Brigade Camp at Romani.

Boundary Posts between Sinai and Palestine.

Hesi. "B" Squadron, under Major Willsallen, came into action across the Wadi with superior forces of the enemy, and, although checked, held its position against several strong enemy counter-attacks. At 2 p.m., "C" Squadron, under Major Barton, was sent to support the 5th, which was holding a long line on our left. They arrived just in time to help beat off a desperate enemy attack. The enemy, doubtless, wished to deny us the water supply of the Wadi Hesi. This Squadron, in conjunction with a Squadron of the 5th, checked all counter-attacks, and retained the position. The enemy was now putting large forces of infantry against what was, early in the day, our single Brigade, but without success. Magnificent work was done by our Hotchkiss gunners and those of the other two Regiments, and without these handy little weapons it would have been almost impossible to hold the ground gained. Later in the day, the 7th Mounted Brigade (two Regiments of Yeomanry) came up on our left, and eased the situation considerably, as a fierce counter-attack was diverted against them, but without success. The arrival, at nightfall, of the 1st L.H. Brigade, and troops of the Australian Mounted Division, on our extreme left, made the position safe, and the enemy attacks ceased.

The determined advance of our Regiment, and the resolute holding of the ground gained about the Wadi Hesi and Tel El Nejile, gave us control of an abundant supply of good water, in springs. The water put new life into our long-suffering horses, which had now been without a drink for 48 hours. The men were able to refill their water-bottles for the first time since leaving Beersheba.

The Brigade and Regimental transport waggons and limbers, which had been toiling along in the rear, joined up at night, and enabled some of the men and horses to get a fresh supply of rations and forage.

"A" Squadron, with the Machine Gun Squadron from Khuweilfeh, rejoined just before dark. Our total casualties for the day were only nine killed and wounded. There was good cover from machine gun fire, and the enemy used very little shrapnel. The line was drawn back slightly at night, and consolidated against enemy enterprise; but the night passed uneventfully.

Bureir, eight miles to the north-west of Tel En Nejile, was given as our next objective. The enemy was now lining the ridges about two miles due north of our overnight position, and a move was made, under cover of broken ground, diagonally across their front, to join up with the remainder of the Brigade, which was swinging well to the left. This movement, as soon as it was exposed, came under distant machine gun fire, the bullets falling like hailstones close to our right flank troops. Lieutenant Donkin, our signalling officer, was the only man hit, and the force of the bullet was so spent that a bruise was the only result. Upon leaving the rough country of the Wadi Hesi, and debouching into the wide plain, which commences about three miles east of Bureir, the Brigade came under heavy shell fire from the north and north-east.

Our two Brigades now made a fine sight as, widely extended, they moved on a parallel front across the plain to Bureir. The 1st was on our left, and escaped the shelling, which, however, did not check progress for one moment.

The Regiment, which hitherto had been fortunate as regards casualties, had now half a troop of "A" Squadron, both men and horses, wiped out by a single shell. At a steady pace the advance was continued. About two miles from Bureir, Lieutenant Snow with two or three men came upon and captured two aircraft guns, but were driven off by considerable numbers of the enemy, who were, however, compelled to blow up guns and retire. Bureir was found unoccupied, and the 5th Regiment made some captures of guns and stores.

Without halting, the Regiment dashed through El Huleikat (where German Headquarters of Kress Von Kressenstein had been) on to Kaukabah, where, at 10 o'clock, it captured an entire enemy supply train of 110 waggons, with horses, mules, donkeys and oxen, and 390 men. The condition of many of the animals was pitiable in the extreme;

they were dying in harness from sheer exhaustion, and lack of food and water. The Turkish Supply Columns had broken down under the too great demand made to supply a wide front, fed by only a single line of railway. The condition of some of the men taken prisoners was not much better than that of the animals; all were suffering from thirst. This capture was made, in the first place, by Lieutenant Zouch, with his troop, who, after handing over the prisoners to the remainder of "B" Squadron, pushed on again to the front.

A halt was made at Kaukabah for breakfast, and to enable the 1st Brigade on our left to link up. Rations and forage, which could not be issued before, were now distributed. Another enemy convoy was observed moving four miles to the north, and as the 1st L.H. Brigade was now abreast and directed on Medjel, our advance was continued. The 5th and 7th Regiments made the convoy their objective, and the 6th Regiment was also sent in by the Brigadier on the right to share the spoil.

Enemy rear-guards were met on the ridges to the south, and covering the village of Ebdis, and although these at first made a stout resistance, they were outflanked, and retired hastily, leaving a battery of 4.2in. Howitzers as a prize to the Regiment. Our Hotchkiss rifles were found to be invaluable for this outflanking work. "B" and "C" Squadrons were now pushed forward with great dash, working with the 5th Regiment, and assisted in the capture of this second convoy of 100 waggons and 300 prisoners.

Enemy rearguards, with field and machine guns, blocked any further advance, either in the direction of Beit Duras or El Kustineh, though the three villages of Suafir were occupied after "A" Squadron had driven out enemy machine gunners and snipers, with some trouble. These retired down a Wadi towards El Kustineh, and were encountered again a little later. "A" Squadron was finally held up on the same line as the 6th Regiment, on our right. That Regiment had not fared so well as the other two, and had been checked two or three times by enemy strongly posted in deep wadis. These were outflanked, and driven from one line to another, but a final check was caused by a strong position and numerous enemy forces with machine guns, near Tel El Turmus.

Enemy guns now commenced shelling the 5th and two Squadrons of the 7th with the captured convoy, the shells falling among our prisoners and causing these to panic. It did not seem to occur to the Turkish gunners that they might kill their own comrades-in-arms.

As darkness had now fallen, orders were received from Brigade to send all the prisoners back to B.H.Q., at Suafir Es Gharbiye, and for the Regiment to withdraw also, concentrate, and place outposts in the vicinity of that place.

Before this could be done, however, our temporary outposts of "B" Squadron challenged and fired upon a body of Turks outside our lines, who attacked with bombs and rifle fire. These proved to be the enemy who had earlier in the day been driven out of the cactus hedges of Suafir Es Gharbiye, and in retiring they had blundered upon our advanced troops. With great promptitude, the men under Lieutenant Waddell, who was in charge of the outpost, shouted out "Tesleem" (Surrender), and after some resistance they threw down their arms and gave themselves up to "B" Squadron, which only numbered forty-six of all ranks at that moment. There were 234 Turks in this lot. With some difficulty, owing to the darkness, a withdrawal to Suafir Es Gharbiye with the prisoners was made, and a line of outposts placed to link up with the other Regiments of the Brigade.

This day (9th November) had been a great one for the Regiment, as well as the Brigade. The Regiment alone had captured six guns, 110 waggons, and over 500 prisoners, and had assisted the 5th Regiment in the capture of 100 more waggons and 300 men. Our casualties for the day amounted to only 21, mostly sustained by "A" Squadron.

For the skilful handling of his Squadron during this day, Major Willsallen received the D.S.O., and a number of other decorations were later on awarded to N.C.O.'s and men, for gallant conduct.

CHAPTER IX.

THE PURSUIT.

THE Regiment, linking up with the 5th and 6th Regiments, placed outposts round the village of Suafir Es Gharbiye; the cactus hedges which overrun this place made excellent obstacles against an attack, but the enemy was too weary and broken to attempt anything, and the night passed quietly. Efforts were made to water the horses, but it was with the greatest difficulty that sufficient water was obtained for the requirements even of the men. The wells were 150 feet in depth, and water was obtained from them by means of a skin fastened to a rope pulled over a runner by a donkey or bullock. The unfortunate Turkish prisoners moaned for water all night; dysentery was rife among them. Nothing could be done for them until daylight. They were then sent in parties of twenty to the wells, but only a few had quenched their thirst when a divisional order was received to send all prisoners back to Medjel, under escort, and to use all speed to get the horses of the Brigade watered.

Our Engineers installed troughing and improved somewhat on the primitive drawing gear at the four wells, but the process was very slow. The villagers also were in straits for water, as the Turks had deprived them of the supply before our arrival; some consideration had to be shown to them.

At the wells we were shelled severely at intervals during the day, from the vicinity of El Kustine, which was still strongly held. No interruption, however, took place, and only a few casualties resulted. As it was necessary to discover the enemy strength in front, composite squadrons of the fittest men and horses of the 5th and 7th Regiments were sent forward, but they were quickly held up by machine guns, strongly posted in a railway cutting about 2,000 yards south-west of El Kustineh. Captain Stevenson, in command of the composite squadron of the 7th, was hit by a machine gun bullet close to the knee, and several other casualties were sustained.

The Brigade had now temporarily run itself out, owing to the famished condition of the horses as regards water, and it was reported to D.H.Q. that any forward movement, or the lack of water for a few hours' longer, would put two-thirds of the horses of the Brigade permanently out of action. By nightfall of the 10th, there still remained a number of the poor brutes that had not been watered, and the more fortunate ones had not had nearly sufficient. It was realised then, that these village wells were inadequate for the 2,000 horses of a mounted Brigade; orders were received that an infantry Brigade was being pushed forward, and as soon as its outposts had taken over our line, our Brigade would withdraw to Hamame, seven miles to the west, close to the seashore, where a plentiful supply of good water was obtainable.

"C" Squadron, under Major Barton, was left to hold the front line at Suafir Es Shemaliye (Northern). As soon as the Ghurka advance guards were in position, this Squadron withdrew, and commenced to move in the wake of the Regiment for Hamame, just before nightfall, and bivouac was made there. Next morning we moved to the edge of the sand dunes, in order to be closer to the water, which was fresh and plentiful within a few yards of high-water mark on the ocean beach. The day was spent in watering the horses and resting. No move was made on the 12th, though all units were held in readiness. On the following day at noon, the advance was continued, the 7th being the advance guard Regiment. A halt was made a mile to the west of Suafir Es Gharbiye, until night, as the Brigade was now in Desert Mounted Corps Reserve.

D.M.C. Headquarters were on the prominent hill close by, from which the bombardment and infantry assault of Katrah, a village ten miles to the north, was being watched. Just as darkness fell the Brigade was ordered to Point 248, three miles south-east of

Suafir Es Gharbiye. Owing to the darkness and difficult wadis, 248 was not reached that night, an outpost position being taken up on the plain about 1,000 yards west of that spot. The Brigade was then directed to move with all speed upon Et Tine, and to come under the orders of the Australian Mounted Division. Hurrying forward, the Regiment, still as advance guard, passed many signs of the enemy's broken and demoralised condition—abandoned waggons, baggage and burnt aeroplanes. Et Tine was reached at noon, and a halt was made until 1 p.m. Forage bags were filled with grain and tibbin from captured enemy supplies. Men of the 4th L.H. Brigade calmly watered their horses at a well more than reasonably believed to be mined.

The advance was continued towards Junction Station, where an infantry assault had taken place on the previous day; an enemy counter-attack was believed to be imminent. The Regiment, still leading, entered the rough country of the Judean foothills, close to the village of Jilia, and passing through Kezazeh came under shell fire on the steep ridges above the Wadi Surar, and overlooking the Jerusalem road in the vicinity of Khuldeh. Junction Station, held by Infantry, with the 7th Mounted Brigade (Yeomanry) on their right, and linking up with us, was about 2,500 yards to the northwest. Advanced troops of the 4th L.H. Brigade were posted on observation points close by; these withdrew as our troops advanced. The enemy's shell fire soon ceased, but a few casualties occurred from well-directed shrapnel. An outpost line was taken up on the high ridges close to Ain Es Sejed, where a good well, with abundant water, was found.

The enemy could be plainly observed in the vicinity of Khuldeh, and straggling wearily along the Jerusalem road; his transport was seen to be parked under the massive shoulder of 850 (Sheik Musa Tellias), but too far away for our guns to reach. His rearguard position was, however, well chosen, with advanced posts in the vicinity of Khuldeh and the rough country to the east, fully covering the Jerusalem road. Every little knob and hill appeared to mount a machine gun, whilst his field guns were well served and wonderfully accurate, quickly silencing our horse battery, which had come up and opened fire.

The Brigade was now ordered to remain in observation and protect the right flank of the line, which rested roughly on the Jerusalem railway line and Wadi Surar to the vicinity of Kh El Bireh. No other course was possible with the numbers available, as a direct attack on the enemy's front would have been disastrous; the turning movement of other mounted Brigades was now progressing, and finally caused the enemy to abandon this strong position.

The outpost line was strongly held during the night, which, however, passed uneventfully. In the morning it was noticed that the greater part of the enemy's transport had got away, and that some of his rearguard seemed to be moving also. The 7th Mounted Brigade now made a demonstration against this, and was supported on the right by "B" Squadron, under Major Willsallen, which galloped forward to the shelter of the low ridges across the Wadi Es Surar, about 3,000 yards north of Ain Es Sejed, coming under heavy machine gun and shrapnel fire.

As it appeared likely that the two Squadrons of Yeomanry sent forward were running into a hornets' nest, they were hastily recalled, and orders were heliographed to "B" Squadron to return. Unfortunately, however, before this could be done, Lieutenant Zouch and a trooper were dangerously wounded by shrapnel. The Turks did not respect the Red Cross on the ambulance sent forward, but opened fire upon it at long range, fortunately, without result. Lieutenant Zouch died at Julis, a few days later. In him the Regiment lost a most gallant and conscientious officer—one whose watchwords were duty and honour. Lieutenant Zouch, whose father also was a soldier and had won the D.C.M. at Elaandslagte, lies buried in the Military Cemetery at Deirel Belah, ten miles south-west of Gaza.

CHAPTER X.

THE PURSUIT CONTINUED.

AS the Yeomanry Squadrons had now withdrawn, "B" Squadron rejoined the Regiment without further casualties; the Turkish fire had slackened.

The plentiful water supply at Ain Es Sejed was a great boon to both men and horses. A considerable quantity of tibben, found in adjoining villages, was requisitioned for the horses. The Mukhtar (Mayor) of the village received a formal receipt, that so many pounds of tibben had been requisitioned; later on, it was found necessary to take greater precautions in giving these receipts, as the Syrian Arab is, as a rule, cunning and unscrupulous. No further movement took place on the 15th, as definite orders were received from Divisional Headquarters that the duties of the Brigade were to be of observation and protection only; on no account was a further attack to be pushed forward.

Orders having been received during the night for the Brigade to rejoin Desert Mounted Corps again as reserve, a move was made through Junction Station and Akir to Ras Deiran, 12 miles south-east of Jaffa. The captured trains, guns and stores at Junction Station were clear indications of the haste and demoralisation of the enemy, and showed how badly he had been hit.

Arabs were flocking from all directions, like birds of prey, to seize whatever they could; their hardihood as looters was astonishing, and they really seemed to consider that the stores abandoned by the Turks became at once their heritage, without reference at all to the troops that had captured them. With greedy, anxious faces they hurried along with their donkeys and women (also beasts of burden), only worried lest others should be there before them. Presumably, the tactical situation did not permit of troops being detailed to guard all captured material and stores; later on, measures were taken to make the Arabs disgorge, but not a tenth part of what had been looted was recovered.

Akir is a Jewish village, and it was possible to buy brown bread and honey there, but at more or less exorbitant prices.

Ras Deiran was reached early in the afternoon, and bivouac made close to a large orchard to the west of this Jewish village, which is of some importance, and apparently more prosperous than Akir. It is pleasantly situated among orange and almond orchards, which run from here almost without a break by way of the villages of Wadi Hanein and Richon Le Zion to Jaffa. These villages are all Jewish colonies, often of Rothschild benefaction; the colonists being, almost without exception, Russian Jews driven by pogroms and persecution to seek new homes in the land of their forefathers. Their neat stone and wooden houses, and fertile and well-kept orchards, form a great contrast to the squalid mud villages and primitive husbandry of the Arabs.

The oranges at Ras Deiran, although not quite ripe, were sweet and refreshing to tired troops. The owners did not seem to be about at first, but once they did come on the scene they appeared to be in great tribulation. Finally, the orchards had to be placed out-of-bounds. October 17th was spent in bivouac, resting at Ras Deiran. Next day the Brigade was ordered to Ludd, 12 miles to the north. Marching through narrow lanes, hedged thickly with acacia, the Regiment passed down the narrow streets and cemeteries of Ramleh, a large Arab town, in the midst of most luxuriant olive groves. Evidences of the fight that the 1st L.H. Brigade had had a day or two previously were seen; many dead horses lay about. There were huge piles of firewood for railway engines; the Turks had caused the devastation of many acres of beautiful olives. The Greek churches of Ramleh, and the ancient "Tower of the Forty Martyrs" are the only imposing buildings in Ramleh; otherwise, it is a squalid Arab village.

Guided by a Syrian, in very baggy trousers, whose English was defective, though he had learnt to swear effectively, the Brigade moved on to Ludd, where Greek Churches again are the outstanding buildings. Under a Latin Church here are said to lie the bones of St. George of England; a shrine, renovated by one of our crusading Kings, marks the spot. Bivouac was made under the olive groves on the northern edge of the town, reached through winding, narrow lanes and paths.

The Turk had now been driven to the rough country of the Judean foothills, about ten miles to the east and north of Ludd, where his rearguard was making desperate efforts to prevent our further advance; his extreme right flank had now been thrown back to Sheikh Muannis, on the coast, about six miles north-east of Jaffa, whilst with his left flank he was doing his utmost to cover Jerusalem. Any further advance on our part along the Maritime plain, north of Jaffa, or the penetration of his line north or north-east of Ludd, would have at once placed his forces covering Jerusalem in a critical position, from whence escape could only be possible by a swift retirement north to Nablus, or Nazareth, or through Jericho, and across the Jordan to the Hedjaz railway, and thence to Damascus. Resistance, therefore, stiffened daily on the front Jaffa to Ludd, and in the hills to the east, and evidence soon appeared that fresh troops were being put into this line.

The Maritime or Philistine Plain from Gaza to Jaffa, with the exception of the coastal sand dune belt, which, in places encroaches on the fertile land as much as six miles, is fine undulating country, evidently capable of growing, under proper cultivation, some of the finest crops in the world. Its depth from the coast of the Judean foothills, the Shephelah of the Bible, varies from about 10 to 15 miles, being at its greatest near Jaffa. Arab, and near Jaffa, Jewish, and two German villages dot the plain at intervals of a few miles. Among these are the modern representatives of the ancient Ashod (Esdud) Ascalon and Ekron, "Cities of the Philistines", now nothing but squalid mud villages. Nothing of the former grandeur of Ascalon, where Coeur de Lion held his court, now remains, Gaza alone of all these famous Philistine cities can claim to be still of some importance. The country is intersected with many wadis, which carry the winter rains from the hills in raging torrents to the sea. The most important of these are the Nahr Rubin and the Nahr Sukereir. Five miles north of Jaffa, the first perrenial stream is met in the Nahr el Auja, fed by springs from the hills, and for a few miles near its mouth a respectable little river. The Plain, almost everywhere, meets the foothills abruptly, and these rise in steep, stony ridges until the backbone of the mountain range is reached, about 20 miles from the coast.

Many Arab villages are perched on, or close to, the top of a number of the lower hills, especially those bordering the Plain. These differ from the villages of the Plain appearance. Olive trees and crops of various sorts are grown on pockets of what appears to be fairly good land among the rocks, but how this mountain country supports its in being built of stone instead of mud, and therefore, have a much more substantial population is remarkable. One suspects that this rugged region supplies many of the recruits to the bands of robbers, who, in normal times, infest Palestine.

The Regiment remained in bivouac at Ludd until the 20th November, when, at 8.30 a.m., a move was made to the front, and a line of outposts taken up in the foothills extending from the railway line near Deirtarif through Beit Nabala to Budros. Troops of the 54th Infantry Division took over this line late in the afternoon and the Regiment returned to camp after an eventful day. Heavy rain at night caused much discomfort as the men had only their thin "bivvy sheets" as shelters. The rain ceased by morning. The Regiment was now ordered to the outpost lines north of Ludd and relieved troops of the 1st L.H. Brigade in positions extending from El Yehudieh to point 265, four miles to the north-west of that place. At 6.30 a.m. on the 22nd, one troop was sent out to the vicinity of Mulebbis, a prosperous Jewish village on the Nahr El Auja, and came in touch with the enemy, who was occupying the heights across the river. Only intermittent sniping took place. At 10 a.m. the Regiment was again relieved, this time by a Camel Battalion, and moved back to where Brigade headquarters were in bivouac just south of Yazur, four miles east of Jaffa.

"C" Squadron was sent on the following day to escort refugees from Mulebbis to Jaffa, as the Jews were apprehensive of ill treatment from the Turks if they regained possession of the village. Nothing of importance happened. On the 24th, two troops were detailed to make a crossing for wheeled traffic over the steep Wadi Nusrah, between the villages of Ibn Ibrak and Yazur; at 11 p.m. on the same day six troops were ordered to escort the Ayrshire Battery, which was to assist in a demonstration by the N.Z.M.R. Brigade, by shelling a bridge over the Nahrel Auja, north of Mulebbis.

The New Zealanders pushed forward well across the river at its mouth and in the vicinity of Sheikh Muannis and our men advanced through the dense orange groves which surrounded Mulebbis, to within 1,000 yards of the southern bank, almost due north of that village. Parties of the enemy, in some strength, were observed across the river, and targets were indicated to our guns, which shelled effectively, quickly dispersing the Turks or causing them to seek cover. No further advance was made, as the duty of the Regiment was simply to cover the guns; a troop, under Lieutenant Suttor, sent to Ras El Ain, three miles east of Mulebbis, encountered no opposition. Darkness caused a withdrawal to the bivouac at Yazur.

The New Zealanders remained in possession of the village of Sheikh Muannis and the Turkish trenches at Khurbet Hadrah, being reinforced by some companies of Infantry of the 54th (West Counties) Division. At daybreak on November 24th, the enemy made a determined counter attack against Sheikh Muannis, and the trenches at Khurbet Hadrah, employing fresh troops. The garrisons were hard pressed, and finally were pushed back and compelled to retire across the river. They reached the southern bank with some difficulty and sustained many casualties from the hot Turkish fire. The Regiment was hurried up to point 275, four miles north of Yazur, and was placed in reserve ready to support the New Zealand Brigade, and a battalion of the Essex Regiment which were lining trenches on the southern bank of the river.

The enemy pushed forward resolutely, and it appeared as if he intended to force a crossing, but he was finally held up by battery fire and machine guns on the northern bank. Late in the afternoon, the Regiment was ordered to relieve a Regiment of New Zealanders who were in close support to the Essex Infantry at "Caves", 1,500 yards north of 275. The relief came under enemy observation and was heavily shelled by howitzers and field guns; cover was good, however, and no casualties resulted.

A quiet night was spent, as the enemy made no effort to follow up his success. Next day spasmodic shelling took place all along the line, the enemy guns making determined efforts to reach us; but the cover was too good, and very few shells burst really close. Brigade headquarters, just in rear of point 275, were not so fortunate; they were shelled by a heavy howitzer just before dark and sustained a number of casualties. Major Bryant, commanding the Ayrshire Battery, who was spotting for his guns on 275, was killed almost instantly by a shell, which must have fallen almost perpendicularly, bursting close beside him.

Beyond shelling, the enemy made no further demonstration on this section of the line, the river evidently presenting too formidable an obstacle. On the 27th, Infantry reinforcements having come up and taken over our positions, the Regiment, less "B" Squadron, was ordered into Brigade Reserve and bivouacked in a shallow wadi, about 1,000 yards south of point 265, a spot indicated by a solitary tree. "B" Squadron, under Major Willsallen, was sent to garrison post No. 7 on the extreme left of the Brigade sector.

CHAPTER XI.

OPPERATIONS NEAR JAFFA.

THE general disposition of the troops, and the line held at this time, was briefly as follows:—

The 54th Infantry Division was based on Ludd with advanced troops near Deir Tarif and covering the pleasant German colony of Wilhelma, six miles to the north of Ludd. In the vicinity of El Yehudeih, this Division linked up with the Imperial Camel Brigade, which held a line running north-west to Bald Hill, a prominent whale-backed ridge, about 1,000 yards east of point 265, already referred to. Point 265 was the extreme right flank of our Brigade and was garrisoned at this time by the 6th L.H. Regiment, an extensive trench system having been almost completed by the 5th L.H. Regiment, which had formerly been in occupation.

Point 265 was the key of the whole position, and any enemy breakthrough there, would have endangered the whole line. Almond orchards in front, intersected with cactus hedges, masked the trenches well and gave good opportunities for our Hotchkiss rifles and snipers against any enemy advance. Post No. 1 was the trench system at 265, with an advanced work at what was known as the Ypres Salient. To the left Post 2 covered the road through the almond orchards to Mulebbis, and was well screened from enemy observation. Posts 3, 4, 5 and 6, were dug actually in the almond orchards on rising ground that gave fair fields of fire. These more or less enfiladed each others front, the front of No. 3 being swept also from Nos. 2 and 4.

On the 27th the 5th L.H. Regiment was garrisoning 3, 4, 5 and 6. No. 7 was an outstanding red mound, rather exposed to enemy observation at Khurbet Hadrah. Any movement brought a blast of enemy shell fire, which was also directed against an orange orchard, half a mile in rear, where an endeavour had been made to water the horses of the Brigade at a good well. Owing to the severity of fire, this had to be abandoned, and horses were sent back to villages in rear, for the most part to Selme.

No. 7 linked up with troops of the 54th Division, established in a redoubt about 500 yards to the north-west. The 161st Brigade of the 54th Division continued the line from here, following roughly the Wadi Auja to its mouth. The siting of the trenches in our Brigade sector, and the greater part of the earlier digging, had been done by the 5th L.H. Regiment, and so well, that, in spite of severe shelling, few casualties resulted during our occupation; any attacks made by the enemy never for a moment looked like succeeding. None of the Posts were further than 500 yards from another, and in the orchards the lateral distance was reduced to 200 so that no enemy troops could filter through without suffering severely.

During November 27, as on the preceding day, enemy movements had been considerable, and just before dark a body of 4,000 Turks was observed, marching from the north towards Mulebbis. On the 28th the enemy commenced to shell the line, from Post No. 7 to Wilhelma, very heavily. Bald Hill, held by a battalion of the Camel Brigade, was especially singled out and spouted 5.9 shells like minature volcanoes. In the forenoon a determined enemy Infantry attack, made in force and supported by heavy artillery fire, drove the Camel Battalion off Bald Hill and appeared to threaten our positions at 265. The attack was not followed up, however, as the enemy did not appear to care for orchard fighting; he had been taken in flank while making this attack and suffered heavy casualties from a Hotchkiss, well handled by Lieutenant Billington, of

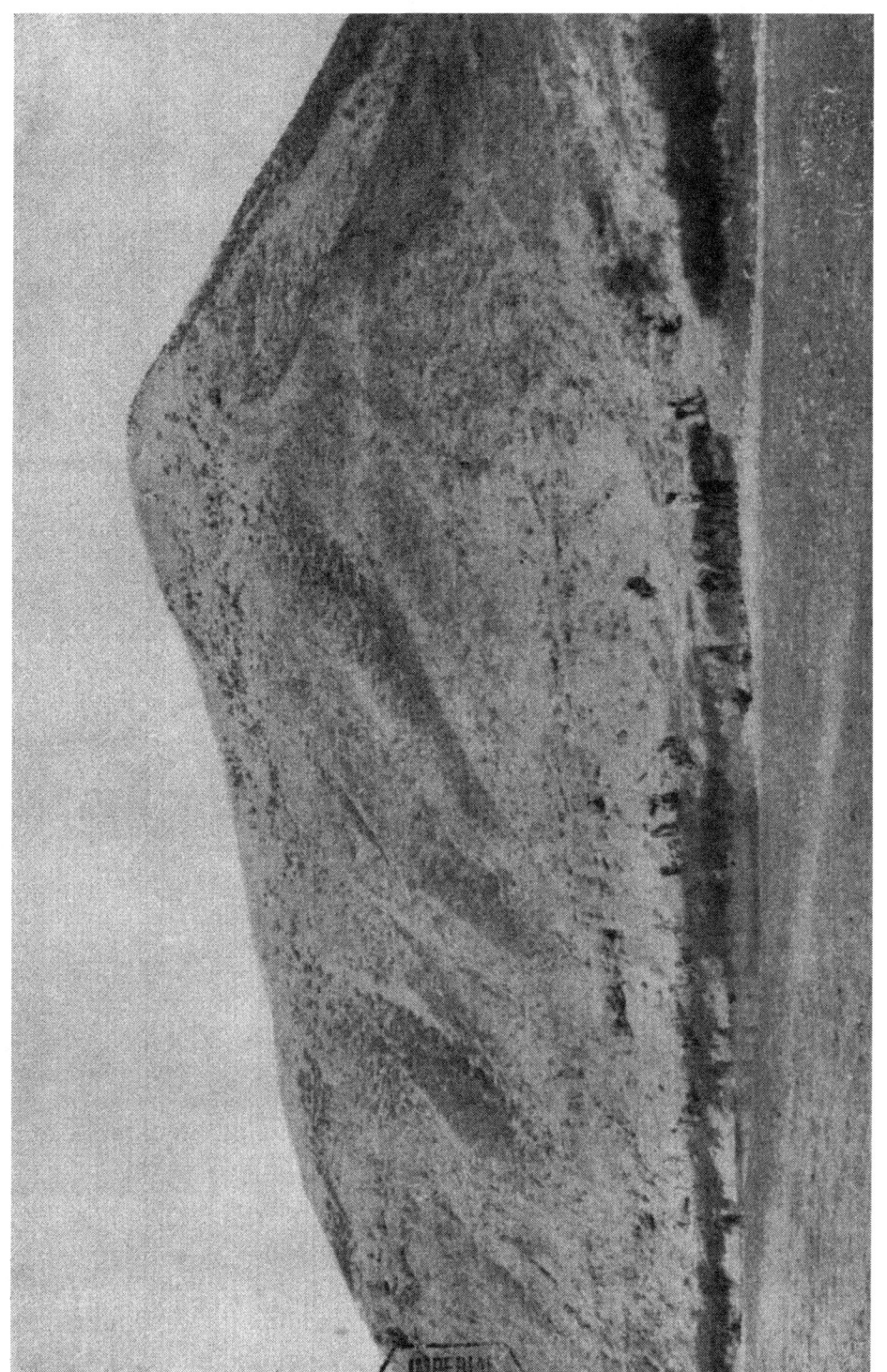

The dimly-seen figures in foreground are washing near the spring at the base of Tel el Fara.

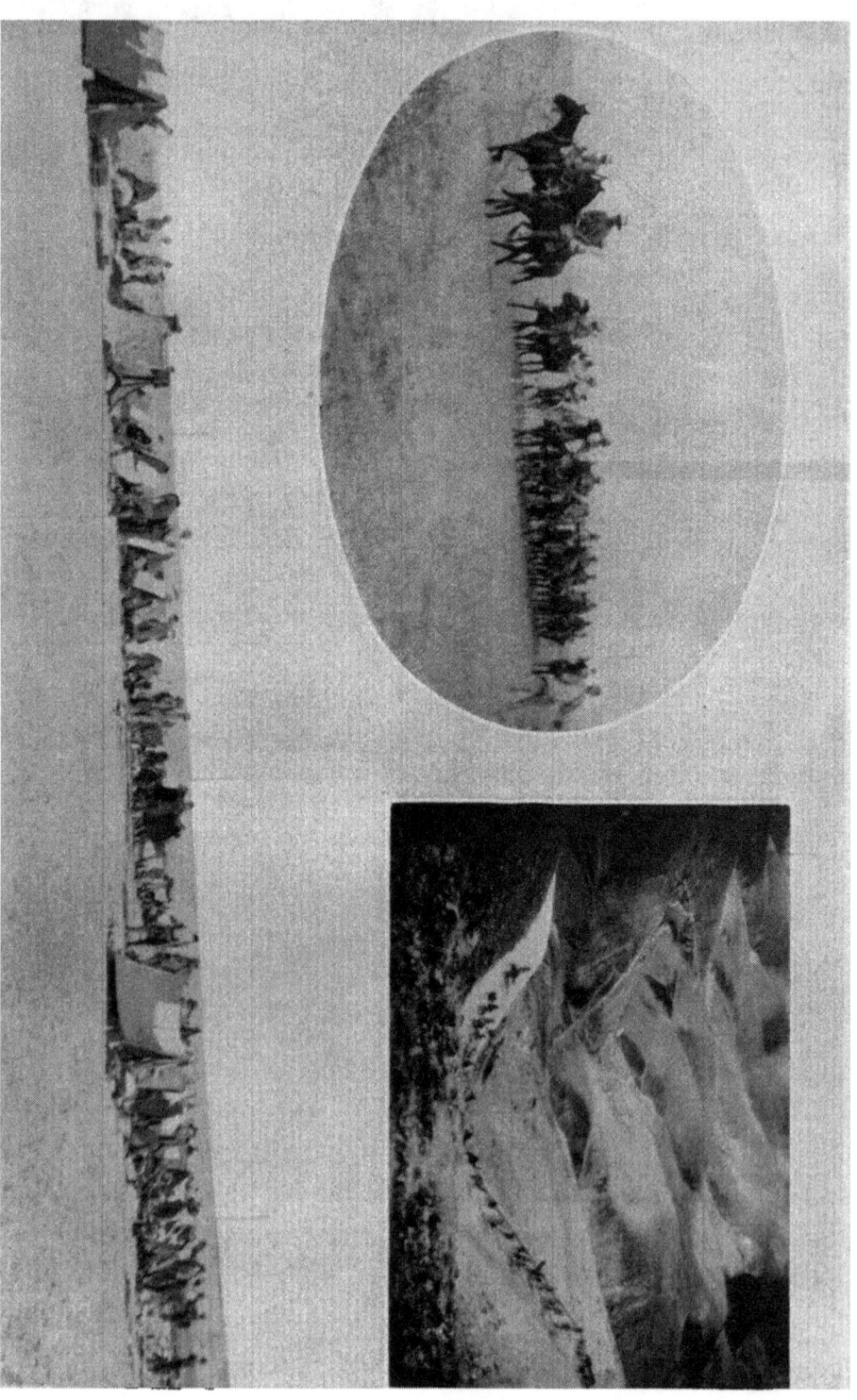

(Top Left)—Troop of Turks captured by "A" Squadron on Beersheba Plain. (Top Right)—Es Salt Road. (Bottom)—Camp at Kilo 7, Kantara.

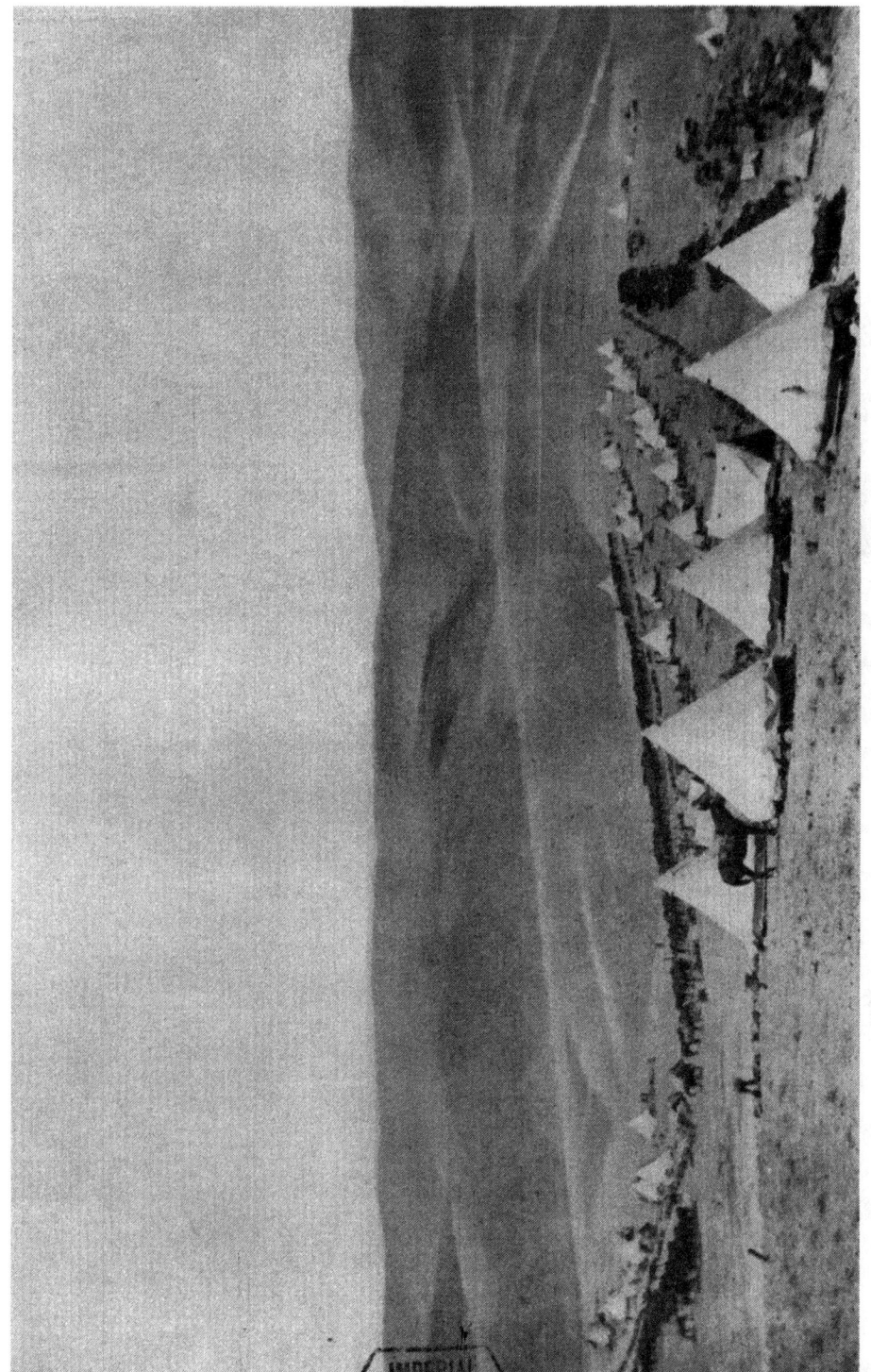

Talaat ed Dumm.

Mosque of Omar, Jerusalem.

the 5th Regiment. The enemy main attack now proved to be moving more to the east and south, where a determined effort was made to break through the 54th Division at Wilhelma, but without success. Furious shelling of the whole line at intervals brought the day to a close without any further attack.

At dusk the 5th L.H. Regiment was relieved in posts 3, 4, 5 and 6 by the 7th Regiment, the whole of our Regiment being then in the front line. The Posts were linked up by telephone to R.H.Q. which remained in the former bivouac position, and every effort was made to improve them defensively. A small amount of barbed wire was obtained and this was placed for trip wire among the almond trees. At night, listening posts were pushed well out in front; but nothing of incident occurred.

Enemy movements in entrenching some distance in front among the trees were observed next morning, and these targets and others were indicated to our guns, whose shelling appeared to be fairly effective. As the enemy gunfire continued to be severe, and his long range guns searched our rear positions, all horses were sent back at dawn to west of the village of Ibn Ibrak, being brought closer up to the redoubts at night. No enemy attack was made during the day. At night the Camel Brigade made a counter attack on Bald Hill, causing some casualties and losing a number of men themselves. The enemy gunfire became intense, the whole countryside being lit up by the flashes of their guns, and ours in answer. The cannonade lasted for some time, and under cover of it the enemy forced the advanced troops of the 6th Regiment out of the Ypres Salient, which had become untenable through being enfiladed from Bald Hill. The firing died down about midnight. Before daybreak on the 30th the rifle and machine-gun fire commenced again, supported to a lesser extent by artillery fire, and it was discovered that a body of Turks, having driven in our listening posts, was making an attack, principally on posts 3 and 4, held by "C" Squadron, under Major Barton. This assault was met by heavy machine gun and rifle fire, and the enemy was quickly checked and commenced to dig in.

When day broke, this party found itself in a bad position, flanks and rear being swept by cross fire from the redoubts. A hot fire was opened from redoubts 3, 4, and 5. This completely broke the enemy's resistance, and, recognising the impossibility of retiring without severe losses, he hoisted the white flag. Lieutenant Finlay, D.C.M. saying, "Well, this will mean a wooden cross or a Military Cross", promptly jumped over the parapet amid enemy bullets fired from troops in rear, and took the surrender. For this act, and gallant behaviour during the attack, Lieutenant Finlay later received the M.C. to add to a D.C.M. well earned at Cape Helles in 1915.

In this little affair, two Turkish officers and 146 other ranks, four Bergman machine guns, and a large number of bombs and rifles were captured. This success did much to offset the unsuccessful counter attack on Bald Hill. On the other hand, the enemy was, apparently, disheartened; for, beyond spasmodic shelling of the line, he made no further attack during the day.

Our guns, which had been reinforced and regrouped, searched the enemy positions with heavy fire, paying particularly attention to Bald Hill and the Ypres Salient, which were registered also for night firing. When darkness fell the 5th Regiment was brought up in close reserve in expection of another enemy attack, and strenuous efforts were made to further improve the trenches and get what little barbed wire was available out in front. The night, however, passed quietly.

December 1st also was a quiet day, with the exception of the usual gusts of enemy fire; any movement in the vicinity of a redoubt was immediately shelled, No. 7 post coming in for more than a fair share. Enemy long-range guns endeavoured to locate our horses and transport, in rear, but without success. Enemy aeroplanes were also fairly active in bombing, and the Camel Brigade lost a number of animals, which were bombed when "barracked" in rather close formation. A long range gun searched our old bivouac area at Yazur and the Jaffa Road close by, which was temporarily a depot for stores brought by motor transport. All supplies had to be brought up at night time, without lights, as the undulating country in rear of the trenches, was well under observation at long distance from the hills near Mejdel Yaba, and the Transport had a strenuous time.

About 9.30 on the night of December 1st, three Turks approached one of our listening posts in front of No. 7 with signals of surrender, and upon being taken into the redoubt, they intimated that a number of others were waiting to surrender further out, but were afraid to approach. Thereupon, Captain Davies, with Corporal MacGuire and Trooper Dobbs, guided by a Turk, went out well in front of the listening posts and close up to the enemy lines and found an officer and 20 odd men waiting, concealed in a thicket. They surrendered readily and were brought in without casualties. For this good piece of work, Captain Davies received the M.C. and Corporal MacGuire and Trooper Dobbs were awarded Military Medals.

Relief of the 6th Regiment by the 5th took place next day in Posts 1 and 2. The day was quiet, except for gusty enemy fire, though this had slackened somewhat. At night again all was silent, and work on improvements to the trenches went on uninterruptedly. The usual burst of artillery fire on both sides took place on the 3rd; our batteries registered Bald Hill, and the Ypres Salient again, in preparation for another night raid. This took place at 8 p.m., the 6th Regiment sending a Squadron against the Ypres Salient, and the Camel Brigade attacking Bald Hill with two companies.

The closest co-operation from flank posts was required. Our Hotchkiss rifles were trained on enemy trenches, and everything possible was done to attract attention. The raid did not go very well, owing chiefly to the faulty firing of one gun in a supporting battery, which dropped shrapnel right into the attacking squadron and held up its advance for two or three vital minutes. However, the Ypres Salient was stormed. Many Turks were bayonetted and five were taken prisoners. The 6th Regiment, however, sustained some casualties, including an officer killed. The enemy guns, which had been re-inforced, opened a heavy fire, and the flashes from both sides lit up the sky as if a most violent electrical disturbance was taking place. We were reminded of the cannonades during one of the raids on Umbrella Hill or Beach Post at Gaza, though Infantry officers, who had been in those affairs, declared that this was more violent.

The attack of the Camel men on Bald Hill met with little success, as the Turkish barrage dropped down upon them as soon as the attack was discovered. The Turks daringly jumped over their trenches to the front and lay down to escape our barrage, and being between the two, probably escaped with few casualties. In front of our posts the enemy fire was severe, but no counter attacks were made. About midnight, the firing, which had gradually slackened, ceased altogether, and the remainder of the night was quiet. Artillery fire from both sides was opened, as usual, at intervals during the next day. That night 33 most welcome reinforcements arrived, to build up the ranks, which were thinning rapidly owing to battle casualties; sickness and exhaustion caused by long marches, and strenuous fighting with little rest under a hot sun, were also taking a constantly increasing toll. Trench digging, which went on almost without cessation, especially at night, was also very exhausting; parties from the Regiment in reserve, however, did the heavier part of this work.

Nothing beyond the usual artillery fire took place on the 5th, and next day word was received that the Brigade would be relieved at night by troops of the 52nd (Lowland) Division. The enemy probably suspected a relief, as, just when this had commenced to take place after dark, a demonstration was made against our posts by bodies of Turks who were, however, quickly driven back by Hotchkiss and rifle fire. At 10 p.m. in cold, drizzling rain, the relief was completed, companies of the 4th King's Own Scottish

Borderers taking over our posts. The Regiment withdrew, pitying the Infantry in the sloppy trenches, and, joining up with the remainder of the Brigade, just west of Yazur, marched to a bivouac site outside the orange gardens of Wadi Hanein, a Jewish village, 10 miles south of Jaffa. This small village, a mile distant from the Rothschild colony of Richon Le Zion, famous for its wines, is surrounded by orange groves and almond orchards. It was just to the south that the N.Z.M.R. Brigade was subjected to a heavy counter attack during the earlier operations, and the graves of many New Zealanders, are situated on the hills close by. Rain continued to fall on the 7th and 8th making things very uncomfortable; the ground, however, absorbed water well.

The Jews were friendly, and oranges, Jewish bread and a small quantity of honey, were obtainable, making a welcome change in the diet. Hot baths at communistic institutions at Richon Le Zion and Ras Deiran (three miles south-west of Wadi Hanein), were enjoyed. Desert Mounted Corps headquarters were comfortably installed in the village of Ras Deiran.

On December 9th came the news of the capture of Jerusalum, an event which must have sounded as a death knell to German hopes and aspirations. Once more the Holy City was in Christian hands.

The next few days were devoted to rest, repairing gear, and cleaning up generally. Thirty-seven badly needed reinforcements arrived to help lighten the Regimental duties.

On the 13th the Regiment moved to a bivouac on the sandhills near Esdud, 15 miles south-west of Wadi Hamein. This move was chiefly to overcome supply difficulties, as the military railhead was now at this village. A dump of stores had been made in possibly the lowest part of a black soil plain, which was quickly flooded by the torrential rains of the wet season, which had now arrived. Consequently, waggons had to go axle deep in mud and water to obtain supplies, and many thousands of pounds worth of valuable stores were spoilt. The sand ridges adjoining the plain, and through which in one place the railway actually ran, formed ideal positions for such a dump. The Regiment bivouacked on the clean sand, a few tents being available. The water supply was good, and everything possible was done to recuperate the health and general conditions of all ranks.

On the afternoon of the 14th, the G.O.C., A. & N.Z. Mounted Division, Major-General Chaytor, distributed ribbons for medals won in the recent fighting. Major Willsallen received the ribbon of the D.S.O., and other presentations were as follows:—

D.C.M.: Sergeant James, A.E.; Sergeant Salmon, W.; Corporal Picton, G.B., and also M.M.

Military Medals: Corporal Turner, W.; Troopers Howard, Ratcliffe, MacGuire, Pullbrook, and Dobbs.

CHAPTER XII.

ESDUD, WADI HANEIN AND NALIN.

AT Esdud a period of rest was allowed—of necessity—only for a few days. A portion of the transport was sent back to draw clothing and equipment at Deir Sineid, the former Turkish Railway Depot, six miles N.E. of Gaza. The wear and tear of the long marches and rough conditions had caused a great deal of clothing to become unserviceable, and as it was now the middle of winter, it was essential that this should be replaced at once. Twenty-eight reinforcements arrived from Moascar, bringing the strength of the Regiment nearly up to establishment. Another referendum upon the conscription issue was taken, keen interest in the result being manifested. Many reasons for and against were advanced, some scarcely logical. One objection urged against compulsory active service was in the language of the camps, "If these cold footers won't come voluntarily, they should not be forced. Old hands have no wish to fight alongside — conscripts."

Training was resumed on the 16th, but only the mornings were devoted to it, the afternoons being given over to games and swimming. Musketry training, gas drill and Hotchkiss rifle classes were proceeded with. The value of the handy little Hotchkiss had been demonstrated, and efforts were made to give at least an elementary knowledge of its action to as many men as possible. On the 28th, Lieut.-Colonel Onslow temporarily took over command of the Brigade, in the absence on leave of Brigadier-General Ryrie. Parties of one officer and 50 other ranks had to be sent daily to unload trains at Esdud. This became an unpleasant duty, as heavy rains now began to fall and converted practically the whole area within half a mile of Esdud station into a quaguire.

In spite of the benefit conferred by rest, evacuations to hospital showed the strain upon endurance that the late operations had entailed. In most cases, of course, these sick men after a few weeks' treatment, rejoined the Regiment. A percentage of these would be able to carry on perhaps whilst conditions were not too severe; when hardships recommenced, though struggling bravely, they would at last be compelled to go to hospital again. In this way each Regiment gradually acquired an increasing number of men who were not quite fit, men who appeared at intervals in the Regiment, when under other conditions they should have been shipped home to Australia without delay. But the slump in recruiting and the rejection of conscription, were beginning to be felt and sick men in Palestine had to be kept with their regiments because healthy men in Australia would not see their plain duty.

Christmas Day and New Year were spent uneventfully in rather cheerless, squally weather. On January 11th a cinema picture of the Brigade and a number of official photographs of the Regiment were taken by Captain F. Hurley of Antarctic fame. Schools of instruction in Cairo, Ismailia and El Arish, had been continued, and during January, the Regiment sent five officers and four other ranks to these. Also, just before the end of our stay in El Arish, four officers and 15 other ranks arrived as reinforcements to fill gaps caused by the evacuations to hospital. The move from Esdud took place on January 12th, the Regiment, with the Brigade, returning to practically the old camp site at Wadi Hanein. The morning broke fine, but with threatening clouds in the east, which came up quickly. Before half the march was over, rain fell heavily, reducing the black soil plains to a horrible sloppy bog. As the whole Division was moving, the march area was soon in a bad state; the transport waggons sank axle-deep, and many belonging to other units remained out all night. Thanks to an early start, all of ours got through and reached Wadi Hanein without great difficulty.

The bivouac area was on ground which absorbed the rain fairly well; and although a cheerless night was spent, in a few days the men were as comfortable as it is possible to be under a "bivvy". This shelter, occupied by two men, consists of two light canvas sheets, each 6ft by 3ft, buttoned together and held up in the usual tent form by light poles or stakes. A "bivvy," if it is well pitched and banked up will keep out the rain fairly well. Something, of course, depends upon the age and condition of the "bivvy" sheets. On the 14th, training was resumed, and on the 17th, the Brigade was inspected, dismounted, by the Corps Commander, Lieut.-General Chauvel.

On the 24th, a most successful Brigade Sports meeting was held; all arrangements were in the hands of a capable committee under Major O'Brien, of the 6th L.H. Regiment, and the result was what a sports meeting should be. Towards the end of the month, 13 more reinforcements arrived from Moascar, to take the place of an equal number of men sent to hospital.

At the end of January, orders were received to be ready to take over a portion of the front line trenches in the vicinity of Nalin, 10 miles east of Ludd. These were occupied by the Regiment of Canterbury Mounted Rifles of the N.Z.M.R. Brigade. The move was ordered for February 4th, and at 8 a.m. the Regiment with one section (4 guns) of the Machine Gun Squadron and a detachment of Engineers and Field Ambulance details, marched by way of Ludd to Nalin. The Canterbury Mounted Rifles were relieved without incident by 1.30 p.m. and practically all the horses were sent back with the horse holders to Wadi Hanein. This was on account of the mountainous nature of the country, which prohibited mounted movement, except along one or two most primitive tracks, suitable only for goats or donkeys. A few G.S. Limbers were retained to draw supplies from Ludd, camels also being used for this purpose.

The trench system taken over was not part of a continuous line, but was held by a number of small redoubts or strong posts. The Regimental garrison actually formed the connecting link between the XX and XXI Army Corps, whose troops were in touch with us on either flank. A Battalion of the Devons was on the left and another of the Leinster Regiment on the right. The line actually held was from Wadi Natuf inclusive, two miles west of Nalin, turning easterly along the high ground to Point 1179 exclusive, the Leinsters being in occupation of this dominating spot. Good water was obtained in abundance from local cisterns, and as the enemy was at least two miles distant, the duties were not exacting, constant watchfulness and a certain amount of patrolling well in front being all that was required.

The country about Nalin, where the foothills finally merge into the backbone of the Judean mountain system is rugged and stony. The natives have, here as elsewhere, terraced the sides of the hills, and have walled in little gardens and plots of land in order to get as much benefit as possible from the small pockets of good soil. Olive trees and figs grow well; wheat too, had been sown on these rough hillsides and was looking well. Beautiful wild flowers, poppies and anemones predominating, grew luxuriantly everywhere; curiously, most of the blossoms were blood red, as if the torrents of blood poured out on these battle grounds had stained even the flowers. The poppies seemed to bear the Crusader's cross in black on a red ground, and were often very large.

Numbers of gazelles roamed about the country well in front, and several were shot by sportsmen from the Regiment, who, at the same time, took a sporting chance of being themselves potted by the Turks.

Lieut.-General Onslow showed great energy in exploring the difficult country in the vicinity and kept most of the officers fit and hard by requesting their company during these walks. Much time was given to improving the trenches and making these capable of standing heavy bombardment. Owing to the rocky ground, sangars or stone barricades had, in many cases, to be restored to; the stone in rear was then blasted out deep enough to give good cover. The sangars were cased with earth and squared up into solid structures, great improvements being also made upon those formerly existing. Parties of men under supervision of the Engineer detachment, were sent daily to improve the roads in rear, particularly a bad grade near Nalin; and before the Regiment left these had been brought into a servicable condition, so that even motors could come right up to Regimental headquarters.

The enemy showed no activity, and only small parties could occasionally be seen far in front. Out patrols worked up to within 800 yards of enemy positions without even drawing fire. Inspections by our Brigadier and by Brigadier-General Howard Vyce (B.G.G.S. Desert Corps) were made on the 18th and 25th respectively. The Australian official artist, Lieutenant G. W. Lambert (famous for his picture in the N.S.W. Art Gallery, "Across the Black Soil Plains") arrived on the 18th and stayed a week with the Regiment, getting local color and making a number of sketches. Enemy aeroplanes flew over us at intervals, but without any bombs dropping. Natives, in their casual way, wandered about the lines and into "No Man's Land"—these were promptly arrested and interrogated as possible enemy spies. Some attempting to escape, had machine guns fired "across their bows" bringing them promptly to a halt.

As a lift forward of the line was shortly to take place, Lieut.-Colonel Onslow, with a small covering party, went out to a high point just east of Shukbah and met Brigadier-General Huddleston, of the 232nd Infantry Brigade, making a special reconnaissance in view of the proposed advance. On March 3rd the Infantry on both flanks moved forward finally occupying a line roughly through Beit Ello and Shukbah, but the Regiment was ordered to remain at Nalin. No opposition was encountered during the advance.

This move left the Regiment in the air, as it were, though without the dangers usually associated with that position; and as no useful purpose was being served, orders were received, to rejoin the Brigade on March 7th. On the 5th an exciting aerial duel, two planes each side, was witnessed. It ended in victory for our planes, one enemy machine being forced down and the other, probably damaged, seeking refuge in flight. On the 6th Lieut.-Colonel Onslow was ordered to proceed, with a number of other Regimental commanders, to inspect the newly-opened school for young officers, at Kelab near Rafa. Next morning the Regiment returned, without incident, to the old bivouac at Wadi Hanein, the horses having been led out the night before to Nalin.

THE 7th LIGHT HORSE, 1914-1919.

PART IV.

THE TRANS-JORDAN CAMPAIGN.

CHAPTER I.

NEW COUNTRY.

THE Regiment returned to the Brigade area to find that all was in readiness for another move; this had long been expected. A month previously the 1st Light Horse Brigade, with the N.Z.M.R. Brigade and the 60th Infantry Division, had captured Jericho, and the Turkish base on the northern end of the Dead Sea. A regiment of the N.Z.M.R. Brigade had been left in this area, based upon Jericho, and it was rightly believed that this would be our next sphere of operations.

Only a few days were allowed the Regiment in which to draw equipment, clothing and the various odds and ends that always seem to be needed after a period in the front line. Orders were received to move off on March 13th at 9 a.m. A party of 56 other ranks was left in the camp area, with details of the other Regiments, the whole being placed under Lieutenant Spencer, to take charge of heavy baggage and to form a Brigade depot or dump. The Regiment moved off with the Brigade, the line of march leading through the narrow lanes of Ludd and Ramleh.

The strictest march discipline had to be insisted upon to prevent a congestion of the traffic, distances of 50 yards between troops and 250 yards between squadrons being maintained. This strung the Brigade out over many miles, and it was impossible to close up units properly until the open country well to the east of Ramleh had been reached. East of that town the soil appears to be of unsurpassed fertility, but it is heavy and traffic is almost impossible away from the metalled roads once the winter rains have set in.

The country generally, as far as Latron, consists of plain, with occasional high ridges and lofty knolls intersecting it. On a knoll within a few miles of the road, are the ruins of Gezer, possibly the oldest known city in Palestine. It is mentioned in papyri of some of the earliest Pharoahs of Egypt, and was given as a dowry for that Egyptian princess who became the wife of the Jewish Solomon. Latron is 10 miles south-east of Ramleh, on the Jerusalem road, and there the Judean hills rise, rock-bound and barren, almost sheer from the plains. Latron, from Latronus, a robber, has been regarded as the birth place of "the penitent thief", without any convincing evidence. The ruins of what was a strong castle of the Crusaders, surmount a high hill above the village, and show that the tactical importance of the place was realised in those days as in these. A large monastry, with extensive gardens and vineyards, is situated close by. The importance of Latron lies in the fact that it commands the pass through which the road to Jerusalem enters the hills, and is the junction of the roads from Ramleh and from Gaza.

A large dump of stores had been made here and fleets of motor lorries in almost endless succession passed, and engaged in keeping up supplies to the front line. Ploughed fields close to Latron had been selected as the Brigade bivouac area, and a halt was made here until the morning of the 17th. Unfortunately, the weather, which had been fine, changed, and the "latter rains" came down in torrents. The ploughed land became a quagmire, in which horses and men sank to the knees. The rain penetrated practically everything, and if it could not soak through from above, it did so from the sodden ground, trenches availing little. Blankets and clothing became soaked and caked with mud, and the horses were plastered, so that it was difficult to groom them.

Mount of Olives. Russian Church with Gilded Domes. Garden of Gethsemane from Walls of Jerusalem.

Jericho from South-West.

Rain fell most heavily on the 16th and during that night there was little rest for anyone as streams of water rushed through almost all the bivouacs. The move forward next morning, though conditions were the same, came as a relief; another camp might become as bad but could scarcely be worse. Under the strictest march discipline, the Brigade moved up the long narrow road to Jerusalem, "snaking out", of necessity, so that at least five miles separated van and rear. Laden camels and fleets of motor lorries made awkward obstacles upon the narrow track, where two vehicles could just move abreast. Considerable engineering skill must have been required in many places to make a road at all, and some of the zig-zags and grades cut in the mountain sides, seemed to show that another hand than that of the Turk had directed things there.

After a tiring and wet march, the Regiment reached a bivouac area close under the walls of Jerusalem, north-east of the city and facing the Mount of Olives. This area was congested, but was fairly dry and as clean as could be expected so close to a great Eastern city. Some of the inhabitants became a nuisance and had to be excluded from the camp areas.

CHAPTER II.

JERUSALEM.

JERUSALEM of the present day consists of the Old and the New City, the latter being chiefly outside the 15th century walls. The greater number of buildings and houses of the New City are clustered close to the Jaffa Gate, the western entrance to the Old City. Some of them provide accommodation for the thousands of almost penniless pilgrims who, in normal times, visit the Holy Places. On the Mount of Olives, a mile to the east of the city, stand modern buildings, the Russian Tower (a hospice of the Greek Church) and the Kaiserin Augusta Victoria Hospice, which was the headquarters of the XX Army Corps.

Reaching first the Jaffa gate one is struck by a massive square stone tower overlooking the city, and, in particular, dominating the road to Bethlehem, which passes to the south of the walls. This is known as the Tower of David, though it is hardly possible that King David had anything to do with it as his city was destroyed by the Chaldeans when the Jews were taken into captivity by Nebuchadnezzar. The older portions of this tower, or, at least, the great blocks of stone which go to form the lower portion, undoubtedly date from the time of Herod the Great; whether they then occupied their present positions is a matter for conjecture.

The City lies "four square," in a way, being built due north and south and the walls, though following the hill features and rising above ravines and valleys, are possibly not greatly different from those of an earlier date. In viewing the modern Jerusalem, one must remember that it stands on the ruins of five earlier cities. The Damascus Gate, not far from the north-western corner of the city, is possibly the finest of all the entrances, and a good example of Saracenic architecture. To the north is Mount Scopas or the Sentinel, where Titus had the main camp of his army. Here the approach is earlier, and it was from this hill that the Romans set up their engines of war to drive a breach in the walls through which stormers eventually forced their way, and sacked the city. On the eastern side lies the Valley of Jehosophat, and the walls of the city rising above it have a most impressive appearance. This valley, with its arms, forms almost a semicircle round the city on the east and the south, where also the walls dominate it. Here is the Mount of Offence and the Pool of Siloam.

Across the Valley of Jehosophat, to the east, rises steeply the Mount of Olives, still clothed in places with the trees which gave it its name. Two magnificent panoramas are presented from certain high points on the Mount, to the west is the Holy City encompassed with walls that, in some lights, are almost golden, with the Mosque of Omar and the Dome of the Church of the Holy Sepulchre standing out prominently. No other city perhaps, presents the same appearance as Jerusalem does from the Mount of Olives.

The view to the east is desolate and forbidding. Fifteen miles away across the sterile mountain ridges which form the wilderness of Judea, a glimpse of the northern end of the Dead Sea is obtained—a flake of bluish green—this peculiar colour evidently is due, among other things, to the haze (caused by intense evaporation) which apparently always hangs over it. Possibly, nowhere can be seen mountains so barren and desolate looking, as those which rise almost precipitously on either side of the Dead Sea. A spot blasted and riven by volcanic fires such as destroyed Sodom and Gomorrah, it now presents an appropriate setting for one of the hells of the Middle Ages, as depicted in Dante's "Inferno." At the extreme northern end, the green of a dense jungle marks where the river Jordan enters, lavishly pouring sweet waters from the snows of Mount Hermon almost at once to become saturated in salt.

Across the Jordon to the east again rises the Mountains of Moab and Gilead, with those of Edom to the south. Turning to the north-west of the Mount of Olives at a distance of about five miles from Jerusalem, one sees the high point known as Nebi Samwil, where the tomb of the Prophet Samuel, is supposed to be. This sport venerated by Christians and Mohammedans alike, was the limit of Richard Coeur de Lion's approach to the city for which he fought so valiantly. It was the scene of much fighting incidental to the capture of Jerusalem in our campaign. The Turks shelled the mosque and shattered it to pieces.

To return to the city proper. The usual entrance is by the Jaffa Gate past the Tower of David; narrow streets, suitable only for pedestrians, branch off David street, about 200 yards inside the gate. This street, which is the only one fit for wheeled traffic in the city, comes to an abrupt end, and then dirty alleyways, often with stone steps and arched over in such a manner as to cause semi-darkness, are followed until the courtyard of the Church of the Holy Sepulchre is reached. The Via Dolorosa, followed towards the east, takes one to the site of Pilate's Judgment Hall, now occupied by the Church of the Sisters of Zion. The famous Ecce Homo arch is built in as a part of the Church. Close by is the ancient temple area, in Herod's day covered by magnificent buildings, but now mostly courtyards for the mosques of Omar and Aksa. The Mosque of Omar or the Dome of the Rock, as it is also known, is considered to be one of the most beautiful buildings in the world, second only to the Taj Mahal at Agra, in India.

The Wailing Place of Jews forms part of the foundations of the Temple area, huge blocks of stone against which the Jews weep for the sorrows of Jerusalem, are all that are left of the former greatness of the city. Mosques, churches and shrines abound; one of the most interesting of these is a German Hospice upon part of the site of the Hospital of the Knights of St. John of Jerusalem, before those champions of Christendom became the powerful military order of later days.

All ranks were keenly interested in seeing the Old City, and in parties of 12, under an officer, the men were allowed to visit practically every place. Indian guards on the Mosque of Omar, and French, British and Italian sentries at the Church of the Holy Sepulchre, showed how the various religions were being considered by Army Headquarters. On Palm Sunday, 300 men of the Brigade attended Mass, celebrated by Captain Mullens (Chaplain attached to the 5th L.H. Regiment) in the Church of the Holy Sepulchre; and later in the day an even greater number of all demoninations marched to the beautiful Anglican Cathedral of St. George, outside the Old City, where the Bishop in Jerusalem conducted a most impressive service.

CHAPTER III.

THE JORDAN.

OWING to unusual floods in the river Jordan, more time was spent at Jerusalem than we anticipated. The river was a fiercely swollen torrent and bridging operations were impossible until it had subsided somewhat.

It was not, therefore, until 5.20 p.m. on March 21st that the Brigade moved off from Jerusalem by the road to Jericho, that old road, now much improved by German engineers, which has been a highway for so many peoples since the days of the Good Samaritan.

Bethany (El Azariyeh), the home of Lazarus, Martha, and Mary, one and a half miles from Jerusalem, is now a squalid village perched upon the mountain side, down which the road twists in wonderful zig-zags to the valley. The road is well metalled throughout, though narrow in places. A number of bridges had been destroyed by the enemy in his retreat, and temporary ones were in position or in course of construction.

Good progress was made and a bivouac site near Talaat Ed Dum (the ascent or Slope of Blood) was reached at 1.30 a.m. on the 22nd. Close by are the ruins of the so-called Inn of the Good Samaritan. The country is wild and rugged, providing retreats for the robbers who, even in these days, prey upon travellers journeying from Jerusalem to Jericho.

The bivouac area was rough, and stony, and great difficulty was experienced in getting suitable sleeping places for the men. The swollen river still caused difficulties, and operations were delayed. At midnight on the 21st, men of a London Battalion managed to swim across the river at Hajla, five miles north of the Dead Sea, though a similar attempt at Ghoraniyeh, where the main bridge (broken by the Turks) had been, proved unsuccessful owing to the strong current.

Rafts were used at Hajla to ferry infantry across, and they came under concentrated enemy machine-gun fire. A bridge head position was gradually formed, and under cover of this the Army bridging sections placed pontoons in positions, and a bridge fit for taking horses was soon thrown over the Jordan.

The enemy fell back to the foothills on the advance of the Auckland Mounted Rifles and Infantry of the 60th (London) Division.

The Jordan Valley is a great chasm or rent in the earth's surface, extending practically from the foot of Mount Hermon, near Damascus, in gradually falling levels through Lakes Huleh and Galilee. After issuing from Galilee the descent is rapid to the Dead Sea, where the Valley is 1,300 feet below sea level. Although the distance from Lake Galilee to the Dead Sea, as the crow flies, is only 60 miles, so tortuous is the river's course, that its actual length is 200 miles.

The low level of the Valley causes intense atmospheric pressure, and very great evaporation, both from the Jordan and the Dead Sea, takes place. Surrounded on the one side by the hills of Judea rising to 3,000 feet above sea level, and on the other by the even higher hills of Moab and Gilead, at an average distance of five miles on either side, the Jordan Valley appears to focus the sun's rays to such an extent, that, in midsummer, the heat is stifling, and even the natives are compelled to seek a cooler climate in the lower mountain slopes.

The mountains everywhere rise almost precipitously from the Valley, and nestling under the very cliffs of those of Judea is Jericho, now a squalid mud village with one or two insignificant European buildings. The ruins of aqueducts and some few spring-fed water channels are all that remain of the prosperity of Roman Jericho, so fair a province, that Antony considered it a worthy gift for Cleopatra, who later sold it to Herod the Great. Springs gush from the mountain sides near Jericho, and these give life to a number of neglected gardens, whose tropical growth show what could be produced by proper attention.

From the village to the river, the country—a plain—consists of whitish clay soil which, when cut up by traffic, is converted into dense dust, which rises in suffocating clouds. In places, deep wadis, which carry the winter rains, intersect the Valley, and along the banks of these low scrub and thorn bushes are plentiful, otherwise coarse sparse herbage of a saline nature is the only thing to relieve the eyes.

Within half a mile of the river, the plain falls about fifteen feet and makes an amphitheatre on either side of ghostly white clay mounds and ridges, devoid of vegetation and of fantastic shapes and groupings. A belt of jungle, from a few yards to half a mile in width, brings one to the river itself, a swift flowing narrow stream. Fords are rare and those marked upon the map were not found to be reliable. Across the river to the east, the country is similar to that already described, though of greater fertility, both in the plain and on the mountains, whose bold heights are clothed with grass and herbage practically all the year round.

The Brigade bivouacked at Talaat Ed Dum, until the bridging of the river had been completed. At 6 p.m. on March 23rd, the march was resumed along the new German-made road, which winds down easy grades in a circuitous route to Jericho. The older road, which dates back to the Roman occupation, traverses rocky and precipitous mountain sides, finally dropping almost by a precipice direct upon Jericho. This road, later on, was greatly improved by our engineers.

An hour's halt was made at midnight at the Hajla Monastery, belonging to the Greek Orthodox Church, about four miles from the Jordan. When the march was resumed, the pace was painfully slow in order to permit of the troops making their way through dense scrub and jungle. They crossed the pontoon bridge two abreast.

Across the river the Regiment formed up just clear of the ghostly clay ridges upon the edge of the wide plain. Daylight revealed evidence of enemy occupation and the shell holes made by our 60 pounders, which had helped to dislodge his covering troops. In the next move forward, the Regiment found itself much split up and its efficiency was affected later on. "C" Squadron was detailed as escort to an Engineer's demolition party, carrying a large amount of explosives. "A" Squadron was right flank-guard to the Brigade, and two troops of "B" acted as left flank-guard, with one troop as rear-guard. As the New Zealand Mounted Rifle Brigade was moving out on our left towards the Nimrin pass, where the main Es Salt-Amman road winds into the mountains, this flank was well protected, but our right was open to a possible attack at any time. The objectives of Shea's Group, as this trans-Jordan force was known, were briefly as under:—

The 60th Division, with the New Zealand Mounted Rifles, were to move against Es Salt, 15 miles from the Jordan, by the main and Ain Es Sir roads. The 1st Light Horse Brigade was left flank-guard of the movement, and was to hold off any enemy attacks made on the wide plain north of the broken Ghoraniyeh bridge, which might cut the line of communications seriously. The 2nd Light Horse Brigade was right flank-guard of the movement, and was to move on the foothills near Khabr Mujahid and then take a road up the Wadi Kefrein, said to be fit for wheeled traffic, which led finally up the mountains to Amman, the important Turkish base on the Hedjaz railway. This railway runs down into Arabia to Medina, where troops of the Sheriff held a formidable Turkish garrison, more or less in a state of siege. If the Hedjaz railway could be cut at Amman, it would further jeopardise this Turkish garrison, and also be a direct menace to Damascus and all the Turkish forces in Judea and Galilee, whose lines of communications would be endangered if a swift movement were then made upon Deraa, the railway junction east of Lake Galilee.

The advance to Khabr Mujahid was made without opposition, the Turks firing only one shell, at very long range, from a mountain gun. Two Turks, wounded in the previous day's engagement, were captured and given over to the ambulance. As the foothills were approached, Arabs, armed with modern rifles and beautifully inlaid swords and daggers, rode down to meet us, protesting their friendship and their alliance with the Sheriff of the Hedjaz. These fellows chased one another in mimic warfare, slashing with their swords in a dramatic manner, and manoeuvring their weedy horses with some dexterity. One or two remained with us to guide the column up the mountains, but the others soon disappeared. Crops of barley, as high as a mounted man's head in places, showed the fertility of the soil, and its possibilities under proper treatment.

The Brigade halted at Khabr Mujahid in order to allow the main body of the Infantry to get into position; owing to the heat and some enemy opposition, this was slow work and many valuable hours were lost. Few of the enemy had been seen on our front and these only at a distance. Later in the afternoon what at first appeared to be goats on a mountain side, five miles away, were discovered to be enemy cavalry, apparently weary and making their way, possibly, from Madeba to Amman. The Divisional Commander was anxious that they should be intercepted, but owing to the distance and the great mountain valleys intervening, this was a physical impossibility.

The advance was resumed at 3 p.m. the so-called road leading steeply up the mountain sides and through narrow and difficult wadis, the Wadi Kefrein being followed for the most part. These roads or tracks leading from the valley to the cool and fertile tableland country of Es Salt and Amman are really fit only for the nimble-footed horses and flocks of the Arab tribes, who alone in normal times use them. In the winter, these people descend to the Jordan, and when the summer heat burns up the pastures and crops there, they make their way to the higher country, where rough grass and herbage can be found during the whole year. High mountains with precipitous intervening valleys are met with at first, but when the top of the pass is reached, after what seems to be interminable climbing, the country gives way to rolling downs with occasional high rocky knolls and low ridges, some covered with loose stones. The tableland country is fertile and grows excellent grain and delicious grapes for which Es Salt is especially famous. The Hauran country, the home of the Druses which lies east of Deraa, is considered to be the granary of Syria. Es Salt was a town of 15,000 inhabitants many being Armenian in pre-war days. Amman is not so large, but is of far more importance tactically; it is the ancient Rabbath Amon of the Bible against which David sent Uriah the Hittite, when he wished to obtain possession of his wife. Roman ruins in a fair state of preservation exist to this day, including the foundations of an old citadel, which formed good harborage for enemy machine guns.

CHAPTER IV.

THE FIRST BATTLE OF AMMAN.

ALTHOUGH our intelligence reports, and the Arab guides declared that our road was good, the guns were in difficulties before a mile had been travelled. Attempts to get these through with double teams only caused delay to the column, which was now strung out to enormous length. Finally, the battery and all wheeled vehicles were sent back to the Valley under escort of two troops of "B" Squadron, and the advance was continued.

Behind our Brigade, followed Divisional Headquarters and the Imperial Camel Brigade with the Hong Kong and Singapore Mountain Battery, their guns and ammunition being carried also on camels. It was well that our wheels had been sent back, for the track soon narrowed, and in a Wadi that had to be passed, we had to move in single file. Then the path zig-zagged up over a high mountain, where also in many places, single file only was possible. A cold, drizzling rain commenced to fall, adding to the discomfort and hindering progress, it increased to a steady driving deluge, which speedily soaked everything. Major White, of the 6th Light Horse Regiment led the advance party, and it was due more to his instinct for country than to the Arab guides that true direction was kept at all.

In many places no track of any sort was visible and men had to dismount and drag their weary horses over huge boulders. It was marvellous how these poor brutes, slipping and floundering over limestone surfaces, were pulled forward. About 3 a.m. on the 25th a halt was called, but sleep being impossible, men sat down in the rain, mud and slush, waiting for daylight. Never was dawn more cheerless; driving mists and rain ushered in a wild grey day. As soon as it was light, the advance was resumed, a halt being made at 7.30 a.m. in a wadi near Ain El Hekr. The top of the pass had now been reached and the rest of the day was spent here. On moving off again at 7 p.m., it was found that the road had considerably improved though it was still waterlogged; the column made better progress.

At 2 a.m. on the 26th, the village of Naaur, a Circassian colony, was passed and just at daylight, after marching under most miserable conditions all night, the outposts of the N.Z. Brigade were met near Ain Es Sir another Circassian village. Moving northward we reached the Es Salt-Amman road at about 6.30 a.m., and a little later bivouac was made in a sheltered spot in a wide valley close by. The sun now shone intermittently. "A" Squadron was sent on patrol towards Es Salt, but saw no signs of the enemy. About 20 enemy motor waggons were found, stuck in the mud on the main Es Salt Amman road; all had been looted by the Arabs. A quiet and much needed sleep was obtained that night.

At 8.30 a.m. on March 27th, the Division moved out along the El Fuheis Amman road to attack Amman. The Regiment was advance guard. It had been reported that Amman had been evacuated during the night, but after two hours' marching, our screen was heavily shelled as it approached the ridges which slope gently to the town. Continuing the advance, the leading squadrons came under heavy rifle and machine-gun fire and were checked. All ranks realised that serious opposition was now to be expected. The enemy was strongly posted on steep rocky hills covering the town, which lies in the bed of the Wadi Amman. The Turks possessed every advantage of cover, besides abundance of heavy and light artillery and machine guns, whilst our only artillery support was the Hong Kong and Singapore Mountain Battery. Moreover, the heavy rain had made the country so waterlogged that any departure from the one metalled road meant that horse or man sank almost to the knees.

Much of the land for some miles west and north of Amman has been cultivated, and in these ploughed fields the soil, with any movement was soon stirred to slush a foot deep. Consequently, any fast movements mounted were out of the question, and our mobility, which makes for at least half the efficiency of mounted troops, was greatly impaired. The enemy shell fire was severe and Regimental Headquarters came in for some of it, the Armourer Sergeant was killed and other casualties in men and horses were sustained.

The Brigade was now deployed for action and the positions for the first attack eventually were as follows:—

The Brigade machine gun squadron, less one section, with an escorting troop of the 6th Regiment, was on the extreme right in position by a ruined castle near El Melful, a mile and a half due west of Amman, being here in touch with the left of the Imperial Camel Brigade. To the left and north of the machine gunners, and blocking rather a large gap, was one squadron of the 5th Light Horse Regiment, the remainder of this Regiment was in Brigade reserve. Brigade Headquarters were almost directly in rear of this squadron on a high hill, somewhat south of El, Weibde. The 7th Regiment was grouped in the vicinity of Arak Er Ruak with the 6th Regiment on its left and extended towards point 2960 to prevent this flank, which was in the air, from being turned.

The plan of attack was an encircling movement of the town of Amman by the New Zealand Mounted Rifle Brigade on the right and 2nd Light Horse on the left, whilst the Imperial Camel Brigade endeavoured to break down any opposition in the centre. For our scanty forces, which could not have numbered, at first, more than 2,000 bayonets, the line was extended to what would have been a dangerous degree against an enemy strong in cavalry. But in this arm, the enemy was very weak, and his horsemen had never shown enterprise; his infantry also had always been content with a defensive attitude when in action against our mounted troops. For various reasons comparatively few rifles were available. In the Regiment it was found that more than a squadron had been taken for duties such as escorts for guns, prisoners and demolition parties. Major Willsallen and about three men were all that were available from "B" Squadron, whilst "A" and "C" were also much below strength.

The enemy was observed to be strongly posted in stone sangars about 2,000 yards north-east of Arak Er Ruak and in the vicinity of the caves at the head of the Wadi En Nueijis. This position covered the Amman railway station and aerodrome, which is 3,000 yards north-east of the old town of Amman itself. The aerodrome, which could be plainly seen, was given as our objective.

It was necessary to dismount immediately, leaving the horses under cover in the Wadi Er Ruak. The two squadrons commenced to advance against sangars which were afterwards found to have been occupied by German troops, with numerous machine guns. No artillery covering fire was available, as the only battery was employed on the right; two machine guns and the Hotchkiss rifles of the Regiment were all that could be relied upon to assist the advance. Marching steadily, no opposition was met until within about 600 yards of the sangars, when the enemy machine guns opened such a concentrated fire that our movement was abruptly checked. In addition, enemy field and heavy guns put up a barrage of high explosives and shrapnel, which soon made the situation very serious. The men were compelled to lie down in the mud, no cover being available. Our Hotchkiss rifles were practically of no use, for as soon as the gunners placed them in position and opened fire their tripods sank deeply in the mud.

Meanwhile the N.Z. Brigade and I.C.C. were advancing on the extreme right, but were also meeting with stiff opposition and making little progress. After nearly three hour's fighting, the whole line was almost stationary, the Canterbury Mounted Rifles alone being able to advance some distance south of the town.

At this stage R.H.Q. was heavily shelled, and suffering casualties, withdrew to another position. Shortly afterwards, the 6th L.H. Regiment, which was operating on the left, was driven back having suffered heavy casualties. This led to a general withdrawal of our centre and left to a position 500 yards in rear. The situation now was critical. "C" Squadron was hard pressed, having had numerous casualties in the ranks; "A" Squadron was suffering severely. The 5th L.H. Regiment was sent from Brigade Reserve to reinforce; but as the enemy did not press his advantage, it was not brought into the line. Soon afterwards, darkness settled down and operations for the day ended. The enemy displayed no activity during the night, and our troops remained in the positions they occupied at sundown.

During the night, the demolition party carrying gun cotton, and escorted by two squadrons of the 5th L.H. Regiment, under Major Bolingbroke, D.S.O., made a dash for the railway line four miles north of the town, and blew up a railway bridge and several lengths of the line, thus blocking all through traffic for several days. This was a dashing affair. The morning of the 28th was quiet, very few shots being fired by either side; preparations were being made for the next attack. A Brigade of mountain guns now arrived for our support and their appearance was greeted by loud cheering from all ranks; a little later the 2-13th London Infantry came up and relieved us, taking over the right of our sector. The 181st Infantry Brigade, less two battalions, had now marched from Es Salt and were sent into the gap north of Es Salt Amman road, thus relieving the squadron of the 5th Light Horse and stiffening our right. The New Zealand Mounted Rifle Brigade was now well to the south and east of Amman and directed upon hill 3039, which dominates the town. This was strongly held by the enemy. The plan for the next attack was for the 2nd Light Horse Brigade to make a dash, mounted, for a position north of Amman and to turn the enemy's right flank. At the last moment this order was cancelled owing to the sodden condition of the ground, and the Brigade was ordered to advance dismounted against the enemy positions facing our extreme left, co-operating also with the attack of the two London battalions, upon the sangars and enemy machine gun nests sheltering in the foundations of the old citadel of Amman just north of the Amman Es Salt road. The Imperial Camel Brigade was to attempt to force its way through to the south of the road, and the New Zealand M.R. Brigade was to endeavour to capture 3039. The artillery support was better now, but unfortunately, care had to be taken with ammunition owing to the distance from our base and the difficulty of getting supplies through except by camel train. The road from Es Salt to Amman had been badly cut up and the late rains had rendered it very boggy in places. Practically all the artillery support went to help the New Zealanders against 3039 and the Infantry against their objectives; none was allotted to us.

At 1 p.m. the attack was commenced. The regiment, with little more than 100 rifles, moved off in two extended lines, 200 yards apart, the 2-13 Londons moving on our right and the 6th Light Horse on our left. Our final objective was, as before, the enemy aerodrome, but many sangars filled with machine guns blocked the way. The first stage of the advance was across a sodden barley field, and for a mile we were under enemy rifle fire, with occasional shrapnel. The movement finally was checked by a concentrated burst of machine-gun fire from numerous sangars on a low stony hill, 300 yards in front. Men fell rapidly, and great difficulty was experienced in getting the wounded out of action. The 6th Regiment had also been checked and was suffering even more severely; one troop was wiped out. Any further advance was out of the question. though these sangars could easily have been silenced by adequate artillery support. Every moment was adding to the casualties; Lieut.-Colonel Onslow had a narrow escape from a bullet, which knocked a map out of his hand. The position was clearly untenable, and indeed, one of great danger, so that the order was given to retire to a long low hill 500 yards in rear.

All the wounded were got away except two, one being Corporal Picton, D.C.M., M.M., who was in such an advanced position that he could not be rescued. The enemy followed up our retirement which was made in good order, though with difficulty owing to getting the wounded back. The two machine guns attached to the Regiment were placed in position on our retiring point, and these, with two guns attached to the 6th Regiment, took heavy toll of the advancing enemy and did much to prevent him pressing too closely. A line was at length taken up on this low hill, which was held until the wounded were in safety. The enemy demonstrated as if to push a counter attack in considerable strength about 800 yards away, but did not come on. The 6th Regiment also had fallen back to a similar alignment, and the final retirement to a good defensive position, high above the left bank of the Wadi Er Ruak, was made before darkness fell. In this day's action out of little more than 100 of all ranks engaged, our casualties were: 2 killed, 2 missing, and 27 wounded. Three officers, Major Barton, Lieutenants Suttor and Finlay had been badly hit on the first day during the retirement. Most of our Hotchkiss rifles had either been shot to pieces or put temporarily out of action by the concentrated enemy fire. The machine guns and remaining Hotchkiss rifles now checked the enemy advance, though he remained in considerable strength, about 800 yards in front, until our final retirement. Owing to casualties, men on escort duty (prisoners, guns, etc.) and otherwise detached, the strength of the Regiment was at a very low ebb that night and at one time was considerably under 50 all told. A good defensive outpost line was taken up, however, and strengthened by four machine guns from 2nd M.G. Squadron. The night passed quietly.

The 29th was a quieter day on the front held by the Regiment, as our attacking power had practically ceased, though the machine-gun fire was almost incessant on both sides, and the Turks shelled our position intermittently. The lack of sufficiently powerful artillery and the shortage of S.A.A. and shells for the mountain batteries was keenly felt. A squadron of the Wellington Mounted Rifles, under Major Bachelor, was attached to the 7th and the whole of the left flank which included the 6th Regiment and two squadrons of the 5th, was placed under the command of Lieut.-Colonel Onslow. Rain fell intermittently, and away from rocky ground or formed roads, horses and men sank to the knees in sodden ground. At night it was bitterly cold.

On the 30th at 2 p.m. another effort was made by the Infantry, I.C. Brigade and N.Z.M.R. Brigade; our role was simply to hold our ground whilst making as great a demonstration as possible. The attack gained some of the objectives, but Turkish counter attacks followed, particularly against the Infantry on our right. These London troops fought with the greatest gallantry and all day long the battle for a low hill (since known to our men as Infantry Hill) continued. Although taken and retaken, the hill finally remained "No Man's Land"; no troops could hold it owing to the concentrated shell fire brought to bear upon it. In this fight the machine guns attached to us, and the Hotchkiss rifles of the Regiment, were trained at long range on the massing Turks, causing numerous casualties, but the nature of the ground did not permit of any other assistance even had our orders allowed it. The enemy made no move against our lines, though he appeared to be massing for an attack on several occasions, but machine gun and rifle fire was continuous all day, with intermittent shelling. The fire all round slackened towards night when orders were received that a retirement would take place at daylight, the 2nd Light Horse Brigade to be rear guard, the Infantry passing through our line, the 7th Regiment remaining in position for this until all had passed, and then swinging back with the 5th Regiment towards the Es Salt road, the 6th Regiment on the extreme left being the pivot. The mountain howitzer battery and the Somerset Battery R.H.A., which had forced its way through on the proceeding day, were to cover the retirement; however, they were not required.

At daylight on the 31st the retirement commenced; the Infantry were exhausted and it was some time before they were all concentrated and commenced to move. The Regiment moved as left flank guard to the retiring column, but the Turks, beyond firing a few shells, made no attempt to interfere with the withdrawal. Rations were drawn at Suweileh and Ain Hemar, where a halt was made for an hour for a meal. The Infantry and guns had passed on, the former to Ain Es Sir, the latter to Salt. Ain Hemar was left just as darkness came, the Regiment being in advance of the Brigade, which was in column of route. The roads were much cut up, the whole country was waterlogged, and it was a bitterly cold night. Es Salt was reached about 1.30 a.m. on April 1st, and the Regiment completely exhausted, bivouacked in a sheltered valley, about one mile north of the town. At 9 a.m. the march to the Jordan was resumed, rations being drawn, also Hotchkiss guns for those damaged in action, about a mile south of Es Salt on the Shunet Nimrin road. The Jordan Valley was reached just before dark, and the bivouac was made close to running water, among thorny bushes that bear Jordan apples or Dead Sea fruit.

One of the most pitiful sights during the whole campaign was the stream of refugees fleeing from Es Salt and Turkish vengeance down the Nimrin road. Many of these unfortunates were weak and old and staggered along. Our men assisted some by mounting them on their horses. After a refreshing sleep at Shunet Nimrin, at 7 a.m., the Brigade moved towards the Jordan. Enemy aeroplanes bombed the bridges and camps in the vicinity, but no bombs fell near us. The Jordan was crossed at Ghoraniyeh, and bivouac was made by the Wadi Kelt, about a mile south-east of Jericho. On April 3rd "A" Squadron was ordered to report to the I.C. Brigade and moved off at 4.45 p.m. and at 6 p.m. the remainder of the Regiment was ordered to move and proceeded to the Wadi Auja, six miles north of Jericho, coming under the orders of Brigadier-General Smith, V.C., commanding the Imperial Camel Brigade.

CHAPTER V.

THE JORDAN VALLEY.
PATROLS AND RAID TO ES SALT.

THE Regiment on April 4th moved to the high banks of the Wadi Obeidah, for better protection. "A" Squadron was sent to patrol the Wadi Mellahah and observed small bodies of enemy cavalry east of the Jordan. A troop, under Lieutenant Riley, reconnoitred the Auja Ford, and another patrol tried to get in touch with the 74th Division on En Nejme, the high peak to the north-west, but found the country too difficult. Owing to the casualties at Amman a redistribution of officers was made, the Squadrons being constituted as under:—

"A" Squadron: Major Easterbrook, M.C.; Lieutenants Dalton, Chapman, Riley.
"B" Squadron: Major Willsallen, D.S.O.; Lieutenants Ducker, Stanley, Dowsett.
"C" Squadron: Captain Johnson, Lieutenants Williams, Waddell, Walker.

On the 5th, patrols were sent to the Auja Ford, and at night, in front of the line held by the Camel Brigade, which ran from Musallabeh to Mellahah, touch was also obtained with the Devon Regiment on En Nemje. The daily routine now was that of patrols to the Auja Ford, the Mellahah, and to the left of the I.C. Brigade line, towards Tel El Truny in which direction a listening post was left at night. Touch with En Nejme was obtained by patrols over rather a difficult track. The enemy shelled every moment and the night-listening post at Truny, under Lieutenant Ducker, on the 7th, was attacked and two bombs thrown. On the other hand, a number of targets were picked up for our guns, which shelled with good results.

Rather unusual enemy movement was observed on the 9th and as there was considerable intermittent artillery fire, the Regiment remained saddled during the night. At 3 a.m. on the 10th, the 6th Regiment arrived, and under heavy enemy artillery fire, moved to the Wadi Auja. Patrols were sent as usual, and after Brigadier-General Smith had inspected the line, two squadrons were sent to the Wadi Abeid, to be ready to reinforce the left flank. At daybreak next day the enemy commenced a determined attack against the line held by the I.C. Brigade, more particularly against Mussallabeh, which spouted shells but was most gallantly defended. At 6 a.m., the Regiment moved to support the left flank of the line, and was heavily shelled, but found fair cover in the Auja. At 8.45 a.m. as the attack had died away, orders were given to return to camp. "C" Squadron on the right reported at 5 a.m. that the enemy was attacking the 1st L.H. Brigade and 5th Regiment outposts at Ghoraniyeh across the Jordan, and witnessed the complete cutting up of that attack by our artillery fire. As snipers were worrying the right post of the I.C. Brigade Line on the Mellahah, Lieutenant Walker was sent with a troop to try to dislodge them, but they were too strongly posted and strengthened with machine guns. The remainder of the Squadron moved that night close up to the Jordan near the same place, to watch enemy movements. One mounted prisoner was captured here at dawn on the 12th. A squadron of the 6th Regiment relieved our Squadron about 6 a.m. the same day.

As the 2nd Light Horse Brigade had been ordered to make a reconnaissance along the Roman Road towards Wadi Fusail, the Regiment concentrated with the Brigade at 12.30 p.m. in Wadi Obeidah and then moved off with "B" Squadron as advance guard. The enemy commenced to shell heavily, especially after the screen had passed Musallabeh, where B.H.Q. and R.H.Q. were established. As the advance guard approached the Wadi Bakr, it was met with machine-gun fire and also from the marshy ground close to the Wadi Mellahah. A Regiment of cavalry was observed about three miles to the north.

Lieutenant Williams and two troops moved to within 30 yards of the Um Es Shert crossing, but were held up by machine-gun fire. As the enemy's line had been found, the withdrawal under considerable shell fire commenced, a post, under Sergeant James, being left east of the Mellahah to watch enemy movements. One O.R. wounded was the only casualty for a day of heavy shelling and fairly intense machine-gun fire. Fifty very welcome reinforcements were received on this day when camp was regained.

Patrols were found as a daily routine, and on the 15th the Regiment moved to a camp site in the Wadi Abeid, known henceforth as Onslow's Farm, owing to the excellent crops of barley in the vicinity. On the 17th Major Willsallen made a reconnaissance of Wadi Bakr coming, as usual, under shell and machine-gun fire. The reconnaissance was satisfactory, although observation was difficult on account of a dust storm. The immediate honours for Amman were announced:—

  No. 210   W.O. & R.S.M. Keen .... M.C.
  No. 3026 Trooper Bell .... M.M.
  No. 2816 Trooper Gillighan .... M.M.
  No. 1070 Sergeant Baly, B. .... M.M.
  No. 1033 Trooper Williams, E. .... M.M.

Captain Davies, who had been doing staff training at Descorps, now rejoined, whilst a few days previously Lieutenant Donkin had reported for attachment to the R.F.C. for instruction in aviation signalling. The reconnaissance of Tel El Truny, Wadi Bakr, Mellahah and the Auja ford was now an unpleasant daily duty; invariably there was a fair amount of shell fire and bursts from machine guns as the troops approached the enemy's lines; fortunately, however, practically no casualties resulted. On the 18th, the Regiment, less two troops under Lieutenant Chapman on the left flank of the I.C. line, concentrated with the Brigade on the right bank of the Jordan, near Ghoraniyeh, for a demonstration towards Kabr Mujahid. The Jordan was crossed at 4 o'clock next morning, and moving out for about a mile, the Regiment came into Brigade reserve for the day. An escort of a troop was provided for the guns and came under heavy shell-fire; the 5th Regiment received the brunt of this but, fortunately, sustained few casualties. At 6 p.m. a withdrawal of half a mile was made, and outposts were for the night found by "C" Squadron.

On the 20th, the Regiment returned to the old camp site in the Wadi Abeid, and the daily routine of patrols and reconnaissance was resumed. Small camps and parties of enemy could often be seen and good targets were reported to our guns, which usually ranged accurately on these. Night patrols between Mussallabeh and the Mellahah were also found. The Cyclists' Battalion of the 53rd Division was now on En Nejme, to which our patrols were occasionally sent, though the track was very difficult. A steady stream of sick men, evacuated to hospital, was hardly counterbalanced by reinforcements. Officers and O.R.'s were now also being sent to schools of instruction. The digging of rough trenches on the left of the line held by the I.C. Brigade was commenced.

On the 28th the Regiment was relieved by the Stafford Yeomanry and proceeded to the Jericho Dump. Major Bird, with "C" Squadron, made a reconnaissance across the Jordan east of Hajla, the C.O. (Lieut.-Colonel Onslow) reconnoitring Kabr Said and Kabr Mujahid. The Regiment crossed the Jordan to bivouac half a mile east of Hajla Ford. Lieut.-Colonel Onslow, with Lieut.-Colonel Eughster, of the 20th Brigade R.H.A., further reconnoitred Kabr Mujahid and Kabr Said, with a view to attack, and selected a spot for Headquarters about 2,000 yards north-east of Kabr Fendi El Faiz. At 8 p.m. on the 29th, the following troops came under the command of Lieut.-Colonel Onslow for an attack and demonstration against the enemy's left so as to mask the real attack and the break-through on his right:—7th Light Horse Regiment, 1 Squadron of Hyderabad Lancers, 1 Section 2nd M.G. Squadron, 1 Battalion Patiala Infantry, 8 guns of the 20th Brigade R.H.A., and Field Ambulance details.

This force came under the direct orders of the G.O.C., 60th Division, and was ordered to seize enemy's advance works near Kabr Said and Kabr Mujahid.

Concentration was made at old Turkish huts just east of the Hajla Ford, and the place of deployment was on the spot previously selected for Headquarters. "A" Squadron found front and flank protection. At 2 a.m. on the 30th, the Patialas (Indians) moved to attack Kabr Mujahid, and "B" Squadron, under Major Willsallen, with two machine guns, to attack Kabr Said. Lieutenant Dalton, with two troops of "C" Squadron, secured flank protection for the attacking infantry; Captain Johnson, with the remaining two troops, formed the escort for the guns; "A" Squadron and the Hyderabad Lancers and 1 Sub-Section Machine Guns were in reserve. Both objectives were taken by 3 a.m. with slight opposition, the Patialas repulsing a weak counter-attack at 4.30 a.m. At 5.30, the Patialas were compelled to withdraw from Kabr Mujahid a short distance, as this prominent feature made a good target for the enemy shell-fire, and at intervals during the day it spouted high explosives like a volcano. The enemy opposite Kabr Said was found to be withdrawn about 2,000 yards into the high ground, and did not attempt any movement during the day.

From daylight the gunfire on both sides was intense and at times swelled to almost a continuous roar, drawing the eyes of everyone from the real attack, which was being carried out on the extreme left—the galloping through of the Australian Mounted Division to seize Jisr Damieh ford and Es Salt. Regimental Headquarters and the gun positions came under heavy fire, but the effect of high explosives from field guns is very local, and the Turk has seldom extensively used shrapnel. As this attack by Onslow's Force was only a demonstration, no further advance was made, and the line was simply maintained during the day.

At 4.30 p.m. the remainder of the Hyderabad Lancers relieved the 7th Regiment which was ordered, with the Machine Gun Section attached, to Butmet Halul, two miles south-east of Ghoraniyeh Bridge Head, where bivouac was made. The casualties for the day were one O.R. killed, and three horses wounded.

At 1 a.m. on the 1st, the Regiment marched to join the Brigade by the Um Es Shert Road at Es Salt, the advance having so far proved successful. The road was a mere goat-track up which horses had, for the most part, to be led, great trouble being experienced with the pack animals. On the latter part of the journey it rained heavily. Es Salt was reached at 11.30 a.m., but the Brigade, which was under the orders of the Australian Mounted Division, had moved to the Amman Road where, four miles out, B.H.Q. was found. The Regiment rejoined Brigade at 1.45 p.m. and put out outposts near Ain Hemar at 5 p.m. At 7.30 orders were received to withdraw, but owing to the darkness and the extended line, the Brigade was not again concentrated until midnight, when march was commenced to a position on the Nimrin Road, one and a half miles south of Es Salt. The 2nd Brigade now received orders to be prepared to move with the 5th Mounted Brigade, soon after dawn on 2nd April, against high ground in the vicinity of Arkub El Khaluf (1460). All ranks were now feeling the effects of continuous movement and lack of sleep and officers and N.C.O's were busily engaged waking men who fell soundly asleep in the saddle.

At 9 a.m. on the 2nd, orders were again received to move down this road, dismounted, to support the attack of the 5th Mounted Brigade against the enemy position in the Nimrin Pass. Then just as this movement had almost been completed a report was received that the Turks were advancing in force from Amman; a counter order was therefore sent from Headquarters, Australian Mounted Division, for the Brigade to return and take up a defensive position from El Awab to Kh Elfokan, and so cover Es Salt from the east. "A" Squadron was placed on the right, "B" on the left, "C" Squadron in reserve in this new position.

At 10.30 a.m. orders were received from Australian Mounted Division to prolong the line to the Amman Road due north of present position. "C" Squadron occupied the high ground in this vicinity by noon, at which hour the outposts of the 3rd L.H. Brigade, which had been well in front, were driven back to this line. The enemy attempted no serious attack, but 300 cavalry made a demonstration, retiring after coming within rifle range. "C" Squadron was relieved at 2 p.m. by the 5th L.H. Regiment, and withdrew to the centre of our line. Small enemy parties could be seen in front, but these were content to snipe at long range. This line was made also the outpost line for the night, which passed quietly.

As all rations had been eaten and it had been found impossible to get supplies through to us, requisitions were made on the country for cattle, the horses being grazed on barley. After daylight on the 3rd, the enemy made an attack on that part of the line held by the 3rd L.H. Brigade and 5th Regiment. The new troops just hurried up from Ammam, who were put into the attack, blundered into a "V" shaped machine gun barrage, and, besides many other casualties, left 350 prisoners (including 9 officers, one a Battalion commander), in the hands of the 5th and 8th Regiments. This disaster to the Turkish forces probably prevented any other serious attack against our weak line during the day, though the shelling was more or less continuous, and small parties of the enemy kept filtering into the positions within sniping distance. It was almost impossible to get at these, owing to the difficult country, which precluded any flanking movements. Further requisitions on the country were made.

4.30 p.m. orders were received that, owing to the presence of large enemy reinforcements, the whole force would withdraw, the Regiment to retire from this line at 10 p.m., and to hold the road immediately covering Es Salt and form rearguard. A difficult track was taken to reach this spot. Lieutenant Riley was sent with a troop to watch for any enemy advance up the Nimrin Road. The rear-guard position was reached at 1 a.m. on the 4th. At 3 a.m. word was received that the whole column had passed through, and at 4.15, the Regiment commenced to withdraw, taking the same rough Um Es Shert Road, as had been used in coming up. About five miles down the road, a regiment of the 5th Mounted Brigade was found in position, and rearguard was passed over to it. Lieutenant Riley, with his troop from the Nimrin Road, had joined up without incident.

During the descent, and especially as daylight broke, the enemy commenced shelling the track, but their fire was very inaccurate. The march was continued straight to the Jordan, which was crossed at Ghoraniyeh, and bivouac was made in the Wadi Kelt, one and a half miles south-east of Jericho. The whole operation had been most exhausting; the men had had only a few hours sleep during the whole period and needed rest badly. It is astonishing that, during all these days of almost continuous fighting, and some heavy shell fire, there were no casualties.

The operations known as the Es Salt Raid nearly ended in a disaster, and much of the credit of the withdrawal from a difficult position must be ascribed to our gallant Brigadier, whose coolness and sound judgment were never more in evidence. The whole plan, which was brilliant in conception, was marred by one bad mistake—the insufficient garrisoning of Red Hill, a prominent landmark east of the Jordan.

When the 4th L.H. Brigade, taking advantage of the diversion caused by Onslow's Force, had galloped through and seized the Jisr Damieh ford, the 3rd L.H. Brigade followed and forced its way through to Es Salt, which was taken with many prisoners. The 5th Mounted Brigade then came up in support, with our Brigade following more slowly. It was now the opportunity of our allies—Arabs of Beni Sakr tribe—who had promised full co-operation, to fall on the enemy's rear and flank between El Haud, at the mouth of the Nimrin pass, and Amman, and cut off all supplies and block reinforcements or retirements. They did nothing.

In the meantime, our old friends of the 60th Infantry Division were to attempt to storm El Haud, and the mounted troops from Es Salt would then enclose the Turkish garrisons in the Nimrin valley in a pair of pincers. The failure to co-operate on the part of the Arabs probably spoilt the operation, in any case, but what nearly caused disaster, was the passage of the Jordan by a large body of Turks, five miles south of the Jisr Damieh ford, and the capture of Red Hill, from which a weak squadron from the 1st. L.H. Brigade was driven.

The enemy then streamed across the plain to the foothills, hoping to close the door against the retirement of the 4th L.H. Brigade. The danger was realised in the nick of time, and this Brigade managed to gallop through a small and rapidly closing gap; but some guns and ambulance waggons had to be abandoned. The enemy endeavoured to follow up his advantage, but the N.Z.M.R. Brigade, which had been in reserve, was pushed forward and a line was taken up to cover the Um Es Shert track, now the only line of retirement for the almost isolated Brigades in Es Salt. The Infantry attack on El Haud—a very Gibraltar of a place—failed, although most gallantly pushed, and the mounted troops from Es Salt were unable to make any headway down the Nimrin pass.

Finally, a general retirement was ordered, and if any disorder, confusion or panic had been evident, especially among the rear-guard troops, the partial destruction of three Brigades might easily have ensued. The Brigadier, as always in a crisis (although a very sick man, who should have been in hospital), was an inspiring example to all ranks and was ably backed up by the Acting-Brigade-Major (Major Easterbrook) and the Regimental commanders. The plan of retirement worked without a hitch, and when morning broke, the enemy found that what had appeared an easy prey, had slipped away.

The 5th was devoted to badly needed rest, but on the 6th, Lieutenant Dalton, with three troops, was ordered to guard and patrol the crossings of the Jordan at El Yehud, Hajla, and El Henu, and to Rujmelbar on the Dead Sea. At 5 a.m. on the 7th, the camp was bombed by eight hostile planes, one bomb bursting with deadly effect, killing eight men and eight horses, and wounding 10 men and 15 horses, all casualties occurring in "B" Squadron. This appeared to be a new type of bomb, which raked the line in which it fell, from end to end. The patrol to the Jordan, under Lieutenant Dalton, returned later in the day. On the 8th, Brigadier-General Ryrie, before proceeding to hospital, addressed the Regiment, thanking officers and men for their good work and loyal support. Lieut.-Colonel Onslow assumed command of the Brigade, Major Bird temporarily commanding the 7th Regiment.

A working party of 34 O.R.'s, under Lieutenant Dowsett, was sent to Ghoraniyeh next day, for wiring purposes. On the 10th, Anzac Mounted Division Headquarters moved to Talaat Ed Dum, and the Brigade came under the command of the Australian Mounted Division. The weather was now almost unbearably hot, and the dust in the Valley, in any place where there was traffic, was frightful. A steady drain of sick men to hospital kept the Regiment well below strength. On the 11th, a day of great heat and dust, the Regiment shifted camp to the camp site of the 12th A.L.H. Regiment on the Wadi Nuameiah, 3,000 yards north of Jericho, an unclean and dusty spot. From this date until the 22nd, the daily routine consisted of road reconnaissance, with road making and trench digging parties for the purpose of improving front line positions on the Auja, and communications thereto.

On the 22nd, camp was changed to a place near Ain Ed Duk about 4,000 yards north-west of Jericho; this was a better spot but very dusty. A plentiful supply of water was obtainable from a spring. Working parties consisting of up to 100 O.R's continued to be requisitioned mostly for road-making purposes; a serviceable road was eventually formed from the Jericho Road, south of Wadi Nuameiah, running round by Ain Ed Duk, to the front line on the Auja, with numerous lateral communications.

On the 25th, the Regiment took over the "W" Posts of the Auja Defence Line, from the 5th Regiment, two squadrons being in the out-posts line with two machine guns, with one squadron and four machine guns in support. The enemy shelled the whole line intermittently with field and mountain guns, doing, however, very little damage. "Stand to" was at 3.30 a.m. when patrols were sent out, one troop going to, and remaining in observation at Truny all day. One squadron then took over the line, the other two, with the machine guns, returning to camp at Ain Ed Duk. Casualties were few, Truny being about the most dangerous spot owing to enemy machine guns

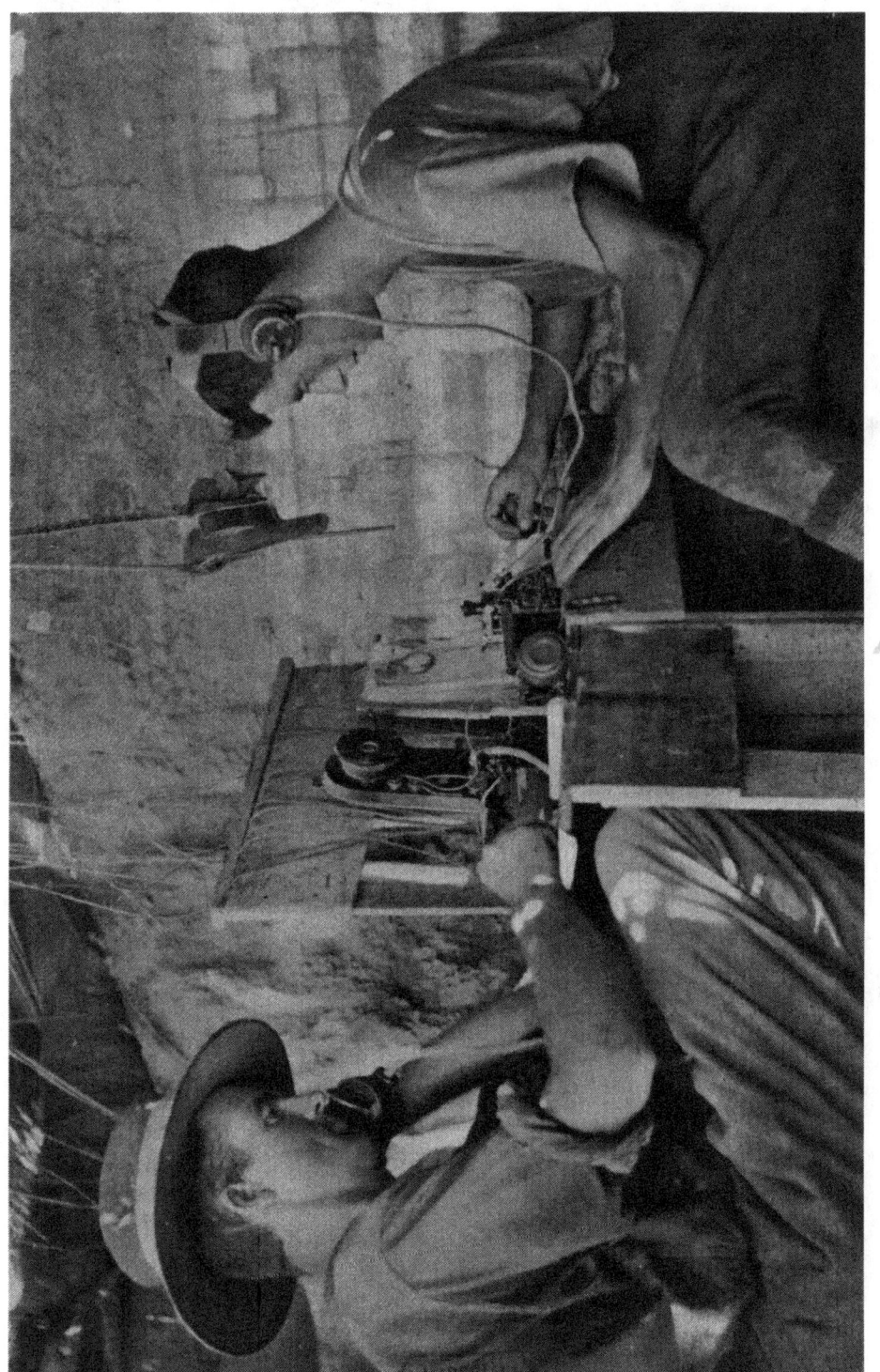

Sig.-Sgt. Laugier and Sig. Harper in Trench, Wadi Mellahar.

(Top)—Turkish Trenches at Shellac, Wadi Ghuzze.
(Middle)—Regimental Officers' Cook and his "offsiders" at Hebron Road Camp.
(Bottom)—Camp at Kilid Bahr, Gallipoli, in 1918.

posted on high ground near Tel El Risheh. At night, digging and wiring was carried on at the different posts, strong working parties coming from the 5th and 6th Regiments. The Squadrons took turns to find the out-post line at night, and the day observation posts and patrols. Practically every day the line was more or less heavily shelled, and any unusual movement near a post caused a few shells to be fired into it. The valleys and roads in rear were also occasionally searched and consequently the Squadrons had to move in to the posts after dark and pick covered ways out before the light was strong enough for the enemy to observe them.

The 5th Regiment, on the 28th, again took over the out-post line, and our Regiment found the large wiring and digging parties at night. The same camp to return to in the daytime, had been retained in the line. On the 31st the 5th Regiment was again relieved in the line. The names of the posts held were Wood, Wild, Wane, Wart, and Wax, these linking up with the "V" posts on the right. The lateral communications between these were now good, and the posts themselves, were practically all dug and well wired. The weather was always hot, but some days were intensely so, though Ain Ed Duk is some hundreds of feet above the Jordan, and therefore, rather a better place than most in the valley. A plentiful supply of good water compensated for a great deal, but snakes, some very venomous, swarmed in the vicinity of the water channels. The Tel El Truny patrol usually came in for a fair amount of shelling, and our batteries shelled the machine gun nest above Risheh and other places in retaliation for this and other shelling of our line. It was a fine sight to see the heavy shells of the big howitzers and 60 pounders bursting on the hillside and the Turks running for cover in all directions.

On June 4th the welcome orders for relief came, and the 9th Regiment took over the out-post line from us. At 7.50 p.m. on the 5th, following B.H.Q. at 20 minutes interval, on account of the dust, the Regiment moved out and proceeded to Talaat Ed Dum on the Jerusalem-Jericho road, where advance parties had been sent earlier in the day. The old Roman road, much improved, was used for the mounted men, the wheeled transport taking the new motor road. Talaat Ed Dum was reached at 10.30 p.m. and bivouac was made on rather a windy spot, which, next day, became enveloped in dust. On the 6th, the Regiment left bivouac at 7.15 p.m. for Solomon's Pools, passing the 1st A.L.H. Brigade at Bethany at 11.30 p.m. Here a great change in temperature was noticed and it became still more marked as the top of the range was reached at Jerusalem. At Bethlehem, the air was bitterly cold, while Solomon's Pools, reached at 5 p.m. on the 7th, were enveloped in driving mountain mist.

Solomon's Pools was not found to be an ideal rest camp, as the long distance from water meant that the men were occupied with the horses during many hours of the day when they should have been resting and preparing for the next term of duty in the Valley. The climate, however, was beautiful, and fresh fruit and vegetables and a good supply of canteen stores were available. Until the 20th, the routine consisted of physical training and bayonet fighting, watering horses, visits in parties, under officers, to Bethlehem and Jerusalem, and ordinary Regimental and Brigade duties. The evacuations to hospital during this period were heavy, as the reaction from the heavy strain of service in the Jordan Valley had set in, and it was necessary to send many men away.

On the 21st at 5.30 p.m. the Regiment again moved out for the weary journey down to the Valley, bivouacked at Talaat Ed Dum at 1.30 a.m., and at 7 p.m. next day moved to a bivouac site on the Wadi Nueiameh arriving there at 10.30 p.m. On the 23rd, the camp of the Gloucester Yeomanry on the Wadi Auja was taken over, and the Regiment came into Brigade reserve, the only tactical duties being two patrols of one N.C.O and nine men each, which were sent out between the left hand post on the Wadi Mellahah and the redoubts on Mussallabeh, to watch what was known as "The Gap." Guards for water areas were found, and large parties were detailed for such duties as canalisation of steams and oiling marshy places to prevent mosquitoes breeding. Lieut.-Colonel Onslow was still in charge of the Brigade, and Lieutenant

Donkin moved to B.H.Q. as Intelligence Officer. The enemy's shelling was severe at this time, but the areas chosen were mostly the Auja Crossing, near El Madhbeh, Mussallbeh, and the Mellahah posts. At night, large working parties were found for wiring Turtle Post, in the scrub in rear of "The Gap", in an excellently covered position, but the actual trenches apparently had been laid out with too close an imitation of methods adopted in France, and were unsuitable here, where a concentrated fire would soon wipe out the whole garrison without hope of support from neighbouring posts or reinforcements from second lines, where deep shelters might have been dug. None of these secondary works were ever constructed to strengthen what were undoubtedly isolated posts, and as the scrub was very thick, snipers would also have been able to pick off the garrison easily.

On the night of the 26th, one of the patrols in "The Gap" was attacked by an enemy party in some strength, and driven in, but being reinforced later occupied the original position. On the 27th, Major Easterbrook, M.C., who had been ill for some time, was evacuated to hospital. Two additional troops were now sent out into the scrub in rear of "The Gap," one, as a rallying point for the two patrols, about a mile north of Turtle Post, and the other to protect the Ayrshire Battery, which was in rear of that place in an exposed position. These troops had to move out and return during semi-darkness, as the enemy's shelling had increased, and even one or two mounted men were considered fair targets. B.H.Q. had been driven out of the scrub by shell fire and into the Wadi Auja, where there was fair protection.

The usual routine was of working parties, patrols and escorts for camels carrying R.E. material for defense purposes from Jericho, until July 3rd, when the Regiment moved out to the Mellahah to relieve the 6th Regiment in the "T" Posts. As advance parties had been sent earlier in the day to take over stores, signals, etc., the relief was completed without a hitch, by 10.30 p.m. At 11 p.m. the enemy, possibly hearing something of the relief, or wishing to define our line, made a demonstration by a forward patrol using rifles and machine guns, while upon flares being sent up, their artillery opened, shooting badly.

No reply was made to this, though the demonstration continued intermittently until midnight. The remainder of the night passed quietly. As no movement was possible on any of the posts in the day time without causing a blast of shells, it was necessary that all work improving trenches and wiring should be done at night. R.H.Q. was changed from a place which seemed likely to get the "overs" fired at the trenches, to a spot in the front line, from which lateral communication with all posts was more or less covered. The daily routine was mostly that of observation and to this end special observation posts were established.

Enemy movements were plainly observable, especially along the old Roman Road leading to Beisan. The enemy's shelling was almost daily increasing, and it was fairly evident that some concentration of troops was proceeding. Our guns fired a good deal in retaliation and at any targets which could be picked up, and the moral effect of the burst of the 60 pounders was noticeable. At night patrols were sent out and "No Man's Land" was made ours, whilst the work of digging, wiring and sand-bagging posts was carried on continuously. That the Turkish morale was not good, was clearly seen by the number of deserters coming in, averaging almost one a day, either to our posts or to those of the 5th Regiment on our right. The swamps in front of the posts claimed much attention, as breeding grounds for malaria-carrying mosquitoes; parties were constantly employed draining and oiling the water whenever possible. Unfortunately, however, whenever the wind blew from a northerly direction, it brought mosquitoes from undrained swamps in "No Man's Land" and Turkish territory, and these insects were responsible for most of the malaria that occurred. Our patrols at night left a good deal of propaganda in places where the Turks might be likely to pick it up. Occasionally, the enemy made a demonstration from the vicinity of his posts, firing Verey lights, giving bursts from his machine guns, and then his field guns would open. This would last for perhaps half an hour, and the remainder of the night would be quiet.

Supplies for the posts had to be brought out at night, and as the track was often shelled, it was fortunate that there were no casualties among the waggons and limbers. The weather was intensely hot, and the powdery nature of the soil in the Mellahah made conditions miserable for all ranks. The slightest effort produced profuse perspiration, which the ever-present dust quickly caked on the skin. Our snipers were pushed forward during the day, especially to a prominent feature called "Shark's Tooth," and easily kept down enemy sniping. It was no pleasant duty, however, lying all day in the hot sunshine.

On the 8th, at 6 p.m., the enemy fired about 40 shells in the vicinity of our posts, and close to R.H.Q., but although several burst right over some of the trenches, no damage was done. Lieutenant Waddell and eight men went out on patrol at 7.30 p.m. and after a good reconnaissance, returned at 2.30 a.m., having observed no enemy movement. About midnight, enemy firing commenced again, but nearly all the shells went well over and towards Auja. The shelling—a mixture of 5.9's, 77's and mountain guns—came from two directions, Wadi Fusail and Um Es Shert. The 9th was a quieter day, though there was still some intermittent shelling. Four cadet officers arrived on this day— Second-Lieutenants Worthington, Croll, Teschner and H.G.H. Waugh, all non-coms., who had been granted commissions after a long period of excellent service.

Lieutenant Walker on the night of the 10th, took a patrol of 8 men to examine a trench to the north-west of Tool Post, believed to be occupied by the enemy during hours of darkness. This trench, since known as Donkin's Mistake, was found to be unoccupied, but had evidently been one used when the Camel Brigade held the line. The day and night was quieter, though our guns did a good deal of registering in the afternoon. On the 11th, there was more shelling, Thin Post being especially singled out, and a number of shells falling close to R.H.Q. General Chaytor inspected the line in the morning of a day of most intense heat, accentuated by the white banks of the Wadi, and the confined nature of the ground which prevented any breeze. Until the 14th, nothing unusual beyond increasing shell fire occurred; the patrols moved unhindered at night in "No Man's Land," and the work of improving positions went on steadily. However, it was evident that a concentration against our front was in progress, particularly in guns, and the number of heavy shells which fell close to our trenches, or screamed overhead towards the Auja daily became greater. The ration track at night came in for many of these, and the enemy had an unpleasant habit of battery-firing for two or three minutes at any time, from about 10 p.m. until midnight. This rather spoilt the rest of the men who were unable to sleep during the day, on account of intense heat.

At 2.30 a.m. on the 14th commenced the Second Battle of Mussallabeh, for it was principally around that point and Abu Tellul, in the vicinity, that the main attack was made, though the 5th Regiment, on our right had a fairly serious attack launched at them, which was easily beaten off and brilliantly countered. The enemy's advance was heralded with a storm of shell fire, mostly directed against Mussallabeh, and Abu Tellul, but a fair share also came our way, particularly on Tool and Tool Counter Post, and the scrub in the rear of "The Gap" was searched with 5.9's, with the object evidently, of hitting the Ayrshire Battery, concealed there. In front of our line only small bodies of German troops appeared, about 40 of these occupying Shark's Tooth and giving us some good shooting. The Hun is not nearly so clever as the Turk at concealing his movements, or at sniping. The enemy main attack had been broken by 10 a.m. and the enemy in front of us merely contented himself with sniping from his bare and uncomfortable positions, on a day of intense heat from which he must have suffered severely. These German troops wore caps, and had come within the last few days from the pleasant climate of Es Salt and Amman.

This abortive effort on the enemy's part was probably intended to thrust us off the high ground about Mussallabeh, Abu Tellul and El Madbeh, and to gain the good water supply of the Wadi Auja. Three or four German Battalions were pushed forward as storm troops, possibly to show the Turks how the work should be done. These were to be supported by two Turkish Divisions, but if any support was given it was done in such a half-hearted manner that it was useless, and when the Germans rushed forward they were quickly left well " in the air." Their attack on the extreme right came against the 5th Light Horse Regiment, but was quickly crushed, and fluttered out altogether after counter bombing attacks had been brilliantly made by parties of the 5th, in which a number of prisoners were taken.

The attackers on the left moved past Mussallabeh, swarmed up the whaleback ridge of Abu Tellul, and attacked the "V" posts, held by the 2nd Light Horse Regiment. These Posts were well dug and wired, and the garrison had no trouble in holding out, though the enemy artillery fire was intense and excellently directed. The Germans rushed like waves on a rocky shore against these, and although they captured some beer at Regimental Headquarters, it was their only capture, and they were quickly shot down or driven to cover. A counter-attack by the Reserve Regiment of the 1st L.H. Brigade completed their defeat, and many prisoners were taken. A number of these were suffering from sun-stroke and were semi-comatose, while a few were showing the effects of the beer which they had drunk.

The night was quiet. Next morning, as the Germans were still on Shark's Tooth, Lieutenant Walker and 20 men were sent to try and dislodge them, but though they drove in advanced snipers the nature of the country and the numbers against them prevented this being done. Any attempt at a flanking movement was met by hot machine-gun fire down Wadis that had to be crossed, so that at 2.30 p.m. orders to withdraw were sent out to the patrol, which returned at 5.30 p.m. coming under hot fire as it did so. Our casualties were two killed (Sergeant Hill and Trooper Weatherall) and two wounded; the known enemy casualties were six killed and four wounded, all Germans. The men on our patrol, who returned, were much exhausted and famished for water.

Later, our guns shelled Shark's Tooth, and dislodged all the enemy there. For gallantry and the excellent handling of his Hotchkiss, Trooper Cartwright received the M.M. on this day. On the 16th, enemy snipers and machine guns were still active on our front, and our men again did some excellent shooting. Our field guns opened on targets found for them by our observers with good results dispersing bodies of the enemy and inflicting casualties. The night was again quiet. Next day, soon after dawn, the Ayrshire Battery fired 30 shells against the enemy on our front, dispersing several parties. Enemy guns did not open up until 5 p.m. and little movement was observed during the day; apparently a withdrawal of guns and men from advanced positions was in progress. Our 60 pounders shelled targets reported. On the 18th, there was rather more shelling as if enemy guns were registering from new positions, and evidently they feared a mounted attack through "The Gap" as many shells fell in that place where there were no posts at all. A number of 77's and 4.2's fell close to our R.H.Q. and Tool Post.

Lieutenant Waddell, who had done a great deal of the night patrol work, took out another patrol at 7.30 p.m. to Shark's Tooth, returning after midnight finding no enemy. Our snipers now gained possession of Shark's Tooth.

Until the 21st, the enemy contented himself with spasmodic shelling, while our guns were very active, the 60 pounders paying a lot of attention to the Um Es Shert Ford. The usual night patrols went out and the repairing and improving of outposts continued. On the 21st, however, not a single enemy shell was fired and there was scarcely any sniping. On the 22nd his guns again opened up and 5.9's fell close, three of them fortunately being duds. A few shells also fell close during the day.

Lieutenant Waddell again took the night patrol to Shark's Tooth, finding no enemy, and went out on a similar mission next day. As the R.F.C. had reported some enemy movements on the 23rd, constant patrols were sent out, but nothing unusual was reported. On the night of the 24th, about 50 shells were fired at intervals against our line, mostly landing wide at Tea Post. It is possible that the enemy hoped to catch some of our ration parties. No horses or wheels, of course, could be left in the Mellahah in our sub-section during the day, and although there were emergency rations and water in all the posts, the ordinary rationing had to be continued, as usual, by night. The usual spasmodic shelling took place on the 25th, but otherwise things were quiet and little movement, except that of small parties making towards the Jordan was noticed. The enemy was having a bad time through lack of water in any of his posts away from the river, and various deserters stated that one water bottle had to last them, in some cases, for nearly 48 hours—and the Turk is a great and improvident water drinker. For about an hour, from 5 p.m. on the 26th, the enemy shelled our line heavily with large and small shells, many falling close to R.H.Q. but no damage was done. The night was quiet. The usual night patrols ventured well out into "No Man's Land," Lieutenant Waddell taking the majority of these, and work on the trenches was carried on every night.

The welcome news of relief at last came, and on the 27th Captain Williams and a party were sent to Talaat Ed Dum to take over the camp site. On the 28th at 11 p.m. a quiet night, the Regiment was relieved by the 6th Cavalry Regiment (Indians), everything going smoothly, and then proceeded to the Regimental transport and horse lines in the Wadi Obeideh.

A most trying period had been spent on the Mellahah, and one that many men, who developed malignant malaria in spite of all precautions, will have reason to remember for the remainder of their lives. The discomfort was extreme, and the heat so intense, that the men did not eat half of their rations, while constantly craving for water. Sandflys, mosquitoes, flys, scorpions, and spiders were always in evidence, while the dust on the roads in rear was amazing. The enemy's shelling was severe at times, and the mental and physical strain reduced the condition and vitality of the Regiment, to perhaps, a lower ebb than at any time since Gallipoli days.

At 7.30 p.m. on the 29th, march was commenced for Talaat Ed Dum, which was reached at midnight, the dust during the early portion of the march being stifling. At this place the Brigade came into Corp's Headquarters Reserve, and this new site was a much better one than the former one at Talaat Ed Dum, being close to water troughs and on better ground.

CHAPTER VI.

THE END IN SIGHT.

ON the 31st, one officer and 25 O.R's proceeded to Port Said Rest Camp for a month's leave. The evacuations to hospital during this period were numerous; many men broke down, now that the strain was over. On August 2nd, Lieut.-Colonel Onslow returned to Regimental Command—Brigadier-General Ryrie having come back to the Brigade. On the 9th, the Corps Commander, Lieut.-General Sir Harry Chauvel inspected the Regiment with the Brigade. It was a hot and trying morning and the long waiting was exhausting to men whose strength had been sapped by malaria or general debility; some of them had to leave the parade.

The same day the march to Solomon's Pools was commenced on the 9th. At 7.30 p.m. we followed the long and tiring road to Bethany and Jerusalem, thence to Bethlehem. The camp area, about four miles beyond Solomon's Pools was found to be much better than that previously occupied, as a good water supply was available close by.

Near this spot a number of springs come to a head; these were known in Herod's day, and many of the old aqueducts are in a wonderful state of preservation; one known as that of Pontius Pilate was now being repaired by the Egyptian Labour Corps. Pilate is supposed to have been recalled to Rome owing to a too lavish expenditure on this work. The new water supply of Jerusalem developed by the Royal Engineers, comes from this place.

Officer's picquets in Jerusalem and Bethlehem had to be found in turn with the other Regiments; otherwise there were few duties and as much time as possible was given to resting. On the 19th, the Divisional Commander inspected the Regiment with the Brigade, and found everything in good order. On the 23rd, this resting and recuperating period came to an end, and at 4 p.m. the Regiment again moved off on the long march to the Valley. A halt, was made at Bethany to allow the 3rd L.H. Brigade to pass, the march being resumed at 3 a.m. on the 24th. Talaat Ed Dum was reached at 6.30 p.m. A windy and dusty day was spent here and at 4 p.m. on the 25th, the final stage of the march to the Valley was commenced. At a camp site near Tel Es Sultan, a mile from Jericho, the Regiment rested until 3 p.m.; a move was then made to another camp in the Wadi Nuameiah. This proved to be a good place, with abundant water, and plenty of bushes to make shelters against the heat of the day. The Regiment was in Brigade reserve and only usual camp and Brigade duties were found.

On the 28th, the Commander-in-Chief, Sir Edmund Allenby, at D.H.Q., presented ribbons to Major Richardson, D.S.O. (Brigade-Major 2nd L.H. Brigade), Major Bird, D.S.O., Captain Williams, M.C., and Sergeants Ford and Guy, M.M. The Commander-in-Chief made rather a dramatic entry on a pig-rooting horse, and was abrupt and to the point as usual in a fine soldierly manner.

Officers' patrols were sent to the 11th Cavalry Brigade to make reconnaissances east of the Jordan, from Hajla to Ghoraniyeh, over country in which the Regiment in future would most likely be working. On September 1st orders were received to move to the Monastery at Yehud, five miles east of Jericho and half a mile from the Jordan. The march was commenced at 6.30 p.m. on a rough track and we arrived at our destination at 8.30 p.m. Two waggons had been overturned and smashed. Our own camp was left standing and dummy camps and lines were formed, in order to deceive the enemy, so that the cavalry withdrawal from the Valley and the concentration against his right flank on the coast might not be observed. Dummy horses were made out of stakes and old blankets, and apparently served their purpose well, for the enemy maintained his strength against our line in the Valley, and up to the last moment apparently was uncertain as to where the real attack was to be launched. His aeroplanes reported increased cavalry strength in the Jordan Valley, whereas three Cavalry and one Infantry Division had been gradually withdrawn to the coastal sector.

Bivouac at Yehud was fairly good, though very dusty; officers were quartered in the Monastery, which required some cleaning. The sand-flies, however, were a dreadful pest, and in spite of mosquito nets, it was almost impossible to sleep at night. The Regimental Quartermaster suffered intensely. News was now received that Lieut.-Colonel Onslow, who was away on leave, had been appointed to the command of the 5th Light Horse Brigade, with temporary rank of Brigadier-General. Major Richardson, the Brigade Major, was given command of the Regiment, obtaining temporary rank of Lieut.-Colonel, on the 9/9/'18, this being made substantiative two months later. Major Easterbrook was appointed Brigade Major in his place.

The making of dummy horses and Regimental routine were now the chief duties, though from September 3rd onwards strong night patrols and outposts in front of the infantry line at Makhadet Hajla had to be found; also a patrol of troop strength from El Henu to the Dead Sea. The infantry trenches at Makhadet Hajla were garrisoned by a battalion of Patialas (Indian Imperial Service troops), and our night outposts in front of these were to give warning of any serious enemy advance. These night patrols and outposts were found in turn with two regiments of the 12th Cavalry Brigade (2nd Lancers and Central India Horse), under whose command the Regiment had temporarily been placed. A day reconnaissance by two troops followed; these usually worked along the Wadi El Rameh to Kabr Fendiel, Faiz, thence towards Mashrah Kefrein, the enemy occasionally shelling when the patrol came under their observation.

Eighty cases of gifts arrived on the 5th and were much appreciated. It is to the credit of those in charge of the A.I.F. Comforts Fund in the later days of the War that, under great difficulties, a regular supply of goods was sent forward right to the front line, and materially helped to keep up the health of the troops under trying conditions.

Shortly after daylight on the 6th, an enemy advance to Kabr Fendi El Faiz, about two miles from the Hajla Bridgehead, was reported and his guns commenced shelling the vicinity of the pontoon bridge and a dummy camp in the rear, on the western bank of the river. The Central India Horse had sent two squadrons on patrol that morning, and these soon came in touch with the enemy troops, but as the shelling continued for some time, and the enemy seemed to be in strength, the Regiment was ordered to move rapidly across the river and endeavour to interrupt his retreat. However, by the time the river had been crossed and the outer wire reached, it became apparent that his columns were nearly back in the high ground, being followed up by the C.I. Horse. After standing by for about an hour, orders were given to return to camp. The Regiment found all outposts for that night.

Spanish influenza, in addition to the other hardships incidental to a campaign, now began to make its appearance, and many evacuations to hospital ensued.

The Regiment now commenced to find the outposts both day and night, until the 5th Regiment came to our assistance on the 16th. Little was seen of the enemy, though our patrols were vigorously shelled if they came under observation within range. On the 9th, the Regiment again came under its own Brigade, which had headquarters in the Hajla Monastery; General Ryrie was the G.O.C., Right Sector from Ghoraniyeh Bridge (exclusive) to the Dead Sea. From this time onwards, the vigorous pushing forward of our patrols began, Tel Er Rameh, just under the eastern foothills, being a daily object of reconnaissance, and a dangerous one also; this place was sometimes held and sometimes not, whilst wire and other obstacles prevented it from being rushed. On the 16th the Regiment moved down to Ghoraniyeh and crossed at 5.30 p.m., making as much movement and dust as possible to attract the enemy's attention. The demonstration was then continued along the Kabr Mujahid Road, to the vicinity of Khurbet Kefrein, when, after pushing patrols well out, the Regiment returned to Butmet Halul to bivouac, and during the night patrols were frequently sent well forward. The object was to make the enemy think that a reconnaissance for attack was in progress, and so to keep his forces tied down in the Valley instead of being hurried to the coast, where the real attack was pending. At about 2 a.m. on the 17th the Regiment returned to camp, leaving a post at Butmet Halul.

From this date, turn was taken with the 5th Regiment in finding day and night outposts. On the 19th orders were received to be ready to move at very short notice. All spare gear was packed and placed in a dump at the Hajla Monastery. On the 20th, as D.H.Q. wished the situation to be cleared up, believing that the enemy was withdrawing, the Regiment, less "B" Squadron, made a demonstration against Kabr Mujahid. Kabr Said was occupied and R.H.Q. established there. Captain Maddrell, with "A" Squadron, rode to within 1,000 yards of Kabr Mujahid, being then met by a blast of machine-gun fire; only one horse was wounded. The enemy's line had now been found, and it was clear that he was in some strength, as at least six machine guns had opened from practically one spot; the Regiment was not shelled at all, which was unusual. Tel Er Rameh was occupied by a patrol that morning, and a Turk and his horse were wounded. These had approached to within 700 yards. At 1 a.m. on 22nd, "A" Squadron, with Captain Maddrell, made a demonstration against Tel Er Rameh and the high ground in the rear, then moving north towards Kabr Mujahid. Tel Er Rameh was occupied without opposition, but pushing on, the Squadron came under machine-gun fire, and later, when withdrawing, was heavily shelled.

"C" Squadron, under Major Johnson, found outposts on the night of the 22nd-23rd, and having concentrated at 1 a.m. next day, moved against Kabr Mujahid from the north, firing Verey lights when close up to draw fire. As there was no response, Kabr Mujahid was occupied at 4.30 a.m. and three green lights were sent up to show that the enemy had withdrawn. The remainder of the Regiment immediately saddled up and, leaving camp at 5 p.m., moved to Tel Er Rameh, pushing patrols well into the hills to the east. Only small parties of the enemy were met, and sniping continued during the day. R.H.Q. was established at Tel Er Rameh, B.H.Q. having moved to Kabr Fendi El Faiz.

Although it was evident that there was no serious opposition in front, no advance was made until 8 p.m., at which hour the concentration of the Brigade was ordered at Kabr Mujahid. Some hitch had occurred in getting supplies through to our Regiment and all ranks were placed on half rations.

With the 6th Regiment leading, and 7th following the 5th, the long trail up the mountains of Moab for the third and last occasion was commenced at 8.30 p.m., over a track difficult enough, and impossible for wheels, but better and under less disagreeable conditions than on the two former well remembered occasions. The track to Thoghra and Wadi Ramle was especially difficult. All pack animals, including the 32nd Indian Mountain Battery, which was following in rear of column, had a rough march, and the latter was left very much behind. After marching all night, a halt was made at Bardawil, a well-watered little village, at 9 a.m. on the 24th for breakfast and to feed and water the horses. At 11.30 a.m. the march was resumed up this pleasant little valley to the well-known Circassian village of Ain Es Sir, which was occupied by the 6th Regiment and B.H.Q. Here a good deal of shell-fire from mountain batteries was encountered, but after a short halt, the Brigade again moved, the 6th Regiment taking up an outpost line covering Ain Es Sir, the 5th Regiment a similar one covering Ain Hemar, and the 7th Regiment holding the gap between the two. It was a fine sight to see the Brigade, in shell-fire formation, moving to take up these positions; only a few shells at very long range were fired by the enemy; they burst close to R.H.Q.

The Regiment was now short of officers and the C.O. was the only one left of field rank, as Majors Bird and Johnson had been evacuated sick on the previous day. Major T. L. Willsallen, D.S.O., who had been doing duty as an instructor at the Cavalry School at Richon, was retained by Descorps as a liaison officer when the advance commenced. At 11 p.m. on the 24th General Chaytor advised that Amman would be attacked on the morning of the 25th. The night passed quietly, and at dawn on the 25th Lieutenant Finley was sent out to gain touch with the enemy on the Ain Es Sir-Amman Road. This he did about three miles from Amman, where enemy cavalry and mule mounted infantry were found to be holding a position with mountain and machine guns.

At 6 a.m. the Brigade moved to the attack of Amman, the 7th Regiment being on the right, the 5th Regiment on the left and the 6th Regiment in reserve; the N.Z.M.R. Brigade, which had come by Es Salt, attacked on the left of the 5th Regiment. The enemy opened with shell-fire from his mountain guns, but no check was made, and the 5th Regiment, moving with great dash, with our "C" Squadron, under Lieutenant Dalton, as our advance guard, well in touch with them, occupied a position within a few hundred yards of the Turkish line. The Indian Mountain Battery now opened and found the range, after placing one or two shots dangerously close to the men of the 5th Regiment. The enemy, probably disheartened by recent events, quickly hoisted the white flag, though two officers and some men of the 5th Regiment were hit upon advancing after this surrender had been made. Lieutenant Finlay, in charge of the screen of "C" Squadron, moved on immediately and captured a mountain gun, two machine guns and about 50 prisoners, as well as 20 horses and 15 mules.

The Regiment followed fast in the rear, and the advance guard, having been again held up, came under some heavy machine-gun fire at about 1,000 yards; fortunately only a few horses were hit. The enemy was probably badly rattled, as his marksmanship should have been better. Cover was found in the large Wadi running into the Wadi Amman, close to the old ruined castle of El Melful, where R.H.Q. was established. The section of machine guns, which had been attached to us, was brought up here and placed in good positions to bear upon the enemy's sangars and trenches, eight hundred yards in front. An observation post for the Indian Mountain Battery was established on top of the old castle. Good shooting was done. Several demonstrations, covered by the fire of the four machine guns, were made to test the strength of the enemy in front of us, and to define his position, and it was evident that the sangars were strongly held with plenty of machine guns in position. "C" Squadron attempted to work round the enemy flank up the Wadi Amman from the south-west, but was held up by fire from the Circassian village of Ain Amman.

"A" Squadron, under Captain Maddrell, was sent to try to get right round to the rear of the enemy's positions east of the town, but moved too far out and was of little use for the remainder of the day. The country here was found to be very difficult. "B" Squadron continued to work down the Wadi from El Melful towards Amman with the 5th Regiment, which had come up, under shell-fire on their left. Lieutenant Stanley made a daring and successful reconnaissance by which he discovered some dead ground, which led to within about 80 yards of the enemy's lines. Captain Williams and Lieutenant Stanley then led about 35 men across this and made a rush upon the Turkish trenches. The enemy evidently was completely surprised and made only a feeble defence, which a Hotchkiss quickly silenced, and 9 officers, 97 O.R.'s, with 7 machine guns, surrendered to this gallant little party. The 5th Regiment, advancing simultaneously on our left, after some minor opposition from machine guns in caves and a certain amount of sniping from the ridges opposite, entered Amman, and this key to the Hedjaz railway was at last taken.

The strength of the enemy's position was clearly seen afterwards, as about 5,000 prisoners were taken in the town, or just out of it, attempting to get away. There were quite sufficient troops and guns to garrison the place, if there had been heart in the men to make a determined stand. The failure to cover just a strip of dead ground was, however, undoubtedly the direct cause of the quick capture of this important town.

At 5 p.m. the Regiment moved down to the beautiful spring-head at Ain Amman and watered and fed up, finding five troops for outpost for the night, from the Wadi Dhraam Es Sawarli to the Nauur Road. The night was quiet. The transport had come up by Es Salt on the 26th and rations were issued, tibbin being requisitioned at the village. A quiet day was spent. On the 27th "B" Squadron, less one troop, proceeded to Leban Station to observe enemy movements from the south and to get in touch with the Sheriffian forces. A wounded Turk, found at Leban, reported that the enemy was in strength at Ziza, part of a force of 5,000 moving up from Maan, south-east of the Dead Sea. A good reconnaissance was made.

Orders were received on the 28th to change camp to the hill above the former camp, which was situated too close to a Circassian cemetery; the adjoining village seemed to have an unusually heavy death rate, probably due to Spanish influenza. Patrols were found along the telephone line from Amman to Suweileh, and one to the cross-roads one mile east of Ain Es Sir. On the 29th Lieutenant Riley, with one troop, proceeded to Nauur at 6 a.m. to watch for any enemy attempt to break through from the south.

Reports were received at 1.10 p.m. on the same day that the Turkish force at Ziza was surrendering to the two squadrons of the 5th Regiment, which had been sent down on observation, but that there was great danger of the Arabs of the Beni Sakr Tribe attacking the surrendered men; the whole Brigade was ordered to move at once and take over their protection. As the matter was one of great urgency, the Regiment moved out 35 minutes after receipt of orders, and proceeded with all speed towards Ziza, 15 miles away. Since urgent messages were received to move faster, pack horses were finally dropped out, and the Regiment galloped across the great plain of Ziza, doing possibly five miles at this pace, and reached the 5th Regiment just in time before dark.

The 5th Regiment was concentrated waiting, whilst the Turks, in their trenches, were standing to arms, holding off the Arabs with shell and machine gun fire. The vulture-like appearance of these latter, who had spoilt our operations at an earlier date and who were now willing that the British should do the fighting and they the looting, will not readily be forgotten. It was getting dark as orders were received to gallop in and take the surrender, the 5th Regiment being on the left and the 7th Regiment on the right. Moving fast by squadrons and brushing the Arabs well out of the way, the Turkish positions, with the Turks kneeling with their caps on their fixed bayonets, were quickly gained, their garrisons were taken charge of and brought in to the Brigade concentration point near the railway station. "C" Squadron was placed on outpost, and several times during the night had to use Hotchkiss rifles to prevent Arabs trying to break through; before morning a number of these birds of prey had been accounted for. That night will never be forgotten. Owing to the extent of the position, a considerable number of the Turks had also to be used to keep off the Arabs, and these were sandwiched with various units of the Brigade and held the line during the night, using their machine guns freely. For once all enmities were forgiven and our men and the Turks boiled their quarts and made "Chapatties" over the same fires. When daylight broke on the 30th the Arabs, baulked of their prize and greedy for the capture of rifles, became bolder and had to be machine-gunned. The Turkish Commander left Ziza at 5.30 p.m. on 29th for Amman with Major-General Sir E. W. C. Chaytor. No attempt was made to collect the prisoners during the night. The Turks in the line fired machine guns almost continuously until daylight. The Turkish officer remaining in charge expressed concern for the fate of his sick and wounded, but on being assured by General Ryrie that we would not leave them to the Arabs, his gratitude was very apparent.

The New Zealand Brigade arrived at 5.30 a.m. and took over the protection of Ziza, and the 5th Regiment, less one squadron, and "C" Squadron of the 7th Regiment, were detailed to escort the prisoners to Amman. These were counted past like sheep and besides over 4,000 who were fit to travel, there were about 600 sick, who were later taken on in waggons.

All ranks, as soon as the prisoners had marched off, were employed in gathering in the guns, machine guns, rifles and all sorts of gear and equipment, and stacking the spoil on the trains which were standing at Ziza Station. During the Amman and Ziza operations the following prisoners and material were taken by our Brigade:—

- 254 Officers, 4978 other ranks.
- 17 Guns.
- 45 Machine guns.
- 2 Auto rifles.
- 3 Railway engines, 25 trucks, 8 water tanks.
- 8 Gun carriages, 1 ammunition waggon, 2 trollies.
- 1 Wireless plant, large quantity of shell, S.A.A.

It was a great capture for the Brigade and a dramatic close to the Great War, so far as our unit was concerned, for the Regiment never fired a shot after this, in Palestine or Syria.

At 3 p.m., having completed the gathering up of the booty, and having handed it over to the New Zealanders, a start was made on the return journey to Amman, which, after a rather confusing ride when darkness set in, was reached at 10.30 p.m. As the railway line had been blown up in several places by our engineers before the surrender at Ziza, it was some days before the captured trains could be got through to Amman.

On October 1st the welcome news of Bulgaria's surrender was announced. Orders were received that the Regiment was to form the escort for 3,000 prisoners to Jericho. The day was spent quietly and an opportunity was taken to erect crosses over most of the graves of men of the Regiment who were killed in the first battle of Amman. At 5.30 a.m. on October 2nd, the Regiment moved off to take over prisoners from the A.P.M., A. and N.Z. Mounted Division. Considerable difficulty was experienced in counting the prisoners, and many fell out before half a mile had been travelled. Thirty cacolet camels were supplied for genuine sick cases, but these animals had to be kept well out of sight, or they would have produced malingerers at once.

During these operations no particular difficulty was experienced as regards rations. Authority was obtained on 26th September to consume our "iron ration," and rations for men were delivered daily after that. Owing to the large quantity of grain and tibbin which had been stored in different places by the Turkish Government, our horses fared well. Water was fairly plentiful throughout, but owing to the number of dead horses and cattle left by the enemy, the streams were badly contaminated, except at the springheads.

The prisoners consigned to our charge were exactly like a mob of sheep; all the strong men surged to the front and were anxious to move, and the frontage often spread over one hundred yards; on the other hand, the weaker ones tailed out on occasions for miles. As there were over 3,000 altogether of weak and strong, frequent halts had to be made. These Turks seemed to have no idea of conserving water and they would empty all their water bottles within half-an-hour of starting. Fortunately, after the first day, there was an abundance of water available in the running streams from Es Salt to Nimrin and the Jordan. The vitality of these unfortunate men was much impaired by previous forced marches from Maan, in which 1,000 are said to have died or have been killed by Arabs, out of the 6,000 which started; in addition, they were afflicted with malaria and Spanish influenza. Altogether they were in a pitiable condition.

Ain Hemar was reached on the first day, shortly after noon, and although the water supply was much reduced in this place, yet sufficient was available for all requirements. Bivouac was made here until 8 o'clock on the morning of the 3rd, when, after counting the prisoners, a start was made for Es Salt, which was reached at 11 a.m., a bivouac being selected under the fig trees, about a mile further down the Nimrin Road, where there was a plentiful supply of water. Motor lorries here supplied us and the prisoners with rations; issuing to the latter was a difficult matter until they were made to understand the method. One tin of biscuits, 5 tins of bully beef, 5 lbs. of onions, and 2 lbs. of dates were given to batches of twenty men, who scrupulously divided these rations. As there were many ripe figs on the trees, the prisoners swarmed up and sustained some heavy falls through breaking weak branches. A Greek English-speaking officer, also some N.C.O.'s, who were efficient in keeping order, helped considerably; they looked for extra food as backsheesh.

At 8 a.m. on the 4th another start was made, halt taking place for an hour at the Howeij Bridge for the prisoners to get water, and at 1 a.m. for lunch at an old Turkish camp close to El Haud. Nimrin was reached at 5 p.m. and the Turks were again rationed, this time much more easily. One Turk committed suicide by jumping over a cliff during the march, and 21 were evacuated to hospital sick on this day. Every day it had been necessary to evacuate a number of the prisoners, the long march and sickness proving too exhausting for them. D.H.Q. at Jericho were now asked to send as many lorries as could be spared to meet the column on the following day.

The march to Jericho was resumed at 8 a.m. on the 5th; the Jordan was reached at 11 a.m. and a halt made for several hours. The prisoners, excepting sick and tired men, stripped and had a refreshing bathe in the Jordan. When the march was resumed the lorries, appeared, and with the help of these and the camels, all the sick men reached Jericho in good time. Here 1,300 were handed over to the 38th Battalion Royal Fusiliers (Jewish), and the balance to the A.P.M. at Jericho, where they were placed in a compound.

The Regiment marched to join the Brigade at the Hajla Monastery, where it was a great pleasure to find mail, canteen and Y.M.C.A. stores awaiting us. Next day was devoted to cleaning up dumps, collecting spare horses, and making other preparations for moving back. Forty-six reinforcements were picked up and were of great assistance to the much depleted Regiment as, although the casualties at Amman had been small, the daily evacuations to hospital, from malaria and Spanish influenza, were about the highest on record for the Regiment.

At 8.10 a.m. on the 7th a start was made for Talaat Ed Dum, which was reached at 1 p.m., rations and forage being drawn there. Next morning the march was continued and a bivouac on the northern flank of the Mount of Olives was reached before mid-day. This was a good place, though rather too close to a city, whose temptations are many and varied.

Leave, up to 30 men per squadron, was granted until 9 p.m. The Brigade remained here until the 12th, many parties of men visiting the Old City. During the last two days, troops were confined to camp on account of the misbehaviour of a few men. At 8 a.m. on the 12th the Brigade moved off for Latron, which was reached at 3 p.m. after a good march. Rations and fodder were drawn. Next morning the march to Wadi Hanein was resumed, the transport, as on the previous day, leaving two hours earlier. A halt of 1½ hours was made for lunch at Bir Salem, and Wadi Hanein was reached early in the afternoon; a camp site was allotted to the Regiment about half a mile due east of the village.

Until the 31st the routine was that usual in all rest camps, or camps back from the line. Hotchkiss classes were commenced, and working parties started on a rifle range. It was believed that the Division might be sent to the Danube to help in attacking Austria. Cholera inocculation was undergone again, but in the main, the period was one of rest and recuperation. The health of the men improved rapidly, and the condition of the horses also. Swimming parties were sent almost daily to the beach, and football was commenced with the likelihood of having a good team. All villages were placed out of bounds, and there was little trouble as far as the discipline of the Regiment was concerned. A number of robberies, evidently committed by the Arabs, were reported in the Brigade, and the sequel to these later and after the Regiment had left for the Dardanelles, was the burning of the Arab village of Surafend, and the killing of a number of natives. Until November 4th, when musketry for the Regiment was commenced, the routine consisted of the usual Regimental duties, with a good deal of training for sports, football and so on; combined Church parades were held on Sunday. On the 7th the news of leave to Australia for the 1914 N.C.O.'s and men was joyfully received—four officers were, later on, allowed to go also. Under 60 N.C.O.'s and men were left of the nearly 600 who had embarked with the Regiment in 1914, and these were given a send-off by their comrades of later date. These men indeed deserve well of their country, and their toughness and constancy can only be determined rightly, if one reads the history of all the campaigns in which the Regiment took part and the extreme hardships endured in them.

The 5th Regiment left on the 6th for Lake Tiberias, being cheered by the 7th Regiment as it passed, and played out by the Anzac Divisional Band. Word was also received with much surprise that the 7th was to stand by in readiness to hand in horses, and proceed dismounted to Kantara and the Dardanelles. It was felt to be a great honour indeed to be the one Regiment of the A.I.F. to represent Australia in revisiting the graves of fallen comrades at Anzac.

The departure of the 1914 men left great gaps in the ranks of the N.C.O.'s, but these were filled, again and again, as other leave was granted, by men, who, perhaps, had not had the same experience, yet who tried conscientiously to do their duty, and on the whole, did it well. A wire was received on the 9th that the Regiment was to be ready to proceed overseas, dismounted, but with officers' chargers and the greater part of the transport.

At 5 p.m. on the 11th the official news of Germany's acceptance of the terms of the Armistice was received, and there was much rejoicing. All the Verey lights in the area were fired off, those from the batteries making a fine display. The Brigade Staff visited the Messes of the Brigade Units later and was fittingly received. On the 12th a successful Brigade race meeting was held, the C. in C. being present. Showers fell at intervals, and the weather had become much colder. No races were won by the Regiment. Orders were this day received that the Regiment would move for Kantara on the following day, with the Canterbury Mounted Rifles, who were representing New Zealand.

On the 13th horses were handed into the Remount Depot, these being led away by men of the 6th Regiment and machine-gun squadron. These fine old comrades had carried us faithfully under all sorts of hardships, through long marches in the deep Sinai sand, through the steep and rocky Judean Hills, and then, perhaps hardest of all, in those three long and exhausting treks across the Jordan and up the goat tracks of the Mountains of Moab, often going without water for nearly two days at a time, and on one or two occasions for much longer periods. These faithful companions, with a few exceptions, were to see no more service, for after being kept in the Remount Depôt for a few days, the greater number were taken out and shot, a much better fate than to be sold to Egyptians, Syrians, Arabs or Jews.

About this time the horses of the whole Brigade were also graded in three classes—"A," "B" and "C" (later on "A" transferred to the Imperial Remounts for use by the Army of Occupation; "B" transferred to the Imperial Remounts sent to the Veterinary Hospitals to be conditioned; "C" were taken out one morning and shot—720 being so treated, a better end for the old friends than to have been sold to the Arab and Jew farmers in Palestine who were eager to buy them.)

That day was one of the saddest in the history of the Brigade.

The first party for Ludd to entrain moved off at 10 a.m., the second at 1 p.m. The Brigadier addressed the Regiment, thanking it for all the good work done and loyal support given. Cheers were given by other units, and the band played us out, for it was then believed that the Brigade would not meet again except perhaps in Australia. Eleven Officers, 105 other ranks with all the animals, limbers and baggage, commenced to load at noon, but did not leave until 7 p.m., whereas the second party, loading at 3 p.m., being the balance of the Regiment, started out at 5 p.m. Heavy showers fell during the journey, and the men, in the boarded-in trucks, were soon wet, and spent a most uncomfortable night. No. 2 Party reached Kantara at 6.15 a.m. on the 14th, and No. 1 after midday on the same day. A camp site was allotted to us at what was Hill 40, in the old days, quite a fair march from Kantara Railway Station; motor lorries were available for extra baggage.

As plenty of water was to be had from a stand-pipe close by, and troughs for watering the horses were handy, this was a comfortable camp. The Canterbury Mounted Rifles were camped just east of us, and we had some good football matches. Both Regiments came under Canal Zone Headquarters at Kantara. During the stay at Kantara every effort was made to smarten up the Regiment, and many expedients had to be resorted to to obtain new clothing, hats and equipment. Colonel Arnott donated £20 from Cinema Funds for boot and metal polish to brighten up the service-worn gear, and did his utmost in other ways to help his old Regiment. Half-hour runs before breakfast, drill and marching, and numerous inspections by the C.O. soon brought about a wonderful change, and when Kantara was left the Regiment looked perhaps smarter and better than it had ever done before.

CHAPTER VII.

THE OLD BATTLE-FIELDS.

THE men were now very keen, and seemed to recognise the honour of belonging to the Regiment selected to represent the A.I.F. on the old battle-fields. Major Hession did good work in securing clothing and equipment when possibly most other men would have failed. On the 17th 57 reinforcements arrived from Moascar, and the Regiment was built up to strength, but unfortunately at the last moment accommodation on the transport became limited and only 22 Officers and 399 O.R.'s, including Canteen personnel, were able to go. Lieutenants Gibbs and Donkin were detailed to stay behind with the surplus men, but these Officers and Liutenant Worthington afterwards followed via Salonica; Lieutenant Gibbs, who was placed in charge of some wheeled transport of the two Regiments which could not be taken, never actually joined up, though he saw Athens, Salonica and Constantinople.

Lieutenant Campbell, of A.I.F. Headquarters in Cairo, took photographs of the Regiment for record purposes whilst at Kantara. On the 27th a move was made for the wharves at 7 a.m. for embarkation, lorries being available for the baggage: the men marched in and were given coffee and biscuits by the Y.M.C.A., whose representative had been with our Brigade in the old days at Marakeb. Horses were got on board without difficulty, but the luggage and canteen goods for the two Regiments were not loaded till midnight. A properly staffed A.I.F. Canteen, under Captain Frost, with sufficient supplies to last the two regiments for four months, was taken, also through the thoughtful arrangements of Major Anderson (R.M.O.) sufficient Red Cross supplies to equip a small regimental hospital of 10 beds; these later on saved the lives of a number of men. The Australian Red Cross Commissioner in Cairo responded generously and promptly at short notice, making these supplies available. The transport, on which the 7th Regiment and the Canterbury M.R. embarked, was the "Huntscastle," a captured boat which had recently been gutted by fire; though a good horse boat and seaworthy, she was not well fitted to carry so many troops. The three officers who had been allowed at the last moment to go on 1914 leave were Major Hession, Lieutenants Waugh, H.G.H., and Waugh, W., and these were said good-bye to before sailing. Captain Maddrell had already gone. The "Huntscastle" left Kantara at 5.30 a.m. on November 28th, Lieut.-Colonel Finlay, C.B., D.S.O., of the C.M.R., being O.C. Troops. Port Said was reached about three hours later, and the day was spent in taking in coal and supplies; time was lost in repairing some horse boxes on deck, which had badly slipped, when men were being assembled to boat stations. The transport put to sea in fine weather at 6 a.m. next day, all ranks wearing lifebelts owing to the menace of anchored mines in the shallow waters, and these belts were always carried during the voyage. The masts of two vessels which had been sunk a few miles out of Port Said showed the work of enemy submarines. On November 30th the weather changed, and, running through the Sporades Group of the Greek Archipelago, it became squally with an unpleasant choppy sea.

Mudros Harbour was reached at 5 p.m. on December 1st, and presented a very different appearance from that place in other days, when crowded with some of the greatest liners and warships afloat; it was then temporarily, at any rate, one of the most important harbours in the world. Now a couple of tramp steamers and half a dozen trawlers sweeping for mines were all that could be seen. Mudros was left at 10.30 p.m. on the same day, and a round-about track had to be taken on account of the minefields. Imbros was passed at daylight next day; a cloud and mist wreathed Imbros in a stormy sea, instead of, as in the old days, standing out clear cut and beautiful with its background of glorious sunsets. The hill features of Anzac and Achi Baba could be faintly seen in the distance. From Imbros to the Straits and to Chanak the "Huntscastle" was guided by a trawler along the narrow swept and buoyed channel to avoid the minefields. Cape Helles and Seddul Bahr, with the famous collier "River Clyde" looking wonderfully well preserved, were passed at 9 a.m., and the old trenches right to Achi Baba could be easily traced through glasses.

Chanak, the most important town on the Asiatic side, was reached at 11 o'clock on a bitterly cold and squally day; the wind cut like a knife, and was the more keenly felt because the two Regiments had just come from the intense heat of the Jordan Valley. Spanish influenza had again made its appearance in a more severe form among the C.M.R., but up to the time of disembarkation there had been only one case in the 7th Regiment. The rations on board the transport left much to be desired, and had to be supplemented from Canteen and Comforts Supplies. At Chanak, where definite orders were expected, none were forthcoming, and all that was known of us was contained in a paragraph in the London "Times." It was necessary to wait on board, in bitter weather, until December 4th, when the 28th British Division, whose Headquarters were at Chanak, took the responsibility of disembarking the two regiments at Maidos, on the European side of the Straits, whither officers had been sent to look for billets, but found none suitable.

The French, who were in occupation of Kilid Bahr and Maidos, were then asked if they could find us accommodation, and they placed an old Turkish hut hospital at our disposal. This was a verminous place, and a great deal had eventually to be done to make it habitable at all. On December 5th the disembarkation commenced, and proceeded slowly, as the horses had to be slung into a horse boat, and everything had to go by lighter to Maidos wharf, about one mile and a half away.

The unloading of Canteen, Red Cross and Comforts stores took much time also, and the last boatload was not landed until the morning of the 10th. The Turkish Hospital, situated between Maidos and Kilid Bahr, had to be shared by the two regiments; it was inadequate for their requirements, and many tents had to be used. It was fortunate that, with the exception of a few bad days, the weather was good during our stay, as conditions on the Gallipoli Peninsula in midwinter often are wretched in the extreme.

On a few occasions, when the weather was bad, the wind was so keen that it penetrated all clothing, and the mountains over in Asia had their mantles of snow, particularly Mount Ida, famous in the Homeric Legend, though no snow actually fell on our camp. It was fortunate also that plenty of firewood of one sort or another was available, some of the old Turkish barracks being found particularly useful in this way. On the 6th a dismounted party of Australians and New Zealanders marched over to Anzac —the first British troops to visit the old lines since the evacuation. The distance is, however, between eight and ten miles, according to the route taken, and this proved rather an exhausting march for men just off the ship.

The work of cleaning up the old hospital and making it fit to live in and comfortable engaged all attention at first; a suitable building was at once set aside for the Regimental Hospital. Influenza, which had already appeared so seriously in the C.M.R., now commenced to spread in our Regiment, and soon many officers (including the C.O.) and men were suffering from this dangerous disease. The little hospital became crowded, and the R.M.O. and orderlies worked incessantly to combat the scourge and to make things as comfortable as possible for the sick men. A stationary hospital was established at Chanak by the 28th Division, under whose command the Regiment now came, but the voyage across the Straits, in cold or wet weather, was anything but beneficial to sick men, and in the beginning our own little hospital was far better equipped. Altogether there were about 60 fairly severe cases in the 7th Regiment, but only 20 of these were evacuated to the hospital at Chanak, where one death from influenza, that of Trooper Jones, occurred. Lieutenant J. Dalton, an officer who had been with the Regiment almost from the beginning, and who was most popular with all ranks, died from pneumonia. On the other hand, the Canterbury Mounted Rifles, under exactly the same condition as ourselves, evacuated about 140 to hospital and had 13 deaths, including an officer. After being about three weeks on the peninsula the influenza gradually disappeared, and during the rest of the stay the health of all ranks was good, and in the keen, bracing climate the vitality of the men quickly improved.

Just before landing, Mr. E. R. Peacock, a correspondent of the British and Australian Press, joined up; he remained with us during our stay, and contributed many articles to the papers that he represented.

Parties, mounted and dismounted, were sent almost daily to Anzac, and later on to Cape Helles.

Interest in the old battle-fields never flagged, and the later men, who had not been at Anzac, were keen to see all the places whose names were familiar to them. The right flank at Anzac, which had been held practically all through by our Brigade, was, of course, the place of greatest interest. Ryrie's Post, named after our gallant Brigadier, was perhaps most visited by our men, who were anxious to identify old trenches and dug-outs which had been their home for so long, and under such hard conditions. Lone Pine, Quinn's, Pope's and Walker's Ridge—in fact, all the old posts—were traced out; battles were fought over again. The trenches were in a good state of preservation after three years of exposure to the weather, and the positions could be located without difficulty.

Dug-outs and tunnels had caved in here and there, and the whole area was gradually being overgrown with scrub, the holly-oak predominating. Hundreds of young apricot trees, some of fair height, were noted.

There had been no violation of graves, though possibly a few had been dug up in a search for buried arms and ammunition; practically all headstones and crosses had been removed. A number of the cemeteries had been wired in, and it seems to have been the intention of the Turk to prevent any possible desecration. Evidence of what they suffered themselves was seen in the numerous cemeteries behind enemy lines, completely filled with graves. Judged by these alone, their casualties at Anzac were at least three or four times as severe as ours, and from what was heard later in Constantinople, there is little doubt that the flower of the Turkish race perished on Gallipoli.

Imbros and Samothrace stood as boldly as ever, but the sun in midwinter sets far to the south-west of the former island, which in those days, which now seem so long ago, used to make a back-ground for sunsets, which were one of the only compensations of a miserable existence. The Turks had wired the beach in places with two heavy lines of wire, practically from Helles to north of Suvla Bay, and perhaps beyond, and there were numerous new trenches ready to meet another landing. Gaba Tepe was found to be honeycombed with great tunnels, gun roads and dug-outs, and seems to have been a place upon which even the intense bombardment of the warships would have little effect. The Turks had built unsubstantial "victory" monuments on Lone Pine and Walker's Ridge, and these, as transitory as their victory, were already falling to pieces. An Imperial Graves Commission, with an Australian Section, had already commenced work, before our departure, identifying and restoring the graves.

On the 19th word was received that Lieutenant Dalton had died, and on the 21st a burial party was sent over to Chanak. Lieutenant Dalton and Trooper Jones were buried in the little English Cemetery at Chanak, where members of a certain British Consular family have been buried since 1830.

Preparations were made for Christmas, with puddings and billies issued by the Comforts Fund. The day was fine and bright, and was passed fairly cheerfully, though all our thoughts were now centred on getting back to Australia as quickly as possible.

On the 27th leave for officers to Constantinople was granted, and until we re-embarked for Egypt parties were constantly sent to that beautiful and fascinating city. Constantinople was now under the muzzles of the guns of the great warships of the Powers, and garrisoned by Allied troops, who held all the important tactical points. Among other places of particular interest in the city to the men of British stock were Florence Nightingale's Hospital and the Crimean Cemetery and Memorial at Scutari. This cemetery, alas! was already being used again to bury men from the warships and the 28th Division, mostly the victims of Spanish influenza. How few are the corners of the earth that are not hallowed by the presence of our British dead?

The bazaars were of constant interest to officers and the few men who were fortunate enough to see them. The mosques are unequalled, and apart from its beauty and magnificence, San Sophia is of special interest to the Christian world as being the first great Church of the Roman Empire of the East.

The Turkish population, although cowed, was found to be bitterly hostile to Greece, a number of whose troops and marines were in the city, unfriendly to the French, but without animosity towards the British, who were relied upon to obtain better conditions for Turkey at the Peace Conference. The Turkish officers who were, as a rule, well dressed, in great contrast to their men, were distantly polite if spoken to, but not truculent. The Turkish Army apparently had been demobilised by simply telling the men to go home, and many unfortunates were wandering about the country and cities in ragged old uniforms, begging for food and getting very little. Two or three of these derelicts were employed as scavengers to our camp; they did the work that was required of them for a little food and what they could pick out of garbage tins.

In Constantinople, food undoubtedly was scarce and very high priced; it was pitiful to see little children lying on newspapers on the pavements of the main street at night whilst the cold winter rain beat on their pinched faces and saturated their thin garments. One saw real poverty and starvation there, such as cannot even be realised in Australia. Constantinople, between Europe and Asia, and a few days' steam from Africa, is surely the fittest place for a world's capital, if such a Utopian idea should ever become a possibility. The hills on all sides slope gently to the Golden Horn, the Bosphorus and the Sea of Marmora, and with domes and minarets standing up among the buildings of a half-European, half-Asiatic city, make a picture that will never fade from the memory of those who are fortunate enough to see it. It is to be regretted that all our men were not able to visit this place, to gain which such gallant efforts were made in 1915.

By New Year's Day, which was fine and bright, the influenza had almost disappeared, though a few men were still in hospital suffering from the after effects. New Year's Eve was given over to a fine fireworks display, and the blowing of whistles and sirens from all warships in the roadstead. The French in the Kilid Bahr forts made a great display. Our men and these French troops became friendly, and the French band used to visit our camp once a week. In order to keep the Regiment fit and smart, half an hour's run before breakfast and about half an hour's parade at 10 a.m. were part of the daily routine, unless the weather was bad. On January 8th the 28th Division asked the C.M.R. and ourselves to undertake a reconnaissance of the Gallipoli Peninsula from Helles to about the vicinity of Gallipoli town. The sector allotted to the 7th Regiment was from Cape Helles to a line between Gaba Tepe and Maidos. The object of the reconnaissance was to discover any guns, dumps or stores hitherto not reported by the Turks. Our sector was sub-divided amongst the three squadrons, "C" taking the Helles sub-sector with Krithia as headquarters, "B" the intermediate sub-sector, and "A" the northern one.

A start was made on the 10th, and the reconnaissance was completed on the 14th. Though the country was well searched, little additional information was gained.

The weather was beautiful now, and it was a great pleasure to walk about the hills and enjoy the splendid views which the Straits and the hills over in Asia always afforded. Organised parties of men wandered far and wide, going right down to Achi Baba, while others were sent by trawler to Gallipoli Town and to the site of historic Troy, on the Asiatic side opposite Cape Helles. One never-failing interest lay in the shipping that passed up and down the Straits; the flags of almost all nations of the Allied Powers could be seen, with all types of vessels from giant transports and graceful cruisers to minesweepers, trawlers and motor-boats.

The hill system of Anzac, which culminates in the height of Chunuk Bair to the north, slopes gradually downwards in undulating ridges almost to sea level at Cape Helles—the height of Achi Baba being the one outstanding feature, not far from the village of Krithia. But between the village of Maidos on the Straits and the headland of Gaba Tepe lies a level plain of no great width, and on the side farthest from Anzac is the famous "Olive Grove," from which Beachy Bill used to fire with such deadly results. The enemy position, known as Pine Ridge, on the right flank, looks down on this plain, and the gully held by the Turks at the eastern end of Lone Pine opens into it. If this gully and the ridge beyond, as well as Pine Ridge, could have been taken, the valley would have been open for an advance at any time as far as the Kilid Bahr Plateau without any natural obstacle.

But Gibraltar itself does not look half as formidable as the Kilid Bahr Plateau, which rises steeply from the plain. It was found to be criss-crossed with trenches on its dominating heights and flanks, whilst water-torn ravines and numerous folds in the hills gave ample protection for reserves in rear. Under the almost sheer reverse slope are situated the great Kilid Bahr forts, practically inaccessible to any fire except from across the Straits. As natural obstacles, Achi Baba or 971 Chunuk Bair did not appear nearly so formidable, and with this place untaken, there could have been no real command over the Straits. As it could be easily supplied almost without molestation on account of its immense bulwark, from the Asiatic shore, there is no reason to suppose that it could not have held out indefinitely even if Achi Baba and Chunuk Bair had fallen.

Lieutenant James, of the 1st L.H. Regiment, with a special photographic party and men to collect war trophies, had arrived soon after the New Year. They camped near Lone Pine in some old Turkish huts; rations were sent to them in our limbers, and all the trophies in the shape of old gun limbers, shells, etc., were carted back to Maidos Jetty.

On the 15th word was received to be ready to embark on the "Norman" on the 20th. This was rather unfortunate, as arrangements had been made with G.H.Q. at Constantinople to allow parties of men to see the city. Also, since the influenza had ceased, the condition of the men had wonderfully improved, and the Regiment would cheerfully have stayed for at least another month.

On the 19th the "Norman" anchored off Chanak, and re-embarkation commenced. As she was not a horseboat, all horses and vehicles had to be left, with two officers and 70 men, Lieutenant Wikner being in charge. At 4 p.m. re-embarkation was complete, and the "Norman" commenced the voyage for Port Said. Cordial "Good-byes" were sent to the 28th Division, who had treated us throughout like honoured guests, and had done their utmost to help in every possible way. The weather soon became cold and squally. Port Said was reached at 8.30 a.m., the disembarkation commenced at noon. The train left shortly after 6 p.m., Kantara being reached at 10.30 p.m. After a meal at Mrs. Chisholm's (now Dame Alice Chisholm, D.B.E.) Canteen, the Regiment marched to the R.A.M.C. Detail Camp for the night.

Next day we travelled by rail to Rafa, where the Divisional and Brigade Staffs were waiting to meet us. A camp site close to the 6th L.H. Regiment was allotted, and tents brought from Gallipoli were pitched in a hollow square, the three squadrons and Headquarters forming the sides with the quartermaster's stores, regimental recreation tent, canteen and cook-houses in the centre. This became a model camp, and it was praised by all inspecting Field Officers. Special attention was paid to the cook-houses, and £10 to £15 per week, from Regimental Funds, was spent in supplementing the rations, whilst a regimental canteen, where vegetables and cooked eggs could be sold, was established. Tables for each little mess were dug on the inside of the tent lines in regular formation, and it was a fine sight to see the whole Regiment at dinner. The horse lines were placed on the outside.

On the 26th 200 horses were handed over to us from the 6th Regiment and Machine Gun Squadron; the 5th Regiment was still in Galilee. The routine now became one of early morning physical exercises, with an hour and half's parade later on, and two mounted parades a week. An educational scheme was commenced, and lectures and classes were properly organised under Brigade arrangements. Trooper Treloar, of the 7th Regiment, later on was granted a Commission under this scheme. Troopers McMaugh and Young were given the rank of Sergeant, the former also obtaining a commission before embarkation. Race meetings, football matches and sports meetings were carried out, and everything possible was done to relieve the monotony for the men. Preparations were made for early demobilisation and embarkation. Leave parties visitd Cairo and other parts of Egypt, also Jerusalem. On February 3rd, Lieutenants Wikner and Glasson, with the remainder of the Regiment (transport, etc.), arrived after a good voyage. Owing to numerous Divisional and Brigade duties, it was always difficult to obtain large parades, and the Divisional Commander, who was constantly making inspections, found some fault with these.

During the stay at Rafa, small parties of men were granted early repatriation on urgent grounds, and, later on, about 40 were allowed leave to England. Reinforcements arrived at intervals from Moascar, but owing to repatriation and leave to England it was difficult to keep the strength of the Regiment up to establishment. Our race horses did not particularly distinguish themselves at any of the meetings, owing chiefly to the fact that nearly all our best mounts had been handed in, and those returned were not very good. On the other hand, the Regiment was first as regards boxing, and was the only one in the Division that sent a team, later on, to complete in Cairo. A fishing boat to supply the Division with fish was financed by Colonel Arnott and Canon Garland and sent up to Rafa; Lieutenant Wikner was placed in charge of the craft, with a party of men from the Division, but these fishermen had no great success. On February 24th the Corps Commander inspected the Brigade. This was a farewell inspection, and all ranks were thanked for the good work done. The weather was, for the most part good, though occasional wind storms were trying.

On March 12th a start was made handing in our horses, and finally only a sufficient number of transport and riding horses was left to carry on the routine of the Regiment. Preparations for embarkation began in earnest, so that, when the news of the Egyptian outbreaks was heard, the Regiment was actually a dismounted unit, with only officers' chargers and a few transport horses available. Fortunately, rifles, bayonets and ammunition had not been handed in. On the 22nd orders were received for the Brigade to entrain for Kantara, to be hurried to danger points and deal with disturbances. At 3.30 p.m. on the 23rd the Regiment entrained at Rafa, the other units of the Brigade having gone on before, and Kantara was reached at 11.30 p.m., where bivouac was made for the night close to the station. On the 24th, at 6.30 a.m., a start was made for the camp site, near the swingbridge. Mrs. Chisholm provided breakfast for all ranks without charge.

All horses had to be handed in to the Remount Depôt and were then redrawn. The camp site was on the banks of the Canal, and the water was a great boon. On the 25th 193 horses and 214 mules were drawn from the Remounts Depôt, and equipment and gear of all sorts was obtained as fast as possible from Ordnance to place us once again on a mobile war footing. The work of re-equipment was strenuous. Finally many non-essential things had to be done without, as Ordnance simply could not supply them. By the 26th all units of the Brigade, excepting ourselves and most of the M.G. Squadron, had entrained for Damanhur. On the same day, orders were received for the Regiment and one section of Machine Guns to move to Salhia at 6 a.m. next morning. It was a difficult matter getting equipment and ammunition in time, but it was done. Reveille sounded at 5 a.m., and horses and mules were saddled in the darkness; it was remarkable how many mules had changed into horses, since the first allotment. Thirty-two camels were provided, including 12 Cacolet camels, for transport, and our wheeled transport was left with a party, under Lieutenant Glasson. The Machine Gun Section detailed was not ready to join us on the 27th, having no guns, and did not reach Salhia with the two troops as escort until about a week later. Word was received that an attempt was to be made to free 12,000 Turkish prisoners of war, in the large compound at Salhia, combined with a rising of the district. The march was commenced at 6 a.m. on the 27th, and after a halt for lunch Salhia was reached at 2.30 p.m.

CHAPTER VIII.

THE EGYPTIAN REBELLION AND EMBARKATION FOR HOME.

SALHIA is a small native village in the Sharquia Province, 25 miles south-west of Kantara, and lying on the edge of the desert, but in delta country, which forms a tongue of fertile land running from the Nile to Lake Menzala, close to Port Said, and is prosperous and fairly well populated. It is connected to the main Egyptian Railway System by single track line to Abu Kebir and Zagazig. Just east of the railway station was situated a barbed wire compound, enclosing 12,000 Turks guarded by a half battalion of the 1/70 Burma Rifles, and with about 250 British personnel for maintaining order and for executive duties among the prisoners.

Lieut.-Colonel Richardson was made Commandant, and later was appointed O.C. Salhia Sub-Sector, coming under the G.O.C. 3rd Light Horse Brigade, in charge of Zagazig Sector.

No time was lost in constructing small redoubts round the compound to prevent any efforts at breaking out on the part of the prisoners, or any combined attempt with the civil population for their release. These redoubts (which were dug and wired by prisoners under guard), and the show of mounted strength, quickly over-awed the prisoners and the inhabitants of the district. Patrols from one troop to a squadron were daily sent through the area, preferably to El Managat El Kubra, Akiad, Dawana, Quahbuna, Samakin El Gharb, El Akheiwa and to San El Hagar (the ancient Tanis and Zoan of the Old Testament). The latter was a two-days' patrol. All smaller villages were visited, and later on much propaganda literature was distributed. Upon our arrival Salhia was practically isolated, except by camel convoy from Kantara, but the railway was soon repaired—a broken bridge near Faqus causing most trouble—and a regular train service with Zagazig was established towards the end of May.

Five railway posts of strength of one N.C.O. and 10 Other Ranks were placed to guard our section of line as far as Akiad, and these posts were wired and rationed to stand a small siege. An officer was stationed at the post at Akiad and another at Azazi. The 2nd Machine Gun Squadron, less one section, had been placed under the Command of O.C. of this Sub-Sector, and this reinforcement was urgently required owing to the numerous duties and patrols. In the middle of June the railway posts were withdrawn and the barbed wire and other material were taken up and stored at Salhia. The situation became much easier during the month, and there is no doubt that the constant patrolling by mounted troops, and the threats of severe reprisals, in the event of sabotage and rioting, had thoroughly cowed the district.

Most of the Omdahs of villages were friendly, and did their best to maintain order. The Molahez (Chief of Police) of Salhia, an Egyptian, was an efficient officer who understood his people and did his duty excellently. Our patrols thoroughly raked the country, and, acting with the civil police, brought in many offenders who had been active during the outbreak in April. Power to convene a military court was delegated to Lieut.-Colonel Richardson, by the G.O.C., East Delta Area, and Major L. W. Davies, M.C., was appointed president. This Court tried cases according to the Egyptian methods, in a much more summary manner than is usual with Courts Martial, and inflicted punishments varying from 12 months' I.H.L. to 15 years' penal servitude; persons guilty of violence receiving up to 25 lashes. The establishment of this Court also had undoubtedly a good moral effect, and Lieut.-Colonel Kershaw (Legal Adviser, East Delta Area) congratulated the Court upon the efficient manner in which it had carried out its duties. The inconvenience to the natives caused by the destruction of the railway line, and the fact that considerable loss was sustained through their not being able to get their crops to market, made an impression at last on minds often not more developed than those of children. Though outbreaks may occur in the future against Europeans, and particularly against Greeks, who are the money-lenders of Egypt, there will probably be no indiscriminate damage to railway property. Elaborate schemes for the defence of the Sub-Sector and protection of the compound in the event of fresh disturbances were made, but these fortunately were not needed. The work of patrolling was continuous and monotonous, and in order that the native mind might be impressed, the patrols were made in as great a strength as possible. To relieve the monotony, a number of race meetings were held, and a squadron cricket competition was organised, also a boxing and wrestling tournament, in which bouts between men of the Burma Rifles and our Egyptian Camel men caused great amusement. Two cases of smallpox occurred during the stay at Salhia—one in the Regiment, the other in the Machine Gun Squadron. Neither was fatal. All units were immediately revaccinated.

Towards the end of the month the welcome orders to march back to Kantara for demobilisation were received. The Omdahs and notables of the district seemed to regret our departure, and expressed the opinion that the Regiment was the best that they had seen since the beginning of the War. Undoubtedly the behaviour of the men, with one or two exceptions, was very good. On May 29th the Regiment moved off at 8 a.m., the heavy baggage being sent by train, and after a good march reached No. 1 Camel Hospital close to the Remount Depôt, where camp was made for the night. All except 20 horses required for camp duties were here handed in, together with arms and equipment, and next day the Regiment marched on foot to another camp site, across the canal, which had been vacated by the 18th Brigade R.H.A. This, although about a mile and a half from the canal, was a fairly convenient camp, having a good ablution area and shady mess huts and kitchens.

The routine was for rest, though sports of various kinds, such as cricket and swimming were organised, and the Regiment won the Divisional Cricket Competition without suffering a defeat. The cricket team had previously a most successful tour in Cairo. Trooper Middleton, an Old King's School and County Cumberland player, made a most efficient captain for this team.

All preparations were made for embarkation, which was fixed for the end of June. Leave was extensively granted, and some officers were even allowed to proceed to Damascus. On June 25th definite orders were received to embark with the rest of the Brigade on H.M.T. "Madras" on the 27th, and on the 26th camp was struck and tents and other gear returned to Ordnance. The embarkation, however, was postponed until the 28th owing to boiler troubles in the troopship, and the men had to make as good shelters as possible out of blankets, though the mess huts were shady and roomy.

The Regiment marched down to "A" Wharf at Kantara and embarked on the "Madras" at 2.30 p.m. on June 28th, four years after the famous demonstration at Anzac. The embarkation proceeded smoothly. The troop quarters were good on this ship, a British-India boat, though the upper deck space was rather crowded; this was more particularly felt in the heat, while passing through the Canal and the Red Sea. Kantara was left at 5 p.m., the band playing the Brigade off. When passing Ismailia news was received of the signing of Peace at Versailles. Although the weather was hot until Aden was passed, it quickly cooled, as here the south-west monsoon was met. Colombo was reached on the 10th, and general leave ashore was granted on the following day. An organised party of the Brigade proceeded to Kandy in a special train provided by the Ceylon Government. Men who could not go in this had an interesting day in Colombo.

The voyage was continued at 2 p.m. on the 12th. The Australian Comforts Fund had provided a great number of gifts, mostly consisting of food, for the voyage. The rations for the most part were very good. Trophies were also given for sports, and in these the Y.M.C.A. also joined, one of the organisers (Lieutenant Crouch) being on board. The Regiment won the majority of Brigade events. A Regimental Competition was also organised, and the prizes won were presented by the C.O. just before we reached Melbourne. Although no heavy weather was encountered, the sea was seldom at all calm, and long rolling seas caused a good deal of movement at times. Fremantle was reached on the 24th. As there were a number of cases of Malaria, and a good many colds, all men in hospital or with a temperature were disembarked and the ship was kept in quarantine. Fremantle was left at 11 a.m. on the 25th and Port Phillip Heads were reached at 7.30 on the 31st. After disembarking a few more sick men the ship moved on to Port Melbourne, berthing there at 3 p.m. Shore leave was granted. At 8 a.m. the following day the voyage was continued, the weather being fine with occasional showers of rain.

The "Madras" entered Sydney Heads on Sunday, August 3rd, a beautiful, bright morning. The 6th and 7th Regiments were disembarked at 2.30 p.m., and our good old comrades of the 5th proceeded by train to Brisbane next day. The Officers and men of the Regiment were driven in motor-cars to the Anzac Buffet, where friends and relatives were met. All ranks were given leave until the following morning when, after reporting to the Demobilisation Officer, medical examination of all men was made, and furlough, according to length of service, was granted.

Christian Refugees at Jericho after 1st Amman Stunt.

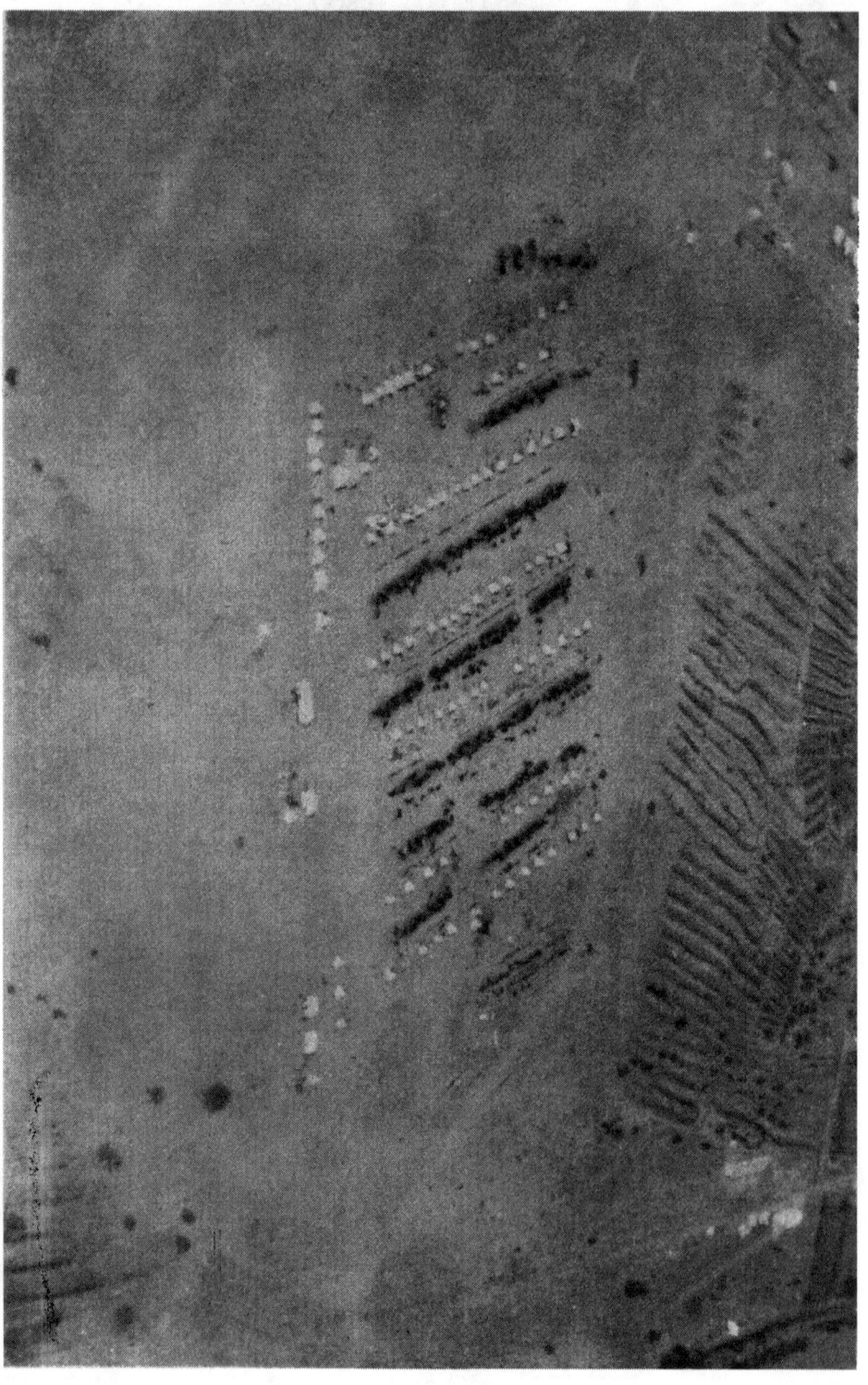

7th Regt. Camp at Salhia, from the air. In the background are depressions in sand for growing vegetables, and in left top corner part of No. 9 Turkish P. of W. Camp.

Samakeen Markets, near Salhia. In the left foreground Lieut. Glasson, Lieut. Carter and Capt. Stanley.

"B" Sqdn. Patrol returning from Samakeen Markets to Salhia Camp.

CONCLUSION.

THUS ended the period of active service of the 7th Light Horse of the Australian Imperial Force. Of all the officers who embarked on that fine December morning in 1914, the C.O. was the only one who returned with the Regiment in August, 1919, and of the N.C.O's. and men of 1914, only five or six remained on the latter date, and these, with only one exception, were now all officers.

Such is the toll of continuous active service. And yet as regards actual battle casualties the Regiment was not unduly unfortunate. But the wear and tear of long, exhausting marches, and the hardships and privations incidental to front-line service, eventually sap away the vitality of the stoutest constitution. The battle casualties, when compared with those in France, were not severe; the class of warfare accounts to a very great extent for this, and of course with mounted troops it is unusual to experience the desperate hand-to-hand fighting that soon cuts infantry battalions to pieces.

The strength of the Regiment during most operations was between 400 and 500 men, and yet from beginning to end about four thousand officers and men passed through its ranks. Undoubtedly, sound training in early days and careful leadership helped wonderfully to minimise the number of casualties, otherwise these might easily have been increased tenfold.

Not counting the operations at Anzac, the Regiment as a mounted force participated in about fifty general engagements, and in smaller affairs too numerous to mention.

One's memory goes back to those varied scenes and battles, and pictures arise that even the years will not efface. The long, hot marches in the desert, the attempted surprise of Birel Abd or Salmana in "the grey dawn," the fog enveloped wadis, and the gallop which captured the Turkish Divisional Commander at the first battle of Gaza; the Turkish Cavalry Division on the Beersheba plain during second Gaza, and the many fights, ambushes and night patrols on that piece of no man's land; the battle of Beersheba and the gallop for the Hebron road; Ebdis, Junction Station, Mulebbis, Jerusalem; the Jordan and the long toiling up goat tracks to the uplands of Moab to fight bloody battles; Ziza with its Gilbertian setting of friends and enemies in a common defence, and lastly the old battlefields of Gallipoli again, and to some few, Constantinople, that so-earnestly-desired city of 1915.

And as a background to all this—Egypt—the same old Egypt which sent its warriors under the greater Pharoahs to conquer the same lands as have fallen to our bow and spear, the same Egypt which saw Saint Louis fail and the great Napoleon checked—the same old sun-baked, fertile Egypt, changeless in the main through all the centuries.

And now, alas, the Regiment is no more; officers and men are scattered all over Australia—old friends—none truer than those who have stood the test of battle—in many cases to meet no more. Yet it is something, and always will be something, to have lived those years, and to have been a soldier of the most efficient body of mounted troops the world has ever known—The Desert Mounted Corps.

DECORATIONS AND AWARDS GAINED BY THE REGIMENT.

(These include only those Awarded to Members of the Regiment whilst actually Serving with it.)

C.M.G.

Colonel J. M. Arnott
Brigadier-General G. M. Macarthur Onslow

D.S.O.

Brigadier-General G. M. Macarthur Onslow
Major T. H. Bird
Major T. L. Willsallen
Lieut.-Colonel J. D. Richardson
Major C. C. Easterbrook

M.C.

Captain C. E. Stanley
Lieut. G. Snow
Lieut. J. M. Carter
W.O. T. L. Keen
Major C. C. Easterbrook
Major L. W. Davies
Major L. L. Williams
Captain G. G. Finlay

ORDER OF THE NILE.

Brigadier-General G. M. Macarthur Onslow
Lieut.-Colonel J. D. Richardson
Lieut.-Col. C. H. Anderson (Med. Officer)
Major T. L. Willsallen

D.C.M.

Corp. C. Kilpatrick
Corp. B. E. Picton
Corp. W. A. G. Smith
Sergt. W. Salmon
Lieut. A. E. James
Sergt. W. D. Archibald
Sergt. L. S. Holmes
Corp. F. P. Curran

M.M.

Sergt. W. S. Salmon
Sergt. G. H. Ford
Sergt. M. T. Gould
Sergt. W. J. Gye
Sergt. G. E. Howard
Sergt. Maguire
S.S.M. W. T. Matthews
Sergt. M. P. Tonkin
Sergt. W. F. Turner
Sergt. E. A. Williams
Corp. H. B. Cartwright
Corp. C. G. Harrington
Corp. B. E. Picton
L.-Corp. H. B. Ratliff
L.-Corp. T. E. Pulbrook
Trooper J. McFarlane
Trooper R. E. S. Heuston
Trooper J. B. Gilligan
L.-Corp. A. Dobbs
Trooper B. Davis

SERBIAN MEDAL.

Lieut. C. E. Holland
Sergt. G. H. Ford
Sergt. M. T. Gould
L.-Sergt. Larsen
Trooper J. McFarlane

MENTIONED IN DESPATCHES.

Colonel J. M. Arnott (4)
Brig.-Gen. G. M. Macarthur Onslow (3)
Lieut.-Col. J. D. Richardson (2)
Major T. H. Bird
Major N. D. Barton
Major T. L. Willsallen
Major C. C. Easterbrook
Major L. L. Williams (2)
Capt. H. O. C. Maddrell
Lieut. C. E. Holland (2)
Lieut. E. L. Zouch
Capt. E. O. Straker
Lieut. C. A. Teschner
W.O. J. Garrood
F.Q.M.S. T. A. Taylor
Sergt. D. G. Small
Sergt. G. F. Bolton
Sergt. W. D. Archibald
Sergt. G. H. Ford
Sergt. M. T. Gould
Sergt. J. H. Manley
Sergt. A. S. Ward
L.-Sergt. Larsen
Corp. F. P. Curran
Corp. C. G. Harrington
Corp. C. Kilpatrick
Corp. Kilgour
Corp. B. E. Picton (2)
Sergt. J. R. Watson
Trooper J. T. Byrne
Driver J. S. Hibbs
Trooper J. McFarlane

COMPLIMENTARY MENTION (ANZAC).

178 Trooper John Campbell

MENTIONED IN DIVISIONAL ORDERS (ANZAC).

Trooper A. Hyde

CASUALTIES.

KILLED IN ACTION OR DIED OF WOUNDS.

(These include only those which occurred to Officers, N.C.O's. and Men actually Serving with the Regiment.)

Lieut. H. W. Gilchrist
Lieut. A. Thorn
Lieut. E. L. Zouch
T. Andrews
C. J. Bateman
N. Beaton
C. A. Benham
C. A. Bennett
W. J. Brodie
F. T. Bull
Sergt. R. C. Butters
J. Campbell
J. T. Campbell
F. W. Cannan
C. Clifford
W. Conn
H. W. Corrick
Sergt. A. Cotter
L. F. Craig
Corp. F. P. Curran
C. H. Daniel
D. Delahunty
L. O. Dobbie
W. M. Drinkwater
P. T. Dunbar
O. W. Duprey
C. E. Eldridge
C. Elton
J. H. Fazio
J. H. Flower
V. J. Foley
F. J. Gannon

T. Gardiner
Corp. W. Geddes
W. J. Gemmell
H. S. Gooch
T. Graham
J. E. Griffen
C. E. Grimshaw
L. A. Guest
Arm.-Sergt. F. P. Hall
J. A. Hampson
T. McN. Harvey
R. E. S. Heuston
Sergt. T. McG. Hill
V. G. Hilton
D. Jacombs
O. Kawlmacker
D. King
E. Kirby
S. Langwell
Sergt. J. G. Lawson
M. Logan
A. V. Louttit
Corp. W. D. Lovegrove
P. A. Madden
Corp. E. L. Magill
E. B. Malone
J. Marshall
Sergt. T. J. Maxwell
—. Melly
Corp. R. G. Moore
G. F. McGuire
W. H. Nicholls

M. O'Loughlin
L.-Corp. C. Parker
B. J. Peel
Sergt. W. A. Peed
R.Q.M.S. L. Perry
P. Poidevin
C. H. Pauntney
A. E. Press
Sergt. E. S. Pryor
Corp. W. Reed
A. J. Sherlock
W. J. Smith
I. Sneddon
F. Stanmore
J. W. Stewart
F. W. Stone
Corp. W. P. Taylor
Sergt. L. Thompson
W. R. Tink
V. Turnbull
C. E. Turner
W. P. Waslin
A. J. Wetherall
J. Wilson
W. J. Woodbury
C. E. Wootten
J. D. Young
R. P. Connelly
V. L. Cooper
—. Steggles
C. D. Tait
J. Taylor

DIED OF SICKNESS OR FROM INJURIES RECEIVED ON ACTIVE SERVICE.

Lieut. J. Dalton
L.-Corp. S. T. Albon
B. Bailey
W. F. Boag
Corp. F. R. Cowdery
A. C. Gentle
W. Gray
E. H. Morris (lost at sea)
Corp. McAree
Sergt. P. C. McBride
J. McFarlane

W. J. McKay
D. McLean
R. L. Styles
E. A. Taylor
C. Throsby
G. H. Ward
R. A. Watson
G. J. White
W. M. O. G. Young
C. H. Frost

W. C. Jones
R. G. Honeynian
Corp. E. E. Keily
G. B. Kendall
E. T. Keogh
J. P. King
E. J. Kinkade
L. Knight
A. J. Laverty
F. S. Miller

ADDENDUM.

WOUNDED IN ACTION.

R. Boag.
H. S. C. Page.

THE 7th LIGHT HORSE, 1914-1919.

WOUNDED IN ACTION.

Colonel J. M. Arnott
Brig.-Gen. G. M. Macarthur Onslow
Lieut.-Col. J. D. Richardson (3)
Major N. D. Barton (2)
Major C. C. Easterbrook
Major E. Windeyer
Major L. Bice
Major C. G. H. M. A. Hession
Captain W. G. Board
Captain K. B. Suttor (2)
Capt. J. O. Stevenson
Capt. G. G. Finlay (2)
Lieut. J. M. Carter
Lieut. R. R. Chapman
Lieut. J. A. Croll
Lieut. E. G. Donkin
Lieut. R. Glasson (2)
Lieut. W. Harper
Lieut. C. E. Holland
Lieut. T. F. Humphries
Lieut. E. K. Maney-Lake
Lieut. G. H. Milson
Lieut. P. V. M. Ryan
Lieut. D. R. Waddell
Lieut. J. H. Walker
Lieut. W. H. Watson
Lieut. H. G. H. Waugh
Lieut. A. Fulton
T. M. Agnew
L.-Corp. S. T. Albon
H. G. Allan
J. D. Allan
Corp. A. Allen
F. Allrich
Sergt. J. Andrews
Sergt. W. H. Andrews
Sergt. W. D. Archibald
Corp. W. Arden
F. J. Backhouse (2)
B. Bailey
J. G. Baldwin
P. J. Barden
Sergt. A. H. Barker
Sergt. H. C. Barnes
N. Beaton (2)
G. Beazley
W. H. Beazley
R. W. Bennett
J. R. Black
Sergt. C. Blight
J. C. Bradford
I. Brewer
I. A. J. Brouff (2)
A. F. Brown
Corp. H. D. Brown
J. Brown
L.-Corp. N. G. M. J. Burton
J. R. Byrne
J. T. Byrne
Sergt. A. Cameron
A. A. Cameron
J. Cameron

A. H. Campbell (2)
H. R. Carmody
Corp. H. B. Cartwright
J. Cawrse
L. E. Charlton
V. R. Chinchin
Corp. E. F. Clarke
S. F. Clarke
C. Clifford (2)
Corp. W. M. Cloey (2)
E. Clutterham
W. E. Clutterham
—. Cole
W. T. Collings
R. A. Collum
W. R. Cotter (2)
C. H. Coupland
J. R. Cousins (2)
L.-Corp. F. H. Coward (2)
R. C. Cowley
J. Coyne
L.-Corp. W. J. Cross
Sergt. P. Cunningham
Sergt. Daggett
L.-Corp. J. N. Dargan (2)
B. Davis
P. L. Dee
L.-Corp. E. A. Dewey
H. A. Donald
Corp. A. A. Dowling
E. H. K. Downes
Corp. E. T. Downes
S. R. Dowton
W. M. Drinkwater
W. B. Duncan
C. E. Dunn
Sergt. W. W. Dunn
O. W. Duprey
L.-Corp. F. G. Dwyer (2)
Corp. W. I. Dwyer
L. D. Edgworth
W. D. Edgworth
J. G. Edmondson
T. Ellis
A. E. Etheredge
L. R. Fairlie
R. Fisher (2)
J. F. Fitzhenry
M. Fitzhenry
J. Fleming
T. W. Foley
C. Ford
J. Francis
F.-Sergt. W. T. Ford
A. W. Fuller
S.-S. J. Geer
A. C. Gentle
G. A. Gibbons
W. Gilholm
C. Girdler
Corp. H. Glover
S. T. Graves
E. D. Green

A. Griffiths
W. Griffiths
Sergt. C. E. Grinter
Sergt. W. J. Pye
Sergt. A. Hamer
L.-Corp. E. D. Hamilton
J. S. Harris
B. J. Hartigan
G. W. Hawkins
S.S.M. R. Hayes
Corp. W. H. Hayes
E. H. Hayman
J. A. Hazelgrove
H. Henderson
R. E. S. Heuston
E. T. Higson (2)
Corp. E. G. Hill
Sergt. T. McG. Hill (3)
Corp. Hodgkiss
H. A. Hollands
E. A. Hollinsworth
G. E. Holms
Sergt. L. S. Holmes (2)
M. A. Holmes
Corp. C. Holt
C. A. W. Holt
R. H. Hore
S.S.M. H. Hotston
Corp. P. V. J. Howard
H. M. Howarth
Sergt. Hume (2)
Sergt. S. F. Hunter
A. Hyde
S.S.M. Inglis (2)
Sergt. J. Inglis
Sergt. W. Jansen
Sergt. W. R. Jardine
J. H. Johnson
S.Q.M.S. Jones (2)
C. C. Jurd
H. Kay
Corp. E. E. Kelley
W. J. Kemp
R. B. Kennedy
S.S.M. H. E. G. Kenny
D. King (2)
H. King
L.-Corp. W. King
C. R. Kirton
G. Kneale
Corp. L. H. Knight
Corp. A. Kotze
L.-Corp. T. A. Lace (2)
Corp. T. A. Lack
Sergt. G. Laidlaw
M. Lamond
S. Langwell
F. J. Leonard
F. L'Estrange
H. Lewis
L.-Corp. R. D. Little
J. S. Livermore
Sergt. W. H. Look

S. F. Clarke
J. Marshall
S.S.M. T. Matthews
F. Maxwell
M. P. Maxwell
R. J. May
R. W. Melville
W. D. Mercer
F. Merrill
W. Metzler (2)
V. F. Michael
Sergt. J. R. Miller
J. Mitchell
M. Moore
F. W. Morgan
W. M. Mulready
A. H. McIhatton
S. F. McCann
Corp. C. J. McCarthy
Corp. McDowell (2)
J. McGann
J. McGrath
L.-Corp. W. T. McHugh
A. N. B. McIntyre
W. A. C. McIntyre
R. B. S. McKinnon
W. McCarthy
W. S. Newton
P. W. Nicholls
R. V. Nicholls
Sergt. D. Nunan
E. S. N. Olsson
F. Osborn
F.-Sergt. J. W. Parr
M. Pascoe (2)
C. J. Paulson
Corp. Pawley (3)
C. S. Perry
Corp. S. P. Perry (2)
F. G. Philps
Corp. E. B. Picton
L.-Corp. A. S. Piper
Sergt. H. J. Piper (3)
C. J. Pittman
J. T. Poppleton

R. Pounsberry
Corp. H. O. Preshaw
S. E. Prosser
P. J. Quinane
Corp. A. G. Ruane
Corp. A. E. Raymond
F. N. Reed
M. Reddy
J. Reeves
J. G. Rew
A. G. Richards
Sergt. J. H. Richards
W. J. Ricthie
F. E. Robertson
T. Rodgers
W. J. Rooke
L. A. Rosewaine
Sergt. D. Ross
R. Rowe
N. C. Royal
A. G. Rane
G. A. Rutherford
P. O. Ryan
Sergt. W. Salmon
T. Salmond
J. Sandys
A. J. Scott (2)
Corp. L. Simpson (2)
W. O. Sinden
J. Skewes
F. Smart
L.-Corp. C. V. Smith (2)
L. H. Smith
M. Smith
Corp. W. A. G. Smith
I. Sneddon
C. Solomon
Sergt. L. W. Spencer
L.-Corp. W. H. Spruce
L.-Corp. J. L. Stirton
W. Straten
R. L. Styles
T. Sullivan (2)
C. Sweny
J. P. Tattam (2)

J. Tetley
J. R. Thomas
A. J. Thurgear
Corp. J. W. Tibbetts
Corp. A. S. Tonkin
F. N. Tuckfield
C. E. Turner
C. H. Veigel
R. P. B. Visser
B. Walford
R. H. Waldron
L. E. Walker
A. H. Ward
A. Waslin
R. S. Waterhouse
Sergt. J. R. Watson (2)
R. A. Watson
H. Wearing
W. R. Webb
S. L. Wells
J. S. Welsh (2)
A. E. Wessell
M. White
W. F. White
W. H. Whitlock
S.S.M. L. R. Whyburn
J. Whyte
F. W. Wicking
W. W. Wild
R. H. Wilkinson
J. E. Willis
E. A. Wise
A. S. Woodward
W. G. Wynne
A. T. Young
Corp. W. M. O'G. Young
E. A. Feltis
E. McKenzie
L.-Corp. H. B. Ratliff (2)
A. Ravenscroft
H. T. Smith
Sergt. H. W. Stace
—. Steggles (2)
P. Tuohy

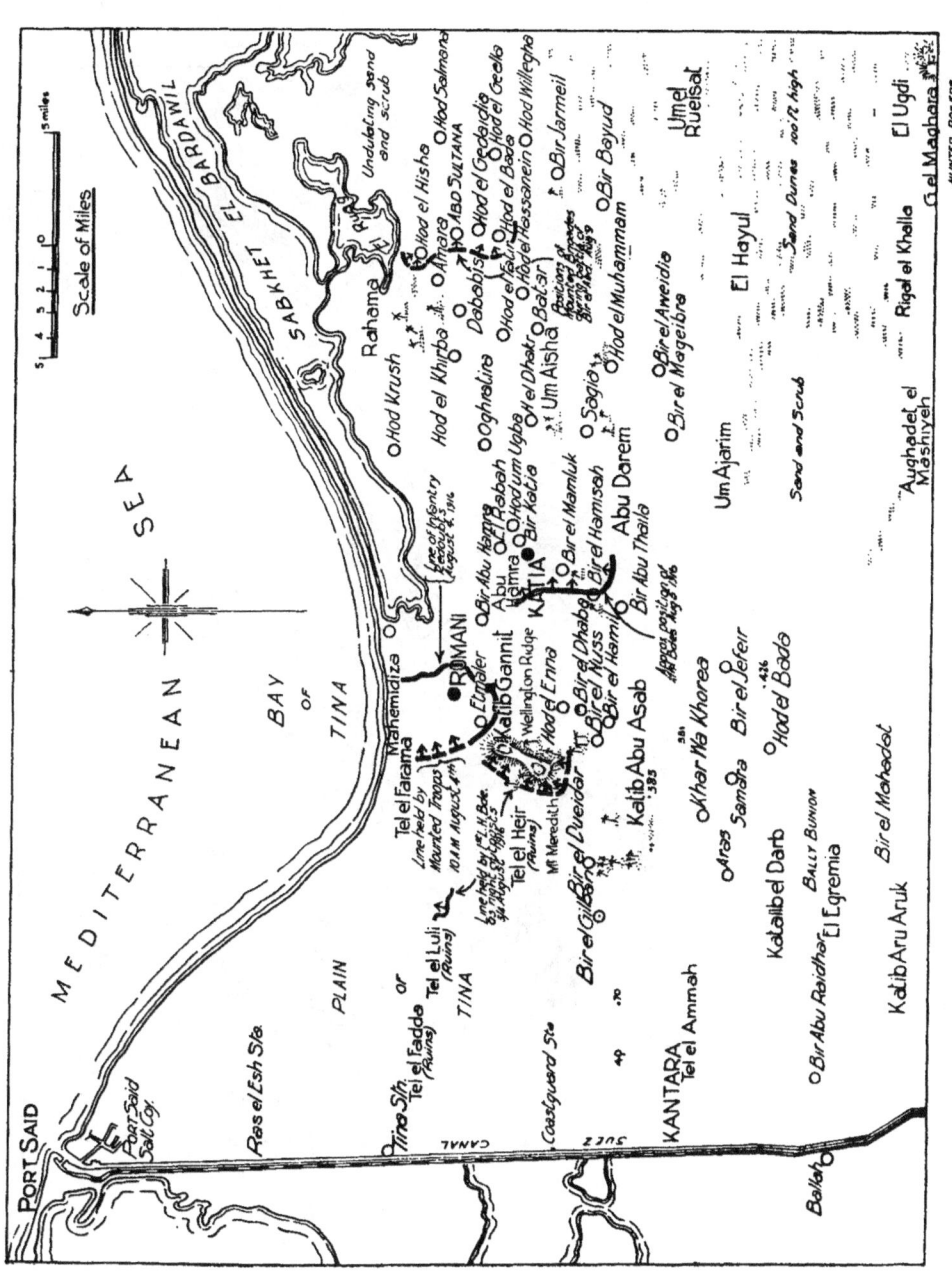

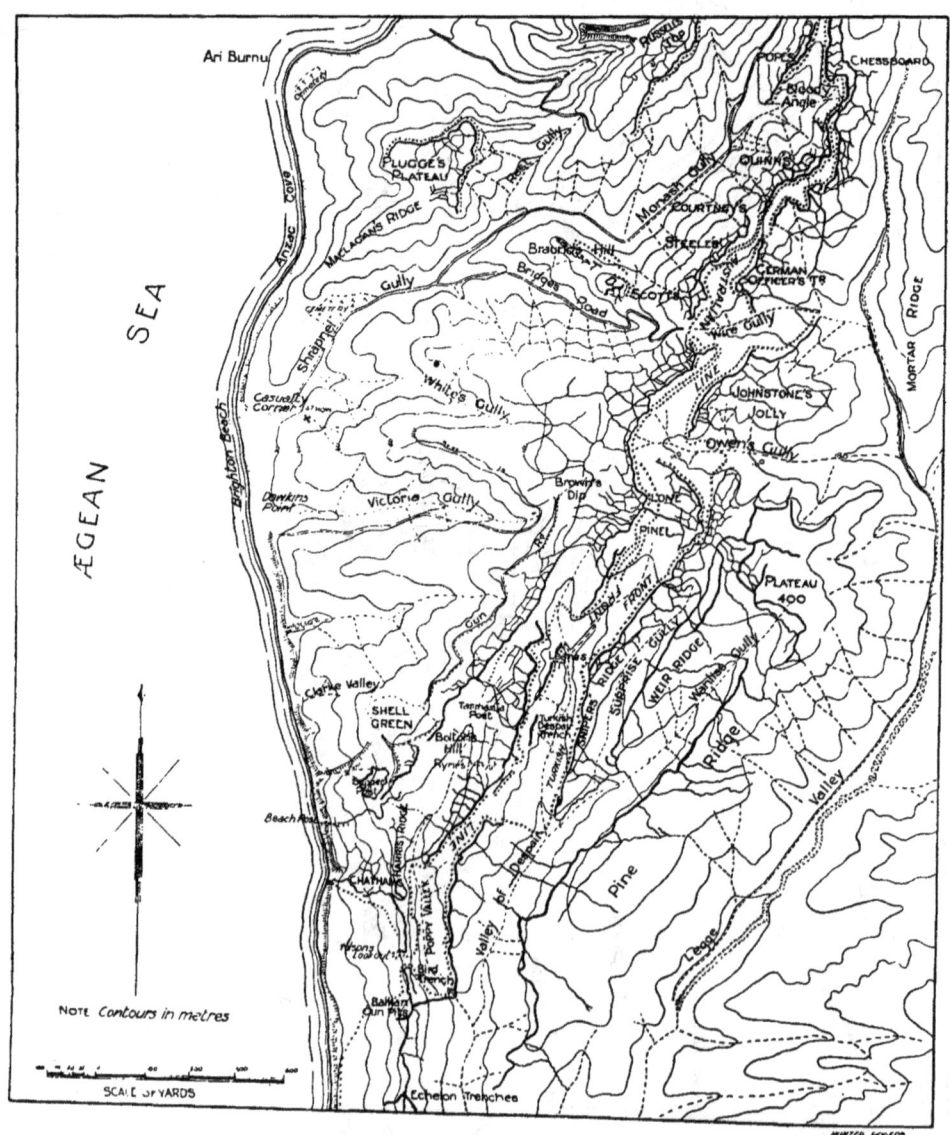

Outline Map, Egypt and Syria, 1 in 750,000, showing Route of 7th Light Horse Regiment. No hill features shown.

(Map by Radcliffe Press, Sydney.)

www.ingramcontent.com/pod-product-compliance
Lightning Source LLC
Chambersburg PA
CBHW080403170426
43193CB00016B/2791